1994

University of St. Francis
G-E 371.91 P481

Education and disability in cr

3 0301 00071953 0

P9-AQQ-545

EDUCATION AND DISABILITY
IN CROSS-CULTURAL PERSPECTIVE

REFERENCE BOOKS IN
INTERNATIONAL EDUCATION
(General Editor: Edward R. Beauchamp)
VOL. 25

GARLAND REFERENCE LIBRARY
OF SOCIAL SCIENCE
VOL. 630

Reference Books in
International Education

Edward R. Beauchamp
General Editor

1. *Education in East and West Germany: A Bibliography*, by Val D. Rust
2. *Education in the People's Republic of China, Past and Present: An Annotated Bibliography*, by Franklin Parker and Betty June Parker
3. *Education in South Asia: A Select Annotated Bibliography*, by Philip G. Altbach, Denzil Saldanha, and Jeanne Weiler
4. *Textbooks in the Third World: Policy, Content and Context*, by Philip G. Altbach and Gail P. Kelly
5. *Education in Japan: A Source Book*, by Edward R. Beauchamp and Richard Rubinger
6. *Women's Education in the Third World*, by David H. Kelly and Gail P. Kelly
7. *Minority Status and Schooling*, by Margaret A. Gibson and John V. Ogbu
8. *Teachers and Teaching in the Developing World*, by Val D. Rust and Per Dalin
9. *Russian and Soviet Education, 1731–1989: A Multilingual Annotated Bibliography*, by William W. Brickman and John T. Zepper
10. *Early Childhood Education in the Arab World: A Source Book*, by Byron G. Massialas and Layla Jarrar
11. *Education in Sub-Saharan Africa: A Source Book*, by George E.F. Urch
12. *Youth in the Soviet Union*, by Anthony Jones
13. *Education in Israel: A Source Book*, by Yaacov Iram
14. *Arab Education in Transition: A Source Book*, by Byron G. Massialas and Samir A. Jarrar
15. *Education and Cultural Differences: New Perspectives*, by Douglas Ray and Deo H. Poonwassie
16. *Contemporary Perspectives in Comparative Education*, edited by Robin J. Burns and Anthony R. Welch
17. *Education in the Arab Gulf States and the Arab World: An Annotated Bibliographic Guide*, by Nagat El-Sanabary
18. *International and Historical Roots of American Higher Education*, by W.H. Cowley and Don Williams
19. *Education in England and Wales: An Annotated Bibliography*, by Franklin Parker and Betty June Parker
20. *Chinese Education: Problems, Policies, and Prospects*, edited, with an introduction, by Irving Epstein
21. *Early Childhood Education in Asia and the Pacific: A Source Book*, edited by Stephanie Feeney
22. *Understanding Educational Reform in Global Context: Economy, Ideology, and the State*, edited by Mark B. Ginsburg
23. *Education and Social Change in Korea*, by Don Adams and Esther E. Gottlieb
24. *Education for Peace: Concepts and Interpretations in Comparative and International Perspective*, by Robin J. Burns
25. *Education and Disability in Cross-Cultural Perspective*, edited by Susan J. Peters

EDUCATION AND DISABILITY
IN CROSS-CULTURAL PERSPECTIVE

edited by
Susan J. Peters

GARLAND PUBLISHING, INC. • NEW YORK & LONDON
1993

© 1993 Susan Jeanne Peters
All rights reserved

Library of Congress Cataloging-in-Publication Data

Education and disability in cross-cultural perspective / edited by Susan J.
Peters.
    p.   cm. — (Garland reference library of social science ; vol.
630. Reference books in international education ; vol. 25)
    Includes bibliographical references.
    ISBN 0-8240-6988-9
    1. Special education—Cross-cultural studies. 2. Handicapped—Educa-
tion—Cross-cultural studies. I. Peters, Susan J. II. Series: Garland
reference library of social science ; v. 630. III. Series: Garland reference
library of social science. Reference books in international education ; vol 25.
LC4019.E3215 1993
371.91—dc20   92-41906
                                                     CIP

Printed on acid-free, 250-year-life paper
Manufactured in the United States of America

G-E
371.91
P481

SERIES EDITOR'S FOREWORD

This series of scholarly works in comparative and international education has grown well beyond the initial conception of a collection of reference books. Although retaining its original purpose of providing a resource to scholars, students, and a variety of other professionals who need to understand the role played by education in various societies or regions of the world, it also strives to provide up-to-date information on a wide variety of selected educational issues, problems and experiments within an international context.

Contributors to this series are well-known scholars who have devoted their professional lives to the study of their specialization. Without exception these men and women possess an intimate understanding of the subject of their research and writing. Without exception they have not only studied their subject in dusty archives, but they have also lived and travelled widely in their quest for knowledge. In short, they are "experts" in the best sense of that often overused word.

In our increasingly interdependent world, it is now widely understood that it is a matter of survival that we not only understand better what makes other societies tick, but that we also make a serious effort to understand how others, be they Japanese, German or Chilean, attempt to solve the same kinds of educational problems that we face in North America. As the late George Z.F. Bereday wrote: "[E]ducation is a mirror held against the face of a people. Nations may put on blustering shows of strength to conceal public weakness, erect grand facades to conceal shabby back-yards, and profess peace while secretly arming for conquest, but how they take care of their children tells unerringly who they are" (*Comparative Method in Education*, New York: Holt, Rinehart & Winston, 1964, p. 5).

Perhaps equally important, however, is the valuable perspective that studying another education system (or its problems) provides us in understanding our own system (or its problems). To step outside of our own limited experience and our commonly held assumptions about schools and learning in order to look back at our system in contrast to

149,823

College of St. Francis Library
Joliet. Illinois

another places it in a very different light. To learn, for example, how the Soviet Union or Belgium handles the education of a multilingual society; how the French provide for the funding of a public education; or how the Japanese control admissions into their universities enables us to understand that there are alternatives to our own familiar way of doing things. Not that we can often "borrow" directly from other societies; indeed, educational arrangements are inevitably a reflection of deeply rooted political, economic and cultural factors that are unique to a society. But a conscious recognition that there are other ways of doing things can serve to open our minds and provoke our imaginations in ways that can result in new approaches that we would not have otherwise considered.

Since this series is intended to be a useful research tool, the editor and contributors welcome suggestions for future volumes as well as ways in which this series can be improved.

Edward R. Beauchamp
University of Hawaii

CONTENTS

ACKNOWLEDGMENTS

The stimulus for this book was provided by Lynn Paine, who suggested to Ed Beauchamp that I might be interested in writing a book about disability from an international perspective. My thanks go primarily to the two of them for their interest and support. In addition, I should like to thank my colleagues who facilitated my work and led me to reappraise some of my theoretical assumptions about disability through their comments on early drafts and through their encouragement; specifically, Roger Cox, Brian DeLany, Jay Featherstone, John Metzler, Richard Navarro, Aaron Pallas, and Jack Schwille. The ongoing support of my dissertation advisor and mentor, Henry M. Levin, continues to be a well-spring of inspiration for me.

Gratitude must also be expressed to Dai-Hua Shen for her work on the initial organizing of the index to this book. I am especially grateful to Lisa Payne for formatting the manuscript, creating tables and figures, assisting with editing tasks, and carrying out the myriad of details needed to see the manuscript to its completed copy-ready edition.

Finally, I owe a special debt of gratitude to the contributing authors for their vision, dedication to disability issues, and for their patience in seeing this book through to its fruition. My father, brothers and sister also deserve a great deal of recognition for their love and support and for believing in me.

INTRODUCTION

This book is a collection of chapters written by scholars who have a wide variety of experiences in the field of disability. Their perspectives reflect these experiences as they write about their own cultures, or cultures that they have spent a great deal of time getting to know. (The possible exception may be the Pakistan chapter. However, the authors of this chapter are careful to present their views taking into account a wide range of Pakistani original sources in their interpretations).

As insiders to the cultures they describe, the authors are able to emulate the central thesis of this book--that is, that disability is a socially constructed and historically mediated phenomenon. Too many books have been written about disability as an objective condition, and thus are dominated by quantitative and behavioral research paradigms. An interpretivist value-based viewpoint is necessary to begin to unravel the "mystery" behind differential treatment and recognition of those perceived to have disabling conditions, especially as these relate to educational issues.

Originally, chapters from Africa, South America, and Russia had been scheduled for inclusion in this book. However, world invents intervened to preclude their contributions. Scholars from these areas of the world whom I contacted were understandably preoccupied with internal environmental, economic, and political upheaval in their respective countries. Initial contacts with scholars from the Institute of Defectology in Moscow were curtailed by its closure during the events of 1991-92. Development of the chapter on the People's Republic of China was made difficult by the Tiananmen Square events in May of 1989, which resulted in a black-out of scholarly exchange of information. In addition, the whole process of completing the book was slowed by necessary translations and editing from several different languages into English, and by the vagaries of overseas postal services. However, the extended time was worth the effort to produce a book that would truly represent cross-cultural perspectives on education and disability.

As editor and contributing author, I have endeavored to provide a theoretical framework for a meta-interpretation of the individual country chapters in the opening and concluding sections of the book. My analysis is entirely my own and is open to debate. I have found a personal catharsis in putting to words the thoughts and concepts that have been fomenting in my mind since achieving the ascribed status of disability in 1974 as the result of a sky-diving accident. This status has opened a whole new world to me which I have viewed as both a challenge and an opportunity to explore the nature of diversity as well as the consequences of being perceived as different. I look forward to your response as readers and interpreters of the experiences and portrayal of persons with disabilities highlighted here.

Education and Disability
in Cross-Cultural Perspective

CHAPTER 1

INTRODUCTION: DISABLED PEOPLE OR DISABLING SOCIETY?

by Susan Peters

WHO ARE THE DISABLED?

A decade ago, UNESCO reported that four hundred fifty million people of the world's population develop a physical or mental limitation at some time in their life cycle (UNESCO *Courier*, 1981: 8). By the year 2000, this number is expected to rise to 600 million (Mittler, 1990: 54). A great number of these people are children who, because of hunger, malnutrition, or lack of adequate health care, are marked for life with a disabling condition. One hundred and forty million children between six and 60 months of age are chronically undernourished--almost 40 percent of the world's children (UNICEF, 1987). The cost to society in terms of lost economic production and other societal contributions cannot easily be measured. However, the world assuredly pays a high price for this loss, especially considering the fact that human capital is the most abundant resource in developing countries.

Recovering from the consequences of disability rests with a society's response to disabling conditions. UNICEF reports that integrated nutrition and early education programs are estimated to provide rates of return ranging from 0.6 to 2.2 percent of GNP (UNICEF, 1987: 9). Both loss of productivity and quality of life are mediated by societal conditions, not only in terms of cause and prevention but in terms of education and rehabilitation efforts. In fact, wide variations in pre-existing disabling conditions and societal response to these conditions characterize the world today.

3

In answering the question "Who are the disabled?" this book challenges traditional views of disability through a shift in paradigms from disability as an innate dysfunction of individuals to a cultural view that takes into account these variations in societal responses. Central to this cultural view is the proposition that the fact of disability cannot be disentangled from the values attached to the disabling condition.

Historically, "Who are the disabled?" has been a persistent unanswered question. The literature on disability cross-nationally has traditionally focused its attention on defining disabled people through "norms of coherence." Norms of coherence are attempts to classify, define and make distinctions among categories of "innate" disability or among concepts built on these categories. Classification is seen as an objective condition with universal application. Thus, most books with an international perspective on special education and disability use a framework of classification such as that developed by the World Health Organization (WHO) in 1980. The WHO framework is organized around four concepts: disease, impairment, disability, and handicap.

All four concepts focus on the individual: the disease rests at the level of active pathology within the body; the impairment is at the level of anatomical structure or function; the disability is a lack of ability on the part of the individual to perform physical or mental activities; and the handicap is an inability to perform according to societal norms or expectations. At all stages, these concepts define people with disabilities by what they are **not**. These concepts are then used to build categories of disability such as "learning disability," "emotional impairment," or "physical handicap."

The WHO framework and similar ones operate within the assumption that disability is an innate dysfunction of individuals. However, these frameworks break down when applied pragmatically. As a result, much time and effort is spent in unproductive attempts to standardize these frameworks across countries and even within a single country. Specifically, a recent study of crude disability rates found a variation across 30 countries from 0.2 to 20.9 percent (Yu, 1991: 63). In the end, those who attempt to classify disability are led to the conclusion that data on classification provide little or no clarity and in fact, a great deal of confusion regarding incidence and prevalence of disability (Biklen, 1989; Yu, 1991).

One of the most dramatic examples of the ways in which these frameworks break down is with the category of "learning disabled," which was initially recognized in 1963 at the first Association for Children with Learning Disabilities conference in the United States (Sapon-Shevin, 1989: 81). This category makes up the largest single group of students identified as disabled in the United States. In the decade between 1976-77 and 1986-87, those labeled as learning disabled grew 119 percent to constitute 44 percent of all students with disability labels in the United States. However, the percentage varied significantly across individual states--from 30 to 67 percent nationwide, and from 0 to 73 percent among large cities (Lipsky and Gartner, 1989: 13). According to some researchers, this variation exists as a result of disagreement on definitions of learning disability and availability of services that are ultimately derived from priorities and decision-making processes inherent in societal values (Lipsky and Gartner, 1989).

In addition to the problem of identifying those with learning disabilities within countries that recognize this category, learning disability as a category is not recognized in several countries. For example, learning disability does not exist as a category in Japan. Although Japan certainly has the technology and the expertise of educators to assess and label students as learning disabled, this category is not socially acceptable and therefore does not exist in the lexicon of educational programs. In addition, many developing countries do not have the expertise and technology to identify such students, even if they should wish to do so.

Because of the variations in recognition of disabling conditions across nation states (of which learning disabilities is only one example but certainly the most dramatic), there is no attempt in this book to provide a cross-cultural standardization of the terms used to refer to disabled individuals within each country. It is this book's premise that these terms must be defined within the context of the individual country. The terms used point to the variations across cultures in defining disability, and thus the need to examine the social and political context within which disability is defined.

DISABILITY IN SOCIAL CONTEXT

The major premise of this book derives from the notion referred to above that disability is to a large extent societally constructed, and that education plays a major role in this construction. Disability, from this perspective, is best defined as: "the expression of a physical or mental limitation in a social context--the gap between a person's capabilities and the demands of the environment" (Pope and Tarlov, 1991: 1). This definition of disability rests on the following assumptions:

1. Focusing on classification misses the critical issue. The critical issue is not labeling, but an analysis of child-environment interaction patterns.

2. Optimal treatment will not be found in a label, but in the analysis of the interaction between people with disabilities and their experiences within the context of the larger community.

3. Disability as a biological condition must be conceptually disentangled from the social ramifications of the condition.

The central concept is that disability is a socially constructed and historically mediated category of experience (Harris & Wideman, 1988: 116). In other words, obstacles to education result not from inherent incapacities, but from the physical and attitudinal barriers socially and politically constructed within the environment. From this perspective, incidence and prevalence statistics have little meaning unless viewed in the context of the political culture and the prevailing ideology of a particular society.

The question, "Who are the disabled?" is best answered, then, by thinking of them as a minority oppressed by lack of acceptance and equal human rights. When Gliedman and Roth first published their book, *The Unexpected Minority* (1980), the idea of people with disabilities as an oppressed minority in the same category with other ethnic and racial groups seemed a novel one. Further, it is an idea that many still seem unwilling to accept (Personal Conversations with Black-American scholars, Fulbright-Hays Group Projects Abroad, 1990). Before Gliedman and Roth, the application of the word oppression to disabled persons had been severely limited. Most literature on the subject of disability was grounded in the discipline of psychology as exemplified by such works as Goffman's which focus on the individual management of spoiled identity (Goffman, 1963). Disabled people have been seen as "the other." They have been dehumanized, desexualized, and devalued for their perceived differences from supposedly "normal" people. However, any disabled person who has read Paolo Friere's *Pedagogy of the Oppressed*, understands that the experience of being disabled or merely "labeled" as disabled produces oppression not unlike that experience by class, race, gender, or age characteristics.

> Dehumanization, which marks not only those whose humanity has been stolen, but also (though in a different way) those who have stolen it, is a *distortion* of the vocation of becoming more human. This distortion occurs within history, but it is not an historical vocation. . . . The struggle for humanization . . . is possible only because dehumanization, although a concrete historical fact, is *not* a given destiny but the result of an unjust order. . . . (Friere, 1983: 28)

Although Friere was writing about peasant classes in developing countries such as his home country of Brazil, his recognition of dehumanization strikes a resounding chord when one considers the separation, stigmatization, and discrimination commonly experienced by people with disabilities. Societies too often dehumanize and devalue people with disabilities. This commonly experienced dehumanization of marginalized groups in society's nation-states necessarily includes disabled people as an oppressed minority.

THE CURRENT SITUATION

Ideally, education is the door to opportunity, the chance to compensate for physical or mental limitations. It should provide the occasion for freedom of choice between a lifetime of dependence and a lifetime of independent living. Schools are the places where education is formalized and validated for most young people in today's societies. However, a recent UNESCO review of the present situation revealed that of 51 countries reporting data, 34 provided for the needs of fewer than one percent of students identified as disabled (UNESCO, 1988: 14). In addition, those people with disabilities who have access to education, like other marginalized groups (ethnic, linguistic, racial minorities, and women) are often disadvantaged in education. Most corrective steps taken in education fail to come up to expectations. Educational inequality has not been alleviated and the gap between the performance of majority and minority students is still considerable (CERI, 1989: 77). Equal opportunity policies have failed. Cloaked in humanitarianism, the movement to provide compensatory programs is more often an effort to remove those unwanted "others" from the "regular" classroom. The numbers of students tracked into separate programs such as special education, vocational education, and bilingual education have increased dramatically as more and more "unwanted" students are added to the rolls of these compensatory programs. (Recall that in the United States alone, numbers identified as learning disabled rose 119% in the years between 1976 and 1986.).

Cross-cultural variability in defining disability is thus carried over into the process of schooling.

> By defining large groups of children as deviant (slow learners, remedial problems, discipline problems, etc.), and giving funding and legislative support for special teachers and for "diagnosis" and "treatment," the state will fund extensive remedial projects. While these projects will seem neutral, helpful, and may seem aimed at increasing mobility, they will actually defuse the debate over the role of schooling in the reproduction of the knowledge and people "required" by the society. It will do this in part by defining the ultimate causes of such deviance as within the child or his or her culture and not due to, say, poverty, the conflicts and disparities generated by the historically evolving cultural and economic hierarchies of the society, etc. (Apple, 1982: 56)

A situation exists whereby schools create certain kinds of disabilities (e.g. learning disabilities). Unwanted children are labeled and sorted into marginalized special add-on programs according to these "needs." As a result, the meaning of disability is better understood through a view of schooling that examines the ideological, political, and economic "needs" of a society.

WHY STUDY EDUCATION AND DISABILITY IN CROSS-CULTURAL PERSPECTIVE?

As education worldwide undergoes massive changes through modernization and technological acceleration in developed and developing industrial societies, educational structure and function can no longer be understood without considering the interconnectedness of people and sensitivity to cross-cultural beliefs and values. Analysis of "special" education must include strong comparative elements (not only within the context of general education but across cultures) to better understand and prepare for the educational needs of citizens and nations in a rapidly changing world. No one country has the one best answer to what the nature of schooling ought to be, the kinds of education children ought to receive, and the responsibilities and roles of governments. Each of these factors is underpinned as well by questions of cultural values of excellence, equality, and occupational expectations for productivity.

Education for all students (including those with perceived disabilities) plays an important role in all societies--those that struggle for an economic foothold in competitive markets, as well as those super-powers experiencing economic expansion or decline. All nations confront questions about what to do with or how to utilize the formerly disenfranchised, under-utilized segments of their population--those commonly classified as at-risk, disabled, or "exceptional." Eighty-five percent of the world's disabled population live in communities where few or no effective education services exist. The need for appropriate educational programs is great and the kinds of responses to this need have important consequences, economically, politically, and socially.

If we are to understand education and disability as socially constructed and historically mediated processes, we must look across countries as well as within them. Cross-cultural study of education and disability is necessary because any move toward educational change in today's world which stays within its own system is parochial and likely to fail. To change, we must articulate our dissatisfaction with the present conditions of schooling for marginalized students, confront past failures, and recognize the invalidity of the current axioms that prescribe unquestioning treatment of these groups of people as deviant and deficient. This book accepts the challenge and is a serious attempt to uncover the existing axioms which drive the perception and treatment of those labeled as disabled. This approach adds to our knowledge of the ways in which education influences the experience of disability.

This approach is necessary because the study of education for students with disabilities, both within countries and cross-nationally, has heretofore typically focused on descriptive analyses of services (mostly formal schooling) and objectification of disability as an innate characteristic of individuals, with its emphasis on incidence and prevalence issues. Moreover, very little research has focused on the world's approximately 600 million disabled. For example, a search of ERIC Data Base reveals eight entries (from over 4000) that address special education from an international perspective. The journals covering the issue on a regular basis can be counted on one hand and are not widely disseminated.

Of all the world organizations concerned with disadvantaged populations, UNESCO has done the most definitive work in the area of disability, beginning around the mid-1970s and spurred on in the 1980s by the declaration of the International Year of Disabled Persons. Most notable among the UNESCO studies are a study of early detection, intervention, and education of 9 countries (UNESCO, 1982) and a report on a survey of 14 countries released in 1986 that focuses on strategies for teacher training (UNESCO, 1986). Findings suggest multiple barriers to education for people with disabilities, including: poverty, shortage of qualified personnel, ignorance, negative attitudes, remaining primitive beliefs and practices. In addition, these barriers exist across levels of economic development. Solutions, however, continue to focus on "model" programs apart from the context in which they might be developed. The final remarks in UNESCO's 1982 report are worth quoting at length:

> ... it can be concluded from the accumulated information reflected in the reports that a considerable amount of knowledge is already available about efficient methods of prevention, detection and intervention. If there were practical conditions to apply this knowledge, immense human gains could no doubt be made. A recent report on mental retardation, commissioned by the World Health Organization, "Mental Retardation: prevention, amelioration and service delivery" (1980) says: "It has been predicted, for example, that the incidence of the more severe conditions (of mental retardation) in the developed countries could be halved before the end

of the century, using present knowledge and techniques." A similar conclusion is probably justified also for other handicaps, and there is no reason to believe that the improvements in the developing countries would be less striking.

The question that begs a response is, "Why, if we have the expertise and knowledge to ameliorate the situation of people with disabilities, don't we do it?" The answer is difficult and complex, but certainly lies in the direction of (re)examining attitudes and cultural values.

Previous approaches to the study of special education lack a theoretical framework that would provide causal explanations of the educational treatment of children with exceptional needs and their ensuing life chances. However, UNESCO took a giant step forward in its final report of May, 1988. This report proposes actions to be undertaken in special education for the 1990s. Its summary of proceedings includes a section on conceptual frameworks and general principles which begin to address the aforementioned question. One principle states: "The development of learning of children can only be understood in terms of the environments in which they are living and learning, namely the environments of home, school and community. Recognition of this ecological perspective represents a definite movement away from a defect-oriented education programme" (p. 9). Proposed solutions in the UNESCO report of 1988 no longer include "model" programs but call for a "major structural and systems change within the field of education" (p. 10). Obstacles have also been redefined: Inadequacy of perceptions in policy formation is very much linked to attitudes, whether they be cultural, religious, political or ideological. Therefore, an "effective" program is "a natural extension of the cultural and education system in a particular country" (p. 13). The report further contends that to accomplish this task, "Education must give disabled persons the tools with which they could manage in their immediate environment and society as a whole. These tools are the skills needed in everyday life. Education must be individual-centered and local-environment oriented, leading to productive work" (p. 15).

Outside of the reports from worldwide organizations such as UNESCO, most smaller scale studies of special education have traditionally derived from the disciplines and paradigms of psychology, which focus on the individual learner. These studies, for the most part, can be characterized as quantitative and behavioral. That is, they tend to objectively describe, predict and control the experience of disability, rather than describe, interpret, and understand it. (James Ysseldyke provides a comprehensive review of the literature in this area in Wang, Reynolds and Walberg, 1987.) In addition, few individual researchers in special education have drawn on the premises and principles of comparative research that have been so well thought out in comparative studies of general education.

Comparative studies in education tend to derive from sociological theories of human interaction. That is, they examine the relationship between processes, structure, and cultural values. "Basic social, cultural, and psychological processes in educational situations are analyzed, rather than the formal dimensions of institutional structuring or the economic resources of education in various settings" (Spindler, 1963:12). The basic principle of comparative education is to take a broad perspective that avoids making culturally limited generalizations about behavior. A comprehensive theory of education takes into account the range of alternative possibilities in educational structure and process across cultures. At its heart, comparative education is ruled by an interpretive paradigm--a way of seeing that attempts to interpret cultural diversity. It is value-based, resists standardization, and encompasses a broad world view.

Irving Epstein's comparison of special education issues in Japan and China is a notable exception in the field of special education. Epstein draws on value orientations and an historical accounting of the development of special education in these two countries that includes an examination of legal and political issues. He observes: "In many ways, the educational system, its treatment of the disabled, simply mirrors external social tendencies" (Epstein, 1989: 14). In addition, a few sociologists (notably Len Barton and Sally Tomlinson from Great Britain) have drawn on sociological theories to study these social tendencies and their effect on special education. To Tomlinson, "Special education is permeated by an ideology of benevolent humanitarianism, which provides a moral framework within which professionals and practitioners work" (Tomlinson, 1982: 5).

While disabled people have been neglected by comparative educational research, objectified by special education research, or assigned to "the other" in theoretical treatises, they have also been forgotten in practice. However, all societies have always had people with impairments and perceived differences from the norm. "Disability" is a human constant that will not go away and, in fact, shows a tendency to increase as modern medicine becomes more skillful at preventing death while at the same time less successful at preventing illness, disability, and disease. The world-wide spread of AIDS is a significant example of this lack of success. Those who have contracted the virus serve as a stark reminder of the interconnectedness of society and the need to address the societal conditions that not only cause disability, but determine its consequences.

In summary, the numbers of people identified as disabled, the appalling lack of services to meet their needs, and the dearth of research cross-nationally support the necessity for cross-cultural discussion of education and disability. UNESCO's agenda for the nineties challenges us to move in this direction. This book is a comprehensive attempt to do so and, as such, includes with each chapter extensive annotated references to help further research in the areas of concern that are identified and discussed.

ORGANIZATION OF THE BOOK

It has been argued here that no policies and practices exist free from context. The following chapter provides an analytical framework for study of education and disability in cross-cultural perspective. The ensuing chapters describe the situation of education and disability in seven countries: England and Wales, Hungary, Japan, Iran, Pakistan, People's Republic of China, and United States. The final chapter analyzes the situation of education and disability across countries and draws conclusions about a new world polity expressed in terms of the theory of disability developed in earlier chapters.

Each individual country chapter begins with a map of education that includes an examination of the state of the nation: political ideology and stability, socio-economic conditions, geographic data and demographic information such as patterns of disability due to climate and access to health care. Examination of national context is followed by a discussion of educational policies and practices. These policies and practices reflect notions of excellence, equality, and productivity, and are related to the institutional frameworks that evolve in support of them. Discussion of these policies provides an understanding of conditions that influence change and innovation.

Inset within these broad national conditions, then, is a map of educational systems. The system components examined in each chapter of this volume were selected from research on developing and industrialized countries (IRT, 1988). These include: 1) goals of the educational system, including selection and promotion of students, identification and assessment, and entrance and exit requirements; 2) school structure, size, and organization (both formal and non-formal); 3) educational planning and regulations, including legislative mandates and administrative and supervisory structures; 4) allocation of financial and human resources; 5) personnel training and supply.

Beyond an examination of the educational system, specific examples of school conditions that represent translation of policy into practice are then described for each country. These examples may include: 1) teacher-student contact (i.e., school and class sizes, number of shifts, length of school day and hours of teaching); 2) student progression and grouping; 3) staff hierarchy (e.g., the existence of a principal and his or her duties and training as well as possibilities for teacher advancement that may strongly affect distribution of resources); 4) access to information (e.g., about instructional strategies, or disabilities); 5) access to physical resources such as libraries, labs, playgrounds, running potable water, and electricity; and 6) community relationships, including legal rights and obligations concerning support and control of schools. Finally, future issues and priorities are discussed to move us toward research and policy agendas.

The countries discussed in this volume represent different types of governmental organization, ancient and modern, super-powers, rich and poor. However, the overriding rationale for inclusion in this volume is the degree of innovation and system-wide change recently undertaken by each. These changes represent evolving belief-systems and adaptations influenced by cultural values and norms, and changing socio-economic conditions.

The chapter authors of the countries included in this book discuss disability and education within the context of their nation's societal beliefs and practice. All authors speak with the critical voice of experience, either as a disabled person themselves, or from significant personal and/or professional relations with disabled individuals. Because their experiences are different, the chapter outline set forth above is not strictly adhered to. Each country, and the authors who describe them, have unique circumstances to convey. Thus we no more attempt to standardize their responses than we do to standardize a definition of disability.

The book aims to tell the stories of how people experience and portray disability. The use of a cultural paradigm to reveal disability as socially constructed, and to apply cross-culturally will prepare the way for richer understandings of the experience, leading to alternative perspectives that will break the chains of oppression regarding disability and education.

References

Apple, Michael W. (1982). *Education and Power*. Boston: Routledge & Kegan Paul.

Biklen, Douglas P. "Redefining Schools" in *Schooling and Disability*. Douglas Biklen, Dianne Ferguson, and Alison Ford (eds). Chicago, Illinois: University of Chicago Press.

CERI (Centre for Educational Research and Innovation) (1989). *One School, Many Cultures*. Paris, France: Organization for Economic Cooperation and Development.

Epstein, Irvin (1989). Paper delivered at the V11th World Congress of Comparative Education. Montreal, Canada.

Friere, Paolo (1983). *Pedagogy of the Oppressed*. New York: Continuum.

Fulbright-Hays Group Projects Abroad (1990). Personal conversations with Black-American Scholars. Harare, Zimbabwe.

Gliedman, John and William Roth (1980). *The Unexpected Minority: Handicapped Children in America*. New York: Harcourt Brace Jovanovich.

Goffman, E. *Stigma: Notes on the Management of Spoil Identity*. Englewood Cliffs, New Jersey: Prentice-Hall, Inc.

Harris, Adrienne and Dana Wideman (1988). "The Construction of Gender and Disability in Early Attachment" in *Women with Disabilities: Essays in Psychology, Culture, and Politics*. Michelle Fine and Adrienne Asch (eds.). Philadelphia: Temple University Press.

Lipsky, Dorothy Kerzner and Alan Garner (1989). "The Current Situation," in *Beyond Separate Education: Quality Education for All*. Dorothy Kerzner Lipsky and Alan Gartner (eds.). Baltimore, Maryland: Paul H. Brookes Publishing Co.

Mittler, Peter (1990). "Prospects for Disabled Children and their Families: An International Perspective," in *Disability, Handicap and Society*, Vol. 5, No. 1, pp. 53-64.

Pope, Andrew M. and Alvin R. Tarlou (1991). *Disability in America: Toward a National Agenda for Prevention*. Washington, D.C.: National Academy Press.

Sapon-Shevin, Mara (1989). "Mild Disabilities: In and Out of Special Education" in *Schooling and Disability*. Chicago, Illinois: University of Chicago Press.

Tomlinson, Sally (1982). *A Sociology of Special Education*. London: Routledge and Kegan Paul.

UNESCO (1988). *UNESCO Consultation on Special Education* (Paris, May 2-6, 1988). Final Report.

UNESCO (1986). *Helping Handicapped Pupils in Ordinary Schools: Strategies for Teacher Training*.

UNESCO (1982). *Handicapped Children: Early Detection, Intervention and Education*.

UNESCO (1981). "Their Handicap is Hunger," UNESCO *Courier*: Paris, France. June 1981.

UNICEF (1987). Progress Review of the Child Survival and Development Revolution 1983-1986.

Ysseldyke, James E. (1987). "Classification of Handicapped Students," in *Handbook of Special Education Research and Practice*, Volume I. Margaret C. Wang, Maynard C. Reynolds and Herbert J. Walberg (eds.). Oxford: Pergamon Press.

Yu, Yeun-chung (1991). "The Demography of Disability," in *Population Bulletin of the United Nations*, No. 30, pp. 61-77.

CHAPTER 2

AN IDEOLOGICAL-CULTURAL FRAMEWORK FOR THE STUDY OF DISABILITY

by Susan Peters

Theory is a necessary myth that we construct to understand
something we know we understand incompletely. (Sarason,
1991: 123)

THE NECESSITY FOR A THEORY OF DISABILITY

This chapter provides a rationale for the selection of a particular analytical
framework and describes its characteristics and degree of usefulness in the
study of education and disability in cross-cultural perspective. As we
analyze problems and practices in educating children with special needs, a
theoretical viewpoint is necessary to provide insights that are grounded in
cultural attitudes and expectations toward persons with disabilities.
Education involves experiences, partnerships, and interactions throughout
individual life spans. These are processes that take on meaning within
the life and work of the society which surrounds it. A theory that takes
into account cultural values and expectations is especially important in an
approach to understanding the structure and function of "special"
education. As a comparatively recent phenomenon in the history of
education, the study of education for special-needs students must be
understood through evolving practice and developing commitment. We
must understand educational goals as they reflect societal values, in order
to better affect positive educational outcomes for people with disabilities.
We must go beyond analysis of systems to the ways in which societies

use these systems and shape them to their own educational goals and values. The framework for the study of disability proposed here depicts models of perception that are useful lenses for understanding the policies and practices that shape outcomes for culturally diverse students identified as disabled or exceptional in some way. This framework provides the means for analyzing the education of people with disabilities in this book.

We conclude from the literature on comparative education that this approach is sensitive to four perennial problems of perspective in the study of cultural diversity: 1) the problem of assuming the nation-state as a homogeneous unit, 2) the need for an historical perspective, 3) scope of analysis that is not limited to two or three countries, 4) linking what goes on with regard to the treatment of people (in this case, students with disabilities) to central ideologies, with a focus on how these ideologies are manifested in educational settings.   Another significant problem of perspective rarely addressed is the critical voice of the people who are themselves affected by the experiences studied. The proposed framework develops a theory of disability that incorporates the perspective of disabled people themselves in order to understand the "other" in their own terms. Their perspective is critical in order to rearticulate ideas of justice and equality.

A theory of disability that takes into account political, economic, ideological, and cultural spheres of influence is necessary not only to understand the circumstances of people with disabilities within the countries discussed here, but to add to our understanding of an emerging "world polity." A concept developed by Ramirez, Boli, Meyers, and others, world polity is defined as a system of creating value through collective conferral of authority cross-nationally. Education has become an important element of the world polity. "Education is institutionalized at the world level and acts as a social imperative for nation states" (Ramirez and Boli, 1987: 171).   The authors argue that world culture is an independent variable with reciprocal causation between cultural, economic, and political structures. Education systems are constituted within these structures or spheres and, as such, carry significant ramifications for the life circumstances of people with disabilities world wide.

THE SOCIAL/CULTURAL CONTEXT OF DISABILITY AND SCHOOL PRACTICE

Societal ideologies shape the definition, structure and legitimacy of education, and also the definition of disability. Therefore, it is important to consider societal ideology to understand the structure of education and perceptions of disability within societies. The proposed perspective on education and disability draws on sociological theory in education. It forces us to think about education in general terms as representing the moral order of society. It is linked most closely to the French sociologist, Emile Durkheim, who defined education as:

> . . . the influence exercised by adult generations on those that are not yet ready for social life. Its object is to stimulate and develop in the child a certain number of physical, intellectual and moral states which are demanded of him by both the political society as a whole, and by the particular milieu for which he is specifically destined. (Williamson, 1979: 4)

Durkheim's work shifted the focus from the individual student to the social context. From his definition, the concepts of "special" education and disability are necessarily thought of in much broader terms than education provided for "exceptional" students in separate school settings. It embraces the notion of any form of education that affects special needs children: family, informal and private community support systems, rehabilitation, medicine, and health care programs. Thus, education and disability as the chosen title for this book is preferred as more all-encompassing than the term special education. It allows us to frame the experiences of disabled people from the broader societal conditions within which they live, learn, and work.

If education represents, and to some extent mirrors the moral order of society, then it makes sense to examine a group's prevailing ideology. Meighan defines ideology as ". . . a broad interlocked set of ideas and beliefs about the world held by a group of people that they demonstrate in both behavior and conversation to various audiences" (Meighan, 1981: 155). Ideologies are "sets of lived meanings, practices and social relations that are often internally inconsistent" (Apple, 1982: 31). Professionals, educators, policymakers, and parents apply these ideologies in their approach to the meaning and experience of disability.

This view of education and disability is a departure from traditional thinking in the field of special education in several respects. First, it views schools as one among many sites of cultural (re)production. That is, the milieu, whether school, home, or community, is viewed as predominantly cultural in its functions and activities through which "different groups produce collective memories, knowledge, social relations, and values within historically constituted relations of power" (Aronowitz & Giroux, 1991: 50). Schools, therefore, are the sites of production for ability, values, and occupational identity (Furlong, 1991). This view is contrasted with the therapeutic function of schools; i.e., diagnosis and remediation based on health needs to effect a "cure" from disease or deviance.

Cultural reproduction in schools is thus defined as systems of meaning that are expressed by patterns of behavior. Current thinking with respect to education of disabled people is dominated by medical, psychological, and administrative approaches. These approaches provide "recipe" knowledge and accept as unproblematic what are in fact very complex and debatable processes involving at least three matters: a) the ways in which disability gets constructed, b) how laws and school practice regulate the social experience of people with disabilities, and c) how the concept of disability is embodied in the world polity.

The second departure from traditional thinking in the field of special education that this book attempts is in its view of cultural values (specifically ways of thinking about disability). Cultural values are believed to be transmitted through the societal mechanism of border creations. Cultural borders are "historically constructed and socially organized with maps of rules and regulations that limit and enable particular identities, individual capacities, and social forms" (Aronowitz & Giroux, 1991: 119). Schools and education perpetuate the moral order through implicit tailoring to positions in the social hierarchy. From this perspective, formal schooling is a form of cultural borders established to sort students according to socially constructed identities based on diverse perceptions of individual capacity.

These borders are often manifested in educational policy. Social and educational policies are guided by systems of beliefs that underlie educational and social ideals. Policy is defined here as web of decisions and actions that allocate values. They are often translated into documents that are backed by political authority and reinforced with power in the form of monetary incentives or disincentives. Writing about educational policy in the United States, Marshall, et al. explain the underpinnings of cultural values in relation to educational policy in this way:

> In state capitals, when policies are formulated to change education systems, the values of *people* are transferred into a set of statements (policy) about the way things *must be done*. We can learn a great deal about a culture by understanding those values, by understanding the iterative process through which they are formed and reinforced, and by understanding the ways in which values are built into policy. (Marshall, et al., 1989: 6)

The third way in which this book deviates from traditional thinking is in its assumption of an overarching cultural framework that is controlled to a great extent by myth and symbol (Meyer, Boli, & Thomas, 1987). These myths and symbols are inherent in the cultural ethos, or system of implicit and deeply interiorized attitudes toward others and may be exemplified in educational practices and in activities such as parental choice of schooling based on expectations stemming from social class. In the American culture, the prevailing notion of disability was so deeply interiorized as to remain virtually unchallenged for several decades. "A child's handicap was seen as an unalterable characteristic of the child. . . Given this, and the conviction that the handicapped were different in kind from the rest of children, it made sense to develop separate educational systems" (Hegarty, Pocklington, and Lucas, 1984: 8).

Fourth, culture is viewed, not as an artifact, but as a terrain of struggle, power, and conflict. Ideologies shape our perception of schooling so that what goes on in education may be linked to central ideologies. These ideologies are often backed by power and authority of politically dominant groups and thus remain resistant to change for long periods of time. However, the overt oppression of people with disabilities will inevitably be challenged, overtly or passively. This challenge is most evident in the high drop out rate experienced in many countries where education does not meet the needs of the people seeking cultural capital.

ANALYTICAL MODEL OF ANALYSIS

This proposed analysis of education and disability departs from study of persons with disabilities as distinctly different from the rest of humanity. It draws on the principles of comparative education research used by Epstein and others, and builds on the theoretical frameworks of sociologists such as Tomlinson and Barton, to understand the treatment of people with disabilities in schooling and in education cross-culturally. A common analytical language is employed through the heuristic construction of four basic models of perception of disability from which to examine the causal relations among: 1) the *structure* within which disabled people experience treatment, 2) the common *ideologies* or values orientations prevalent in a society, and 3) schooling and related services that exemplify these values in *practice*.   In sum, the model depicted below in Figure 1 provides an interactive way of looking at societal structure and ideological influences on the conditions of schooling for children and youth with disabilities.

Figure 1: Analytical Model of Analysis

PRACTICE

* Education

* Schooling

* Services

MODELS OF
PERCEPTION OF
DISABILITY

STRUCTURE

* Political System

* Economic System
  for allocation of resources

* Ecological Conditions

IDEOLOGY

* Sociological

* Political

* Cultural

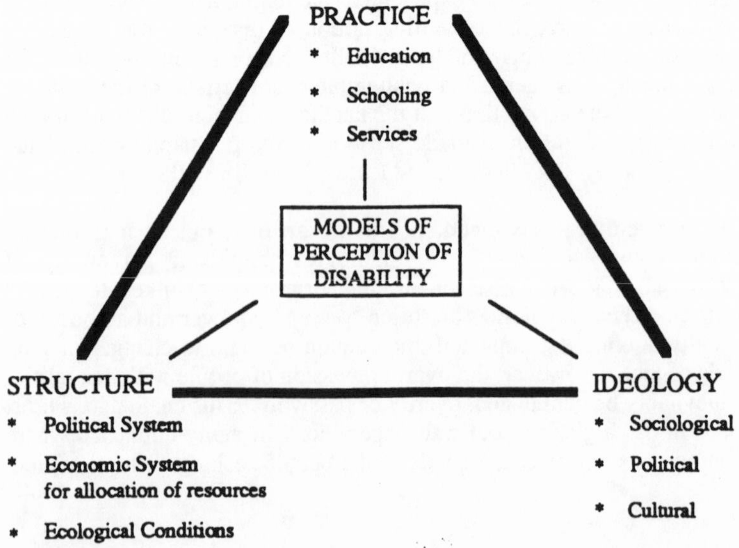

An examination of the causal relations among structure, ideology and practice should be useful in understanding how the task of transmitting values and educational goals for people with disabilities is accomplished, leading us toward a greater understanding of conditions needed to improve their life chances.

APPLICATION OF THE MODEL TO PERCEPTIONS OF DISABILITY

WHO and similar classification systems present a view of disability as linear and progressive. These systems are focused on inputs (innate characteristics), immediate cause, and a one-to-one correspondence between disability and function. By contrast, the framework proposed here is composed of reciprocal relations. Forces in the environment (e.g., cultural values, political ideologies, and economic resources) combine in an interactive manner. The focus is on outcomes and underlying causes.

Analyzing the causal relations between structure, ideology, and practice requires a four-step process. The first step in applying the analytical framework proposed here is to begin with a description of structure, including the political economy, geographic data and demographic information such as patterns of disability due to climate and access to health care, organizational systems, and allocation of financial and human resources.

The second step involves the articulation of practice that is rooted in historical, political, economic, and empirical contexts. Specifically, one examines a particular group's educational system, national goals and priorities related to education, as well as related services that legitimize and support the prevailing ideology.

The third step overlies political ideologies for understanding structure and practice. Several ideologies are possible. Williamson suggests four: 1) capitalist ideologies that are driven by the logic of the need for profit and are necessarily inegalitarian and essentially exploitive; 2) developed socialist ideologies that are "classless," and characterized by centralized industrialization; 3) dependency ideologies that are driven by external domination, and experience poverty and illiteracy; and 4) underdeveloped socialist ideologies that emphasize the development of collectivization and focus on a consciousness change on the part of the masses (Williamson,

College of St. Francis Library
Joliet, Illinois

149,823

1979). Cultural and sociological ideologies underpin and support or challenge the prevailing political ideology. These ideologies are represented in the diverse societal groups in this book. Their practical application and outcome will emerge from the chapters that follow.

The fourth step applies four paradigms (models of perception of disability) to structure, practice, and ideology. These paradigms may be conceived of as ideological/cultural lenses of perception that underlie the consequences for educational practice. They link the relations and tensions between political, cultural, and economic spheres of influence in schools. These lenses are consistent with sociological theories of the relations between social class and structure on the one hand, and practice on the other. They draw relations between people, the kinds of knowledge produced, and the consequences in terms of allocation to positions in society and legitimation of their roles.

This alternative framework leads one to ask questions about 1) the purpose of schools, 2) who benefits from schooling, 3) what should individuals aim for in their lives, 4) how are notions of disability actively learned and internalized, and/or challenged and transformed, 5) what is the relation of culture to schooling and the politics of difference.

MODELS OF PERCEPTION OF DISABILITY: THE PARADIGMS

The four paradigms are explanations of the ways in which cultural values determine how disability is constructed at the societal level through diverse forms of producing knowledge about disability. They make problematic the assumptions upon which the truth claims of disability research are currently grounded. They decenter, while they remap, forcing us to reframe our thinking into terms much broader than individual function.

The four paradigms are ideal typologies. They are conceived of as specific models for the perception of disability defined by assumptions, educational goals, consequences and problems. No one country is likely to represent one type perfectly. In fact, several paradigms may be present simultaneously with varying degrees of intensity, and/or struggling for dominance. However, their practical use lies in their application to the structure and practice of schooling (as well as other forms of cultural borders) in order to understand causal relations that explain the treatment of and attitudes toward persons with disabilities. These paradigms are summarized in Table 1 below. They are discussed in detail in the following sections.

Table 1

Cultural Paradigms of Disability and Education

PARADIGM	ASSUMPTIONS	EDUCATIONAL GOALS	CONSEQUENCES	PROBLEMS
Medical	Individuals have a disease and/or are innately different. The idea of normalcy is the absence of pathological symptoms.	Prescription and treatment are based on health needs to effect a cure. Schools separate students on basis of diagnosis of disease.	Access to services is dependent on diagnosis. Students and their families are passive "patients" dependent on professional "gatekeepers."	Students' social roles are denied. Students and families lack power and rights to help determine appropriate services.
Social	Students deviate from the norm in terms of ability to function in society.	Students receive remediation services by experts through societal filtering mechanisms and educational tracking.	Students and their families are victims of patronizing and sheltering. They are maintained in an inferior recipient status.	Students and families are denied self-determination.
Political	Disabled people are an oppressed minority whose problems are politically constructed.	Integration into the mainstream and equality of educational access and opportunity to reach full potential is stressed. Emphasis is on how schooling affects life chances.	Students' place in society is politically validated. Full participation and full rights are extended to all. Students and their families have expert knowledge and input into educational decision-making.	Rights are influenced by legislation and political power. Pressure groups must be constantly vigilant to maintain rights.
Pluralistic	Normal functioning is relative to cultural values and beliefs.	Differences are recognized as positive influences on all children and are adapted to in classroom environments. Equity is stressed as an affirmative goal. Special help should be provided for diverse groups.	Behavior toward individual differences reflects value of diversity and the belief that everyone has a contribution to make.	Communication of shared values across diverse groups may be problematic. Political inequality may hamper social equity.

The Medical Paradigm

The first ideal typology of perception is the Medical Paradigm. Its assumptions are characteristic of the sociological theory of functionalism. From the functionalist's perspective, individuals are allocated to their places in society according to abilities. Selection involves two components: labeling and separation. Exemplified by sociologists such as Parsons, Dreeben, and Inkeles, the functionalist theory of socialization emphasizes the preparation of societal members for competency as adults. These same attributes are characteristic of the medical paradigm of disability: students are labeled as diseased and separated on the basis of this diagnosis into separate programs where they are made functional for their place in society as a handicapped person. Known as the diagnostic-prescriptive approach to remediation, it concentrates on the individual, at the expense of context.

Persons who subscribe to this paradigm assume that pathological symptoms may be objectively assessed. Application of a label to abnormality reduces ambiguity. We can ascribe physical/mental characteristics to a particular person and thereby foreclose knowledge about the person's history, self-image, character and social status. The disability becomes the paramount characteristic of such a person. ". . . a handicap is considered by others to be integral--'essential'--to the handicapped person's social being is treated differently because of his handicap, and he is expected to behave differently" (Gliedman and Roth, 1980: 20).

Educational goals for those who adhere to this paradigm become focused on health needs to effect a cure. Where a cure is not possible, as is the case with most disabilities, goals are developed that conform to prescribed expectations. Blind people are trained as piano tuners and masseurs, deaf people assemble parts, mentally impaired people learn repetitive and simple janitorial tasks. Special schools for "the blind," "the deaf," and "the physically impaired" are constructed where professionals specializing in their training can assure their successful adaptation to their disability.

The consequences of the medical perception of disability are twofold. First, individual differences are collectivized. Specifically, differences in adaptability, motivation, and interest are washed out and buried under the rubric of "blindness," "deafness," or "mental retardation." The schooling experience becomes a matter of fitting a prescribed characteristic to a task. Second, students and their families must passively accept their fate as prescribed by professionals. In fact, many are made to feel fortunate to be the recipients of these services. Any challenge to the appropriateness of the educational "services" they receive is met with powerful resistance from educators who have been effectively indoctrinated by their profession to sustain their deficit-oriented approach to learning.

Lack of power and social roles are inherent problems within the Medical Model. The right to appropriate education is solely determined by experts. Students are denied choice. Their role in society is prescribed. Limited by their lack of ability to assume social roles, students are consigned to a narrow future position in society.

The Social Paradigm

Social exchange theory tells us how schools function to reproduce inequalities and is consistent with the Social Paradigm of Disability. Social exchange theory includes the perspectives of Levi-Strauss, Christopher Jencks, and Peter Blau, who see education as service organization. The concern is to provide for the welfare of the client.

Students with disabilities are still viewed as deviating from the norm in the Social Paradigm, but in terms broader than innate biological or pathological conditions. Social pathology introduces the idea that a disabled person's function is limited in terms of ability to perform social roles and expectations. Social inferiority of students with disabilities is inferred by others because of the loss of bodily function. This view contains the essential equivalent of the Medical Paradigm in its focus on deficits; however, in a "weaker" form. (The Medical Paradigm strongly insists on innate deficits. The Social Paradigm diffuses the argument with its focus on deviance from *external* norms of functioning.)

The result is to perpetuate educational goals in the narrow confines of remediation through diagnosis and prescription. Many developed countries' practice of labeling students as mildly handicapped falls within this rubric. Students who are difficult to teach, who do not conform to classroom rules, or who seem to be slow learners are labeled as "learning disabled," "socially maladjusted," or "educable mentally retarded." These students lack biological symptoms, or present ambiguous medical diagnosis. They may be well adjusted in home and community settings, but do not fit the mold of schools (specifically, school norms as reflected by societal expectations).

Schools respond by servicing students through societal filtering mechanisms and educational tracking. Students are removed, for all or part of the day, from mainstream classrooms and provided with specialized training by experts. "Typically the client does not know what will serve his/her best interests and is therefore vulnerable and subordinate to the professional who has power based on expertise. The institutionalized norms are such that the professional is expected to exercise this power in the interests of the client, the mechanisms for social control being self policing by the professionals" (Murphy, 1979: 46). The commonly agreed upon goal is to prepare students to reenter the mainstream with functional social and vocational skills. However, this rarely happens. Students are kept in a state of perpetual preparation, never seeming to "catch up" or "catch on" to what is required of them.

The consequences of this paradigm are similar to those of the Medical Paradigm. Students are maintained in an inferior recipient status. They and their families are sheltered from the "real" world. Their civil liberties are often curtailed-barring them from choices open to "normal" children, e.g., the right to attend their neighborhood school with their siblings. Students and their families are denied self-determination in the Social Paradigm. In this respect, they experience many of the prejudices and stereotypes traditionally directed at other minorities who often end up as welfare recipients because of unequal access to quality education.

Both the Medical Paradigm and the Social Paradigm are consensus views of disability. Consistency of disability definitions and continuity of rules governing their treatment are required. They are equilibrium paradigms whereby an individual is locked into a network of social relations, dependent on others for support and cooperation, and eager to earn the good will and approbation of others (Parsons, 1983). The problem with these paradigms is in their failure to explain degrees of competition and conflicting values.

The Political Paradigm

Conflict theory in education, developed most notably by Marx and Weber, studies conflict between groups. While Marx focuses on economic conflict (the bourgeoisie who own the means of production and the proletariats who do not) and Weber emphasizes cultural factors in conflict, the possibility of conflict is inherent in class relations for both. The

Political Paradigm of Disability similarly emphasizes conflict through its assumptions that disabled people are an oppressed minority.

Disability is no longer considered innate from this perspective, either biologically or socially. Those who espouse the Political Paradigm of disability insist that disability as a condition that an individual has must be disentangled from the handicap (the social ramification) of the condition. The central message is that disability is a socially constructed and historically mediated category of experience (Harris & Wideman, 1988: 116). In other words, obstacles to education, employment, and personal relations exist, not because of inherent incapacities, but because of the physical and attitudinal barriers socially and politically constructed by the environment. These socially imposed barriers begin at birth, carry through to the onset of schooling, and subsequently manifest themselves far beyond classroom boundaries.

This ideology has manifested itself in various forms of legislation. Manifestos declare the rights of people with disabilities, not only for equal access to education, but for equal employment opportunities, and access to public buildings and services. This legislation has not been gained without struggle, and has been attained largely through the efforts of disabled people themselves and their advocates who organize in political voting blocs and pressure groups. Opposition has often been stiffest from within the educational community. Educators have viewed assertion of educational self-determination on the part of people with disabilities as an assault on their expertise and professional judgment.

Proponents of the Political Paradigm reject the deficit focus in favor of an emphasis on abilities. The goal is full integration, equality of educational access, and opportunity to reach full potential. Students and their families are no longer passive recipients of educational welfare programs provided by professionals who know best, but are themselves the experts. Their knowledge and input in educational decision-making is not only necessary, but paramount. The model insists on the social validation of disabled people's place in society.

Because their rights are gained through legislation and political power, pressure groups must be constantly vigilant to maintain their rights in the face of open disagreement and conflict from competing groups. In addition, legislation does not always guarantee implementation. Attitudes of classroom teachers, employers, and society in general undermine efforts toward full integration. As a result, many school children with disabilities may be physically integrated in classrooms but remain socially isolated and academically under-achieving due to lack of access to alternative modes of learning within these classrooms. Schools too often become sites of failure rather than equal opportunity.

The Pluralistic Paradigm

Social interaction theory considers that "social reality is a creation of social participants, and that social categories and social knowledge are not given or natural, but are socially constructed--a product of conscious communication and action between people" (Tomlinson, 1982: 19). Socialization occurs within a "context," or a "particular understanding of culture associated with a concept of social place" (Wentworth, 1980: 2). Social processes are complex, and thus carry with them the possibilities of complementarity, reciprocity, antithesis, and rivalry in one structural model of education.

The Pluralistic Paradigm of disability is consistent with social interaction theory. Those groups where the cultural pluralism ideology prevails view normal functioning as relative to cultural values and beliefs. Student characteristics are believed to be both socially constructed and culturally mediated identities. Differences are recognized as positive influences and behavior toward individual differences reflects the value placed on diversity and the belief that everyone has a contribution to make. Many children grow up in a vastly different social world from that manifested in the policies and practices of schools. "The black child who seems maladjusted when judged by the norms of mainstream society may be very well adjusted indeed to the social life that the mainstream imposes on his minority group" (Gliedman & Roth, 1980: 47). By the same token, students with perceived disabilities often exhibit normal adjustment to the injustices of schooling. Rejection of a stigmatizing label through "acting out" behavior may be a healthy attempt to preserve self-determination and self-worth.

Educational goals in the Pluralistic Paradigm stress equality. Differences are recognized as positive influences on all children and are adapted to in classroom environments. In essence:

> The organization of formal teaching as given in schools and
> the concept of the school itself greatly depend on the

cultural model, and on the importance and significance attached in each culture to knowledge and on the actual representation of knowledge within a given society or community. Thus each culture influences in its own way the organization of experience and the formation of cognitive abilities and even generates its own teaching [and learning] model[s]. CERI, 1989: 62

Overall, the educational objectives of the Pluralistic Paradigm are these: 1) to embrace the nature of diversity as a positive force, 2) to foster sensitivities and respect for diverse learners, 3) to recognize the role of cultural factors that mediate the perceptions and treatment of diversity. Cutting across all objectives is the question, "How does culture act as a filter to impede or facilitate the maximum potential of individual students?"

From the pluralistic perspective, treatment of minority children is no longer solely a therapy problem or a legal problem, but involves cultural policy. The notion of diversity is central to cultural policy. Diversity embraces the full spectrum of differences, including such factors as communication, linguistic, physical, sensory, behavioral, affective, and cognitive differences. This view of diversity embraces both individual characteristics and those that exist within and across social/cultural groups, so that students are viewed not as having a particular characteristic or a homogeneous group. Cultural policy goes beyond the concentration on legal issues characteristic of the Political Paradigm. It necessarily must involve all children, or it reverts to the case of compensatory and welfare programs. It is predicated on the assumption that modern societies can survive and thrive only when different cultures coexist.

Both the Political Paradigm and the Pluralistic Paradigm assume conflicting points of view are inherent in cultural values. The Political Paradigm strongly asserts this conflict in its recognition of oppression. The Pluralistic Paradigm is a weaker version of conflict. It strives for equity among diverse groups whose values however, may rest on the need for political equity. When political equity is not accomplished, social equity may be hampered.

SUMMARY

The paradigms of disability, their theoretical underpinnings, and their outcomes are summarized below in Table 2. In addition to the inherent characteristics of the paradigms described above, their world views have several overarching elements. They may be manifest (through schools, teachers, and texts) or latent (through family expectations and conditioning factors such as socio-economic status), political in nature and tied to economic concerns. However, economic form does not totally prefigure cultural form. Economy is not a mechanism, but a social process. Economic allocation of resources involves choices, preferences, and knowledge. All of these elements may be formed by the individual or groups, and may operate at different levels (national, regional, local, family). The ideologies may also be strong or weak in their formation and legitimation.

Table 2:   Paradigms of Disability, their supporting
Ideological/Cultural Theory and Outcomes

PARADIGM	SUPPORTING THEORY	OUTCOMES
Medical	Functional (Dis)ability	Labeling Segregation
Social	Social Exchange Welfare Provision	Educational Tracking Professional Gatekeepers
Political	Class Conflict	Unequal Class Relations Struggle for Political Power
Pluralistic	Symbolic Interactionism	Social Knowledge Individual Difference as Positive Contribution

Overall, the ideological/cultural paradigms proposed for the study of education and disability in cross cultural perspective begin with practice, describing its contours and context. At the next layer of analysis, the official ideology behind this practice is described, focusing on the ideology of the political system (supported or challenged by cultural and sociological ideologies) and its extent of legitimation transmitted by educational policies. The theories underlying the typologies are then applied to discover the connections between structure, ideology and practice and to determine the extent to which ideology masks practice. The ultimate purpose is to begin to describe possible causal relations between public policy and educational practice as it relates to people with disabilities, leading us toward an understanding of the process of education and its outcomes in terms of their quality of life. The central focus on paradigms as prevailing cultural values guides us to ask questions about the meaning of institutions, behavior, and policy. Understanding culture as lived experiences within systems of meaning inform the directions of a worldwide process of nation building governed by an emerging transnational, world cultural system.

References

Apple, Michael W. (1982). *Education and Power*. Boston, MA: Routledge and Kegan Paul.

Aronowitz, Stanley and Henry A. Giroux (1991). *Postmodern Education: Politics, Culture and Social Criticism*. Minneapolis, MN: University of Minnesota Press.

CERI (Centre for Educational Research and Innovation) (1989). *One School, Many Cultures*. Paris: Organization for Economic Co-operation and Development.

Epstein, I. (1989, June). Paper delivered at the *VIIth World Congress of Comparative Education*. Montreal, Canada.

Furlong, V.J. (1991). "Disaffected Pupils: Restructuring the Sociological Perspective," in *British Journal of Sociology of Education*. Vol. 12, No. 3. pp. 293-307.

Gliedman, John and William Roth (1980). *The Unexpected Minority: Handicapped Children in America*. New York: Harcourt Brace Jovanovich.

Harris, Adrienne and Dana Wideman (1988). "The Construction of Gender and Disability in Early Attachment" in *Women with Disabilities: Essays in Psychology, Culture and Politics*. Michelle Fine and Adrienne Asch (eds). Philadelphia, PA: Temple University Press.

Hegarty, Seamus, Keith Pocklington and Dorothy Lucas (1984). *Educating Pupils with Special Needs in the Ordinary School*. Windsor, Great Britain: NFER - Nelson.

Marshall, Catherine, Douglas Mitchell and Frederick Wirt (1989). "A Cultural Framework for Studying State Policy," in *Culture and Education Policy in the American States*. New York: The Falmer Press.

Meighan, R. (1981). *A Sociology of Educating*. London: Holt, Rinehart and Winston.

Meyer, John W., John Boli and George Thomas (1987). "Ontology and Rationalization in the Western Cultural Account," in *Institutional Structure Constituting State, Society and the Individual*. George M. Thomas, John W. Meyer, F. Ramirez and J. Boli (eds). Beverly Hills, CA: Sage Publications.

Murphy, R. (1979). *Sociological Theories of Education*. Toronto: McGraw-Hill Ryerson Limited.

Parsons, Talcott (1983). "The School as a Social System: Some of its Functions in American Society," in *Education, Policy, and Society: Theoretical Perspectives*. London: Routledge and Kegan Paul.

Ramirez, Francisco O. and John Boli (1987). "Global Patterns of Educational Institutionalization," in *Institutional Structure Constituting State, Society and the Individual*. George M. Thomas, John W. Meyer, F. Ramirez and J. Boli (eds.). Beverly Hills, CA: Sage Publications.

Sarason, Seymour B. (1991). *The Predictable Failure of Educational Reform*. San Francisco, CA: Jossey-Bass Publishers.

Tomlinson, S. (1982). *A Sociology of Special Education*. London: Routledge and Kegan Paul.

Wentworth, W. (1980). *Context and Understanding: An Inquiry into Socialization Theory*. New York, NY: Elsevier North Holland, Inc.

Williamson, B. (1979). *Education, Social Structure and Development: A Comparative Analysis*. London: The Macmillan Press Ltd.

CHAPTER 3

DISABILITY AND EDUCATION: SOME OBSERVATIONS ON ENGLAND AND WALES

by Len Barton

INTRODUCTION

Government priorities, decisions, and the values informing them are all part of the public manifestation of the intentions and vision they hold with regard to the form of society they wish to see develop and continue. Thus, the allocation of human and material resources are fundamentally political decisions. Their significance is much more crucial in a societal context in which there are both limited resources and extensive inequalities arising from the existing economic and structural relations. Questions of power and control are central in this situation. The nature of discrimination and its impact on the lives of different groups must be carefully explored and exposed. This will be particularly important where a "blaming the victim" mentality represents the official discourse used to explain these conditions and experiences (Ryan, 1976).

All governments are concerned with controlling human service provision. This includes the issue of funding and the extent to which investment in particular institutions results in the sorts of economic and cultural reforms that are viewed as worthwhile. However, what has been markedly different about the past decade in the British Context, has been the extent and nature of such interventions. Under the guise of a populist rhetoric of freedom of the individual, consumer choice and the value of competition, an unprecedented series of interventions has taken place.

This process covers education, health, and welfare provisions and has involved the introduction of extension legislation. Underpinning these developments has been the application of a free market ideology. Government interest has focused on a radical restructuring of provision and there has been perennial concern with where and how the system is to be managed and what will be the outcomes. The emphasis is on control.

The sheer number, speed and cumulative effect of these changes in definitions, purposes and priorities, the reformulations of the relationship between the individual and the state, the overthrow of trade union dominance, programs of privatization, the introduction of a new morality reinforcing conservative values concerning the family and the role of women and the celebration of excessive individualism through a belief in the centrality of the market, all bear testimony to the significant impact of state intervention (Cultural Studies, 1991; Barton, 1991; Hindees, 1990; David, 1986; Dale, 1990, and Whitty, 1989).

The actions of government have not been without critics and these have covered a range of concerns including: the confrontational manner in which government has conducted itself during this period. Little real consultation has been involved (Simon, 1988); the explicit political interference in, for example, the content of the curriculum and the use of the policy during conflicts with trade unionists (Braid, 1990 and Fine & Millar, 1985); and the deliberate attempts by Government to destroy the role of the local authorities in the administration of and control of education, welfare, and housing provision (Ranson, 1990 and Papadakis, 1990).

In this chapter I will attempt to briefly explore the vision underpinning developments within the field of education and more importantly the values informing these processes of change. This will include the impact of such interventions on the position and experiences of disabled people. The perspective offered in this chapter is not the only one available but it is one which increasing numbers of disabled people support. It is also my perspective on the situation in England and Wales and the definitions offered make no claim to being universally applicable.

Whilst adopting this approach I am reminded of the insightful statement of Apple (1986) in his discussion of alternative perspectives to those informing current policy of education. He maintains that:

The critical power of any social analysis does not arise
from some alleged disinterestedness. This is often
illusory in many ways in the first place. Rather it stems
from the ability of such an investigation to help us pass
judgement upon social realities that seem unjust (p. 180).

For him such insights are shaped by his political actions in various
arenas in education in the United States. This is similarly so for me in
this country. Furthermore, the ideas and issues surrounding the question
of education and disability are not to be viewed as natural or immutable.
They are both complex and contestable social constructions. As such,
they need to be struggled over. This is vitally important in a social
context in which people's understandings, access to knowledge, and
opportunities are unevenly distributed. Thus, the question of whose
interpretation or vision is being seen as significant, with what
consequences and why, must be critically engaged. Too often specific
perspectives supporting the position of more powerful groups are
depicted, and through time perceived to be, both natural and universal
(Eagleton, 1991). These forms of taken-for-grantedness need to be
carefully analyzed and those tendencies within society which would close
down discussion and dialogue between all parties must be resisted.
Finally, in taking this stance it must not be interpreted as a desire to get
back or recapture some golden age of the past. This would be romantic
and counter-productive (Coulby, 1991). Rather, the concern is to resist
complacency and to recognize the degree of struggle still to be engaged
with if rhetoric is to be translated into reality in substantive terms in the
lives of all citizens, including the disabled. Romantic visions and
idealistic rhetoric have too often resulted in human suffering,
disappointment, and disillusionment.

DISABILITY AS A FORM OF OPPRESSION

Disability is a complex issue. Definitions are crucial in that the
presuppositions informing them can be the basis of stereotyping and
stigmatization. One of the dominant influences shaping policies and
practices has been the medical model. From this perspective there is an
emphasis upon an individual's inabilities or deficiencies. "Able-bodiness"

is seen as the acceptable criterion of "normality." A medical model according to Hahn (1985) ". . . imposes a presumption of biological or physiological inferiority upon disabled persons" (p. 89). Terms such as "cripple" or "spastic" reinforce such an individualized medical definition in which functional limitations predominate.

In a powerful critique of the medical model, Brisenden (1986) who was himself a disabled person vividly describes his feelings in the following way:

> We are seen as "abnormal" because we are different; we are problem people, lacking the equipment for social integration. But the truth is, like everybody else, we have a range of things we *can* and *cannot* do, a range of abilities both mental and physical that are unique to us as individuals. The only difference between us and other people is that we are viewed through spectacles that only focus on our inabilities, and which suffer an automatic blindness--a sort of medicalized social reflex--regarding our abilities. (p. 3)

Historically, disability has been viewed fundamentally as a *personal tragedy*, which has resulted in disabled people being seen as objects of pity or in need of charity. They have been subject to discriminatory policies and practices in which the predominate images of passivity and helplessness reinforced their inferior status. One effect of such perspective is that it provides a variety of individualized responses to disabled people. For example, they are often viewed in heroic terms, as being brave and courageous. Their position is constantly being compared against an assumed notion of "normality." Indeed, it is the pursuit of this "which leads to neurosis and is the cause of much guilt and suffering" (Brisenden, 1986, p. 3) on their part.

Disabled people have struggled against such disabilist definitions and the discriminatory policies and practices which are shaped by them. An alternative definition involving a set of different assumptions, priorities, and explanations is provided by Hahn (1986), himself a disabled social analyst. He maintains:

. . . . disability stems from the failure of a structured social environment to adjust to the needs and aspirations of citizens with disabilities rather than from the inability of a disabled individual to adapt to the demands of society. (p. 128).

It is an unadaptive, unhelpful, and unfriendly environment which needs to be examined and changed. Being interested in how disabled people suffer requires an examination of those material conditions and social relations which contribute to their dehumanization and isolationism.

Participation in society is not contingent upon merely the individual limitations of disabled people, but rather, the physical and social restrictions of an essentially hostile environment. Writing on the question of the politics of disability, Oliver (1990) summarizes the essential features of such an alternative position:

All disabled people experience disability as social restriction, whether those restrictions occur as a consequence of inaccessible built environments, questionable notions of intelligence and social competence, the inability of the general public to use sign language, the lack of reading material in braille or hostile public attitudes to people with non-visible disabilities. (p. XIV Introduction).

He maintains that disabled people are involved in a difficult struggle in which they must strengthen their endeavors as a political pressure group. Disability is thus a social and political category in that it entails practices of regulation and struggles for choice, empowerment and opportunities (Fulcher, 1989).

In a society fundamentally organized and administered by and for able-bodied people the position of disabled people in relation to education, work, housing and welfare services is a matter of grave concern (Abberley, 1987; Oliver, 1990). Indeed, in many ways it is a scandal and a reflection of their marginalization, low status and vulnerability as well as an indication of the power struggle in which they are, and must continue to be, involved. Relationships with various professional agencies are often difficult and disabled people have vociferously argued for a range of changes. These include greater choice in the nature and amount of services provided, more control over the allocation of resources, especially in relation to independent living, and new forms of accountability of service providers to disabled people involving clear mechanisms for handling disagreements (Brisenden, 1986; Oliver & Hasler, 1987; Oliver, 1988).

So far I have argued that disability needs to be understood as a form of oppression. Being disabled entails social and economic hardships as well as assaults upon self-identity and emotional well being. However, it would be both disabilist and misleading to give the impression that disabled people are a homogeneous group. Terms such as "the disabled" are a catch-all and give an impression of sameness. But the difficulties and responses to being disabled are influenced by class, race, gender, and age factors. These can cushion or compound the experience of discrimination and oppression. For example, in a study of disabled women receiving care Begum (1990) maintains that:

> . . . . women with disabilities are perennial outsiders; their oppression and exclusion renders them one of the most powerless groups in society. The personal care situation encapsulates so many different dynamics that for many women with disabilities it becomes the arena where their oppression becomes so clearly magnified and distilled. (p. 79)

Supporting this perspective, Morris (1989) illustrates from the lives of a group of disabled women, including her own, that matters of privacy, body-image and sexuality are a source of tension and difficulties in relation to the "care" situation. Also, she highlights the disadvantages disabled mothers experience in having responsibility for the upbringing of the children and general running of the home as well as maintaining some form of outside employment. The degree to which individuals can survive within these conditions will be largely contingent upon their socio-economic circumstances.

Without denying the significance of the different levels of discrimination experienced by individuals, which in itself needs more careful consideration, the fundamental position taken in this brief overview is that all " . . . people with impairments experience discrimination every day of their lives . . ." (Barnes, 1991, preface). Indeed, in the study by Barnes ". . . conceived, sponsored and written with the full co-operation of disabled people and their organizations . . ." (preface) we are provided with a most comprehensive account of the alarming extent of institutional discrimination against disabled people in this country. The research covers education, employment, the benefits system, health, housing and transport, leisure and political life. The overwhelming nature of the case of discrimination leads the author to contend that the struggle for empowerment must include the issue of human rights and the development and implementation of anti-discrimination legislation.

THE CASE OF EDUCATION

Schools are not immune from external influences nor can their activities be described as neutral. Schooling is a system of social practice which gives priority to particular forms of knowledge, evaluative procedures and outcomes. Schools are linked to other powerful institutions which themselves, in complex ways, contribute to the generation and maintenance of social inequalities (Apple, 1990). Thus schooling " . . . is part of a larger process of winning consent to discrepancies in power and opportunity" (Johnson, 1991, p. 77).

Carrier (1990) in an analysis of research findings in the United States and the United Kingdom, is interested in the ways in which pupil performance is understood, how pupils are identified in terms of that understanding and what external forces influence these practices. He maintains that the notions of educational success and pupil failure have been largely taken for granted within the school system and that there has been no demand to articulate them. Within special education such practices are given much greater significance, in that models of difference are essential to the functioning of those institutions. Pupils are defined as bright or failures within a social process and cultural understandings that have, in the United States, influenced the ways "retarded" people have been viewed. They have been seen as menaces needing control, unfortunate people needing services, and members of an under-privileged minority. By identifying the significance of cultural factors in the social construction of categories, Carrier (1990) maintains that, in relation to professionals, we cannot:

> . . . assume that they understand what those pupils do in terms of unproblematic objective assessments, so we cannot assume that those dealings will unproblematically reflect pupil's abilities and disabilities (p. 215).

This raises, therefore, the relevance of social factors in this process and the power of significant others to define the nature of people's abilities and behavior. External forces play their part in shaping the nature of these interactions and outcomes. For Carrier, these include the rise of industrial capitalism, the growth of egalitarianism and individualistic beliefs and the spread of mass compulsory schooling. They have contributed to the development and maintenance of special education and to its primary function of legitimating the distinction between the "special" and "normal" child.

Various arguments have contributed at different historical periods to providing the impetus and maintenance of segregated schooling, particularly for those pupils with severe learning difficulties. Whilst these are not in any order of priority they include the following perspectives. First, this population is viewed as immature, childlike and thus in need of protection from hostile and damaging aspects of the environment. These include mainstream schools and the impersonal nature of their size, their emphasis on academic learning and competitiveness, and the exposure to the cruel and taunting activities of their "normal" peers. The obverse side of this coin is that, firstly, segregated schooling is much more benign. Secondly, the teachers in these schools are depicted as possessing particular qualities, including dedication, love, and patience. It is these which make such teachers special and more fitted to meet the "special needs" of these pupils. Thirdly, the justification has also included the significance given to the special curriculum provided within special schools. Finally, support is offered on administrative/efficiency grounds. The centralizing of specialist equipment, support services, and specialist teachers is seen to be a most effective deployment of resources. Thus, this form of provision is depicted as being in the best interests of these children and young people.

Part of the difficulties with this type of discourse supporting segregated provision is that it depoliticizes the issues involved and does not engage with the wider socio-economic context in which discussions concerning schooling need to be located. Increasing numbers of disabled people are expressing their criticisms of segregated provisions (Reiser & Mason, 1990; Oliver, 1990 and Barnes, 1990). Not only do these refer to issues of low expectations and over-protective attitudes on the part of staff, but also the contribution these schools make to the powerful means of legitimating stereotypes often based on ignorance. Morris (1990) illustrates this conviction in the following remarks:

> People's expectations of us are informed by their previous experience of disabled people. If disabled people are segregated, are treated as alien, as different in a fundamental way, then we will never be accepted as full members of society. *This is the strongest argument against special schools and against separate provision* (p. 59).

Or again, the extent and intensity of the criticisms can be seen in some of the concluding remarks by Barnes (1991) on the topic of segregated "special" provision. He maintains that:

> . . . many young people with impairments have little choice but to accept segregated "special" education which is both educationally and socially divisive, and which fails to provide them with the necessary skills for adult living. Moreover, by producing educationally and socially disabled adults in this way the "special" education system perpetuates the false assumption that disabled people are somehow inadequate, and thus legitimates discrimination in all other areas of social life, particularly employment (p. 227).

Being excluded from daily interactions with their contemporaries means their knowledge of the social world is limited and hardly constitutes a good preparation for participation in society (Fish, 1985).

Sociologists have been critical of those arguments which depict "benevolent humanitarianism" as the sole grounds for government responses in the form of segregated provision (Barnes, 1990; Tomlinson, 1982; Ford et al., 1982, and Barton & Tomlinson, 1984). From a systems perspective, they have maintained that such provision has been an essential means of removing objectionable, unwanted pupils and thereby enabling the mainstream system to function more effectively. This form of interpretation involves a consideration of the socioeconomic, race, and gender composition of the pupils in special schools. This is also an approach that is receiving increasing sociological and historical support in other countries (Soder, 1984; Lewis, 1988; Carrier, 1986; and Skrtic, 1991).

Some educational psychologists have also offered critical commentaries on special schools. Much of their work has been based on a desire for a truly comprehensive system of school provision (Dessent, 1987; and Booth, 1983). The continuation of segregated schooling is attributable mainly to the weaknesses of current policy on comprehensive schools and Dessent (1987) also contends that:

> Special schools do not have a right to exist. They exist because of the limitations of ordinary schools in providing for the full range of abilities and disabilities among children. It is not primarily a question of the quality or adequacy of what is offered in a special school. Even a superbly well organized special school offering the highest quality curriculum and educational input to its children has no right to exist if that same education can be provided in a mainstream school (p. 97).

This perspective is a good example of the level of commitment that some analysts bring to this issue. It also relates to a particular meaning of integration. Supporting this perspective, Booth (1981) maintains that integration is about questions of power and of enabling pupils to have greater participation in the life of the school. This involves challenging notions of selection and ability and being engaged in the establishment of schools which do not exclude children.

The Warnock Report

In 1974 a government-appointed Committee was established with the following terms of reference:

> To review educational provision in England, Scotland and Wales for children and young people handicapped by disabilities of body or mind, taking account of the medical aspects of their needs, together with arrangements to prepare them for entry into employment; to consider the most effective use of resources for these purposes; and to make recommendations (D E S, 1978, p. 1).

The Chair of the Committee was Mary Warnock, a Senior Research Fellow from Oxford University. The Committee's findings were published in an official report in 1978 which became more popularly known as the Warnock Report (D E S, 1978).

Opinions differ strongly as to the extent and nature of the significance of the Report. It was, however, historically unique by virtue of being the first Committee of Inquiry into the "Education of Handicapped Children and Young People." As a major review of existing provisions and practices, its influence was to be felt in various ways. It challenged, for example, medical notions of handicap and introduced the concept "continuum of educational needs." It confirmed the perspective that the purpose and goals of education for all children are the same. Education was thus viewed as a matter of right and not charity. Finally, it emphasized the centrality of service provision and the role of multi-professional teams in this process. Particular aspects of future legislation reflected these and other insights from the Report.

The Warnock Report provided a challenge to orthodox models based on the identification of defects. The Report emphasized the importance of context and resources and proposed a service model based on delivering the goods. It introduced:

> . . . a new conceptual framework within which special educational provision should be made. This entails a continuum of special educational need rather than discrete categories of handicap. It embraces children with significant learning difficulties as well as those with disabilities of mind or body (Warnock Report, 1978, p. 327).

The notion of "special educational need" applied to more than the 2% of children within special schools. According to Warnock, it related to approximately 20% of all children at school. One in five school children would, from this perspective, have special needs at sometime in their school career. The Committee sought to focus positive attention, not on defects, but on what a child needs if he or she is going to benefit from education.

Within the academic world the Report has acted as a stimulus for debate, critique and research. Several important criticisms have been made of the Report. These include the predominantly professional make-up of the Committee, resulting in the membership of a former pupil of a special school and the one token parent member. Professional definitions and priorities are thus maintained to have taken precedence over issues of human rights (Kirp, 1983). Secondly, Lewis and Vulliamy (1981) are critical of the significance given to psychological presuppositions and categories, and of the emphasis on administrative systems including the creation of an elaborate bureaucracy staffed by more "experts." They also maintain that the Committee neglected seriously the issue of social factors in the creation of learning difficulties. Lastly, criticism has focused on the limited consideration given to the question of the curriculum and the conservative and politically expedient values involved (Wood and Shears, 1986).

The question of the position of the Warnock Report in relation to integration is a contentious one; opinions clearly differ. We would concur with Booth (1981), that it is difficult to derive from the Report any unambiguous support for a fundamental shift in educational policy on this issue. Part of the reason for this relates to the strong lobby by supporters of segregated provision. Indeed, Wilson (1981) notes that:

> The bulk of the evidence submitted to the Warnock Committee clearly favoured the retention of special schools as part of a broader spectrum of special provision. (p. 7-our emphasis).

Warnock's failure to address the question of integration in relation to curriculum issues was a lost opportunity to challenge exclusive forms of discourse and practice and to contribute to the realization of a more equitable, or at least less divisive, system of educational provision. For Fulcher (1989b) the Warnock Report represents a conservative political perspective in which there is a celebration of the centrality of professionalism and a form of discourse on disability that serves to deflect rather than engage issues of justice and equality.

Since the Warnock Report (1978) numbers of special schools have shown a small reduction as can be seen from the following table (taken from Barnes, 1991).

Table 3.3   Numbers of Special Schools in
                       relation to Mainstream Schools

	No. of schools in mainstream sector*	No. of special schools
1978	29,059	1,591
1979	28,960	1,599
1980	28,869	1,597
1981	28,602	1,593
1982	28,195	1,571
1983	27,858	1,562
1984	27,362	1,548
1985	26,990	1,529
1986	26,682	1,493
1987	26,489	1,470
1988	26,305	1,443
1989	26,097	1,414
Total Change	-2,962	-177

*Includes maintained nursery, primary, secondary and
independent schools.
Source: Adapted from Table A30.89, pp. 175-6, DES, 1990.

However, Swann (1991) in an analysis of segregation statistics highlights
the varied nature of Local Education Authorities' special education
policies and provision. Whilst some LEAs:

Since 1982 . . . have considerably reduced the level of
segregation into special schools, . . . a smaller number
have done the opposite (p. 6).

This is also the case in relation to children sent to independent special schools.

Whilst the degree of government support for integration remains a highly questionable one, voluntary or independent organizations such as the Centre for Studies on Integration in Education have made an unequivocal stand by producing an Integration Charter. This contains the following points:

THE INTEGRATION CHARTER

Ending segregation in education for all children and young people with disabilities or learning difficulties.

1. We fully support an end to all segregated education on the grounds of disability or learning difficulty, as a policy commitment and goal for this country.

2. We see the ending of segregation in education as a human rights issue which belongs within equal opportunities policies.

3. We believe that all children share equal value and status. We therefore believe that the exclusion of children from the mainstream because of disability or learning difficulty is a devaluation and is discriminating.

4. We envisage the gradual transfer of resources, expertise, staff and pupils from segregated schools to an appropriately-supported and diverse mainstream.

5. We believe that segregated education is a major cause of society's widespread prejudice against adults with disabilities or difficulties. De-segregating special education is therefore a crucial first step in helping to change discriminatory attitudes, in creating greater understanding and in developing a fairer society.

6. We believe that efforts to increase participation of people with disabilities or difficulties in learning in community life will be seriously jeopardized unless segregated education is reduced and ultimately ended.

7. For these reasons we call on Central and local Governments to do all in their power to work as quickly as possible towards the goal of a de-segregated education system.

This type of call has had a mixed response nationally. However, the hope for the realization of a system of school provision which has an inclusive mentality underpinning policy and practice, one in which difference is positively valued and celebrated, has been seriously threatened by the introduction of a market approach to education.

EDUCATION AND THE IMPACT OF A MARKET IDEOLOGY

We are in the midst of an extensive restructuring of educational provision and practice. Centralized control is being accomplished through the articulation of a new vision over what schools must achieve and how that success and effectiveness is to be defined and monitored. A new set of values is being advocated. Central to this approach is a belief in the importance of competition and consumer choice. In a powerful analysis of the growing differentiations within school provision, Ball (1990a) maintains that:

Taken together this emerging stratification of schools not only rests upon a competition between schools, it also creates the basis for a large-scale return to competition for places between pupils. The competitive self-interest of families is underlined and the logic of Thatcherist individualism is ramified in the education system. The education market will tend to weaken social bonds (the social engineering project of comprehensive education is anathema to conservative thinking) and encourages strategies of exclusion and social closure; that is the generation of boundaries of positional hierarchy (p. 93).

An effective market must involve a range of products for consumers to choose from. This necessitates an increased diversity of school provision (Ranson, 1990). Within this climate pupils with special educational needs are not viewed as politically significant and questions of social justice and equity become marginalized. Thus the possibility of establishing a comprehensive integration policy becomes more difficult. Indeed, the whole question of integration may well become an increasingly contentious issue.

In this world of enterprise culture a new management language is being applied to schools which includes such key concepts as: efficiency, cost-effectiveness, targets, performance indicators, competencies, and appraisal. In this highly pressurized world, the task is to market or sell yourself. This will intensify competition throughout the system and serious questions need to be asked about the vulnerability of particular groups in this process. The diverse aspects of a market-led system could give greater legitimation to the demands for segregation.

The traditional relationship between Local Education Authorities and schools is being broken with delegated powers including finance being given to individual schools. The increased diversity of school provision is leading to a more hierarchical, sharply differentiated system of schooling. Thus, a discourse of the market is not only informing policy and practice but also changing the nature of public debate within which education is conceived. As Ball (1990b) contends:

Notions like equality and opportunity have been replaced initially by standards and quality and more recently the ground has shifted again to efficiency and value for money (p. 98).

Questions of entitlement, empowerment, meeting individual needs have to be set against the realities of existing unequal social conditions and relations. The real worry is that winners in such a context will be at the expenses of others. Family background, and geographical location, for example, will be influential factors in terms of the nature and extent of the benefits pupils receive in a diverse system of school provision (Coulby, 1991).

How resources are socially distributed, who has access to them, with what consequences are crucial political decisions. They raise fundamental questions of social justice and equity. What is of significance here are the values which inform both the policies and decision-making of government. In a discussion of the question of understanding "active citizenship" solely in economic terms, Ware (1990) is pessimistic about the implications of this for those people with multiple handicaps. Indeed the values underpinning much of the changes emanating from the 1988 Education Reform Act lead her to conclude that:

. . . it is hard to be anything other than extremely pessimistic about the future of education for children with multiple handicaps. Indeed, it may not be exaggerating to suggest that in the 1990s and 2000s they may once again be both segregated from their peers and catered for by unqualified and untrained staff (pp. 174-175).

This perspective not only illustrates the differential statuses within the disability community itself, but also the very real possibility that such differences, in terms of life chances and quality of experience, will be increased as the implementation of the 1988 Education Reform Act impacts on provision and practice.

DIVERSIONARY RHETORIC

Official documents and policy statements contain a great deal of high platitudes, good intentions and appealing rhetoric. Sociologists have argued for the importance of recognizing the *real* as opposed to the *stated* outcomes of such material relating to special education (Tomlinson, 1982; 1985; and Ford, et al., 1982). In an analysis of human services and their policies, Wolfensberger (1989) makes a distinction between manifest and latent functions. The manifest functions of such services contained in an avalanche of documents are:

> . . . that services are beneficent, charitable, benign, curative, habilitative, etc. (p. 26),

however,

> . . . while services may be some of those things some of the time, they also commonly perform latent functions very different from these proclaimed ones, including ones that are competency-impairing, destructive of independence, that are actually dependency-making and dependency-keeping, health-debilitating and outright death-accelerating, and thus killing (p. 26).

Wolfensberger sets this argument within the context of what he calls a "post-primary production economy." In this contemporary historical period human service systems produce dependency. An important aspect of this process is persuading disabled people and society at large to recognize that recipients of such services ought to be grateful for what they receive. By this means the workings of service systems are depoliticized. Whilst the previously outlined position may be viewed as extreme and mainly negative, from the perspective adopted in this chapter it has an important advantage. It confirms that discussions relating to the experiences and well-being of disabled people *must* be part of a socio-economic and historical analysis. Questions of social justice, equity and human rights will be central to this approach.

EQUAL OPPORTUNITIES

Political action is required if disabled people are to exercise control over their lives and their own agendas in relation to full participation in society. This is both a serious and urgent task. Writing on the question of the implementation of "Local Authorities' Equal Opportunities

Policies" Leach (1989) captures these sentiments in the following contention:

> Disabled people's issues are still seen, across much of the political spectrum, as largely non-political. Paternalism and the exclusion of disabled people from participation in decision-making, is still largely the norm (p. 75).

Given the nature of the definition of disability that this chapter has been concerned to briefly outline, it is essential that this issue is seen as an *integral* part of an equal opportunities perspective. This is for several reasons. First, because the experience of disability is part of the wider and fundamental issue of prejudice and economic inequality in which ideologies perform a socially divisive role. An equal opportunities approach will provide a stimulus for the crucial task of establishing connections between other discriminated groups in order that some common struggles can be engendered. Secondly, it will offer a basis for the identification of those features of the existing society, policy and practice that are unacceptable, offensive and need to be challenged and changed. Thirdly, it will be means of critiquing individualized and deficit models and interpretations. It removes the emphasis from one of being depicted as a personal trouble, to that of a public issue. Finally, it will contribute to such policies being non-disabilist by redressing the extent to which disability has been excluded from them, or merely attached as a bolt-on, tokenistic gesture (Leach, 1989, and Rieser & Mason, 1990).

In presenting this type of perspective it is important to be aware of how "equal opportunities" can mean different things to different people. It is not about gaining access or being able to compete against able-bodied people on equal terms. The stakes are much higher than this. What is required is a direct challenge to the status quo. The struggle for equal opportunities is one of disabled people being able to set their own agendas, define their needs and have real choices and rights. Thus as Findlay (1991) also argues:

> Equal Opportunities, therefore, means a struggle by people with disabilities to set a political and social agenda. We must demand that the idea of "disability" as a

"welfare issue" is scrapped. The power structures as well as the material structures which disadvantage and marginalize us, must both be up for discussion. It is not just an issue of having more choice in what is provided for us, but it is also about having the chance to control aspects of the services too (p. 14).

The breaking down of structures and their ideological supports which exclude, debilitate, and control disabled people must be part of a process which seeks some ultimate liberation and empowerment. We have no room for complacency in that we currently do not have any anti-discriminatory legislation in which the rights of disabled people are enshrined. Disabled people and their organizations are at the forefront of this struggle which is becoming more bitter and could increasingly lead to confrontations with law enforcement agencies and other authorities.

CONCLUSION

Underpinning the approach adopted in this chapter is a recognition that dominant ideologies and the practices emanating from them are neither natural nor unquestionably right. They are a social creation and thus amenable to change. This must not be taken to mean that economic and social relations and conditions can be thought away or that fundamental change can be easily achieved. What is important is the collective struggle for alternatives and as Williams (1983) maintained:

Once the inevitabilities are challenged, we begin gathering our resources for a journey of hope. If there are no easy answers there are still available discoverable hard answers, and it is these that we can now learn to make and share (pp. 268-9).

One of the difficulties to be engaged with if such a journey is to be effective are the fragmentations within and across disadvantaged groups.

This will include the gender, race and age factors which compound and even exacerbate such divisions.

In a critique of the predominate individualistic and deficit view on special needs in education Ainscow (1991) is concerned about the damage we do to children by conceptualizing "educational difficulties" in specific ways. He maintains we do not successfully teach all children and reinforces the question of the centrality of values in terms of our vision of education. Whilst recognizing the difficulties of much of the changes taking place in education today he nevertheless calls for a re-examination of the presuppositions informing current practice within schools.

Such a critical reflection does raise serious questions about the nature and purpose of schools. For example, how can we create schools that are inclusive and welcoming to all children irrespective of their class, gender, race, or disability? This raises the question of the extent to which particular perceptions of difference provide a basis for diversity or a mechanism for exclusion including discriminatory questions (Brah, 1992).

Full inclusion in society is a profound concern. It is a human rights issue involving participation, choice and empowerment. Prejudice, discrimination and oppression must be identified, challenged and ameliorated. For increasing numbers of disabled people this includes a critique of those unacceptable and offensive practices within special education. As Barnes' (1991) research and analysis illustrates:

> By producing socially and educationally disabled individuals, the "special" education system perpetuates and legitimates discriminatory practices in all other areas of social life, particularly employment. Therefore, if institutional discrimination against disabled people throughout British society is to be eliminated, this system must be eliminated too (p. 61).

A journey of hope involving such a project will be difficult and demanding. Whilst not easy, it is nevertheless necessary.

References

Abberley, P. (1987). "The Concept of Oppression and the Social Theory of Disability," in *Disability, Handicap and Society*, Vol. 2, No. 1, pp. 5-19.

Ainscow, M. (1991). "Effective schools for all: An alternative approach to special needs in education," in *Cambridge Journal of Education*, Vol. 21, No. 3, pp. 293-308.

Apple, M. (1986). *Teachers and Texts: A Political Economy of Class and Gender Relations in Education.* London: Routledge & Kegan Paul.

Apple, M. (1990). *Ideology and Curriculum.* London: Routledge. (2nd Edition).

Ball, S. (1990a). *Politics and Policy Making in Education and Explorations in Policy Sociology.* London: Routledge & Kegan Paul.

Ball, S. (1990b). "Markets, Inequality and Urban Schooling," in *The Urban Review*, Vol. 22, No. 2, pp. 85-100 (Special Issue).

Barnes, C. (1990). *Cabbage Syndrome.* Lewes: Falmer Press.

Barnes, C. (1991). *Disabled People in Britain and Discrimination. A Case for Anti-discrimination Legislation.* London: Hirst and Company.

Barton, L. and Tomlinson, S. (Eds.) (1984). *Special Education and Social Interests.* Beckenham: Croom Helm.

Barton, L. (1991). "Teachers Under Siege: A Case of Unmet Needs," in *Support for Learning*, Vol. 6, No. 1, pp. 3-8.

Begum, N. (1990). "Burden of Gratitude: Women with Disabilities Needing Personal Care," in *Social Care: Perspectives and Practice Critical Studies.* Warwick: University of Warwick.

Booth, T. (1981). "Demystifying Integration," in Swann, W. (Ed.) *The Practice of Special Education*. Oxford: Blackwell.

Booth, T. (1983). "Integrating Special Education," in Booth, T., & Potts, P. (Eds.) *Integrating Special Education*. Oxford: Blackwell.

Brah, A. (1992). "Difference, Diversity, Differentiation," in Donald, J. & Rattansi, A. (Eds.) *Race, Culture and Identity*. London: Sage.

Braid, M. (1990). "Determined to Make History a Matter of Fact," in *Independent-Education Section* 5.4.90. p. 23.

Brisenden, S. (1986). "Independent Living and the Medical Model of Disability," in *Disability, Handicap and Society*, Vol. 1, No. 2, pp. 173-178.

Carrier, J.G. (1986). *Learning Disability, Social Class and the Construction of Inequality*. New York: Greenwood Press.

Carrier, J. (1990). "Special Education and the Explanation of Pupil Performance," in *Disability, Handicap and Society*, Vol. 5, No. 3, pp. 211-226.

CIES. *The Integration Charter*. London: CIES (undated).

Coulby, D. (1991). "Introduction: The 1988 Education Act and Themes of Government Policy," in Coulby, D. & Bash, L. (Eds.) (1991) *Contradiction and Conflict: The 1988 Act in Action*. London: Cassell.

Cultural Studies (1991). *Education Limited. Schooling and Training and the New Right Since 1970*. London: Unwin Hyman Ltd.

Dale, R. (1990). *The State and Education Policy*. Milton Keynes: Open University Press.

David, M. (1986). "Teaching Family Matters," in *British Journal of Sociology of Education*. Vol. 7, No. 1, pp. 35-58.

DES (1978). *Special Educational Needs. Report of the Committee of Enquiry into the Education of Handicapped Children and Young People.* (Warnock Report). London: HMSO.

DES (1990). *Educational Statistics: Schools.* London: DES (Referenced in Barnes, 1991, p. 43).

Dessent, T. (1987). *Making Ordinary Schools Special.* Lewes: Falmer Press.

Eagleton, T. (1991). *Ideology: An Introduction.* London: Verso.

Findlay, B. (1991). "Disability, Empowerment and Equal Opportunities," (Unpublished paper).

Fine, B. and Millar, R. (Eds.) (1985). *Policing the Miners' Strike.* London: Lawrence & Wishart.

Fish, J. (1985). *The Way Ahead.* Milton Keynes: Open University Press.

Ford, J., Mongon, D. and Whelan, M. (1982). *Special Education and Social Control: Invisible Disasters.* London: Routledge & Kegan Paul.

Fulcher, G. (1989). *Disabling Policies? A Comparative Approach to Education Policy and Disability.* Lewes: Falmer Press.

Hahn, H. (1985). "Towards a Politics of Disability," in *Social Science Journal,* Vol. 22, Part 4, pp. 87-105.

Hahn, H. (1986). "Public Support for Rehabilitation in Programs: The Analysis of U.S. Disability Policy," in *Disability, Handicap and Society,* Vol. 1, No. 2, pp. 121-138.

Hindees, B. (Ed.) (1990). *Reactions to the Right.* London: Routledge.

Johnson, R. (1991). "A New Road to Serfdom? A Critical History of the 1988 Act," in *Education Group 11. Education Limited, Schooling, Training and the New Rights in England since 1979.* London: Unwin Hyman.

Krip, D. (1983). "Professionalization as a Policy Choice: British Special Education in Comparative Perspective in Chambers," J. & Hartman, W. (Eds.) *Special Education Policies: Their History, Implementation & Finance.* Philadelphia: Temple University Press.

Leach, B. (1989). "Disabled People and the Implementation of Local Authorities' Equal Opportunities Policies," in *Public Administration*, Vol. 67, No. 1, pp. 65-77.

Lewis, J. (1988). "So Much Grit in the Hub of the Educational Machine: Schools, Society and the Invention of Measurable Intelligence," in Bessant, B. (Ed.) *Mother State and Her Little Ones.* Melbourne: Preston Institute of Technology.

Morris, J. (Ed.) (1989). *Able Lives. Women's Experience of Paralysis.* London: The Women's Press.

Oliver, M. (1990). *The Politics of Disablement.* London: Macmillan.

Oliver, M. (1988). "The Political Context of Educational Decision Making: The Case of Special Needs," in Barton, L. (ed.) *The Politics of Special Educational Needs.* Lewes: Falmer Press.

Oliver, M. & Hasler, F. (1987). "Disability and Self-Help: A Case Study of the Spinal Injuries Association," in *Disability, Handicap and Society*, Vol. 2, No. 2, pp. 113-125.

Papadakis, E. (1990). "Privatization and the Welfare State," in Hindees, B. (Ed.) *Reactions to the Right.* London: Routledge.

Ranson, S. (1990). *The Politics of Reorganizing Schools.* London: Unwin Hyman.

Rieser, R. & Mason, M. (Eds.) (1990). *Disability Equality in the Classroom: A Human Rights Issue.* London: ILEA.

Ryan, W. (1976). *Blaming the Victim.* New York: Vintage Books.

Simon, B. (1988). *Bending the Rules: The Baker "Reform" of Education.* London: Lawrence & Wishart.

Skrtic, T.M. (1991). *Behind Special Education: A Critical Analysis of Professional Culture & School Organization*. Denver: Lowe Publishing Company.

Soder, M. (1984). "The mentally retarded: ideologies of care and surplus population," in Barton, L. & Tomlinson, S. (Eds.) *Special Education and Social Interests*. London: Croom Helm.

Swann, W. (1991). *Segregated Statistics. English LEAs: Variations between LEAs in levels of segregation in Special Schools, 1982-90*. London: CSIE.

Tomlinson, S. (1982). *A Sociology of Special Education*. London: Routledge & Kegan Paul.

Tomlinson, S. (1985). "The Experience of Special Education," in *Oxford Review of Education*. Vol. 11, No. 2, pp. 157-165.

Ware, J. (1990). "Severe Learning Difficulties and Multiple Handicaps: Curriculum Developments, Integration and Prospects," in Evans, P. & Verma, V. (Eds.) *Special Education: Past, Present and Future*. Lewes: Falmer Press.

Whitty, G. (1989). "The New Right and the National Curriculum," in *Journal of Education Policy*, Vol. 4, No. 4, pp. 329-341.

Williams, R. (1983). *Towards 2000*. London: Chatto.

Wolfensberger, W. (1989). "Human Service Policies: The Rhetoric versus the Reality," in Barton, L. (Ed.) *Disability and Dependency*. Lewes: Falmer Press.

CHAPTER 4

EDUCATION AND DISABILITY IN HUNGARY

by Tamas Kozma and Sandor Illyes

CONDITIONS OF SCHOOLING IN HUNGARY

The Economy

From 1945 to 1948, Hungary created a comprehensive and compulsory secondary education system together with other countries in the region. Clearly, the action was a political and not an educational (or even an economic) decision.

Comprehensive and compulsory education, however, is always costly. It means, namely, that the state takes care not only of the public--forcing the children to go to school--but also of the schools, taking responsibility for their budget. Comprehensive and compulsory education was especially costly in Hungary, because there was no financial support to restore war damages (school buildings, facilities, serious teacher demands) after World War II.

Costs of compulsory schooling have also increased for the 6-16 year olds as a result of the 1961 Education Act. This, again, was a political rather than an educational decision, and expensive for two reasons. First, two more age cohorts were retained in the system; and second, these cohorts were out of productive work.

Again, for political reasons, vocational education has been overstressed while academic studies underestimated. Because of financial reasons (different budgets for academic studies form the Ministry of Education while training is paid for by the Ministry of Labor) no one realized the high costs of vocational training in comparison with the low costs of academic instruction. Also taken into consideration is the fact that half or more of the pupils leaving general schools have been oriented to the more expensive form of upper secondary schooling.

The increasing numbers of upper secondary school leavers increased the proportion of those who applied for higher education. Although higher education was and still is closely controlled by the state budget (few places are available for full-timers), the applicants' increasing numbers forced the state to increase the places available. This, in turn, made higher education costs more expensive.

All in all, these are the components of an increase in the educational budget, which, on the other hand, met with decreasing economic possibilities in Hungary. After a period of boasted socio-economic growth--that is, the 1970s--one might ask the reasons for this rapid decrease and the roots of the Hungarian complaints.

Part of the reform after 1956 and during the 1960s was to develop the socialist welfare state. Parochial as it was, the state promised several services like education, transportation, pensions, health care, leisure activities, sports, mass communication, as well as cheap food supply, housing and child care. To build up a welfare state is expensive too, and the region's countries were not really rich enough for this. In particular, they were not wealthy enough to subsidize production on the one hand while offering welfare state services on the other.

Hungary, as well as its neighboring countries, had not enough resources for financing an unproductive industry together with the welfare state services. The main practice was (and still is) a highly centralized state accumulation of money upon which decisions are usually made from the political and administrative centers. In addition to that, different resources have been used (sometimes even exploited) in the course of the decades. For example, during the 1950s, heavy industry was mainly financed from the agricultural production.

In the period of the 1960s, new labor forces were involved in the production sphere to increase both the amount of the production and the level of productivity (particularly for women and youngsters). Hungary, as well as other Eastern European countries, has a 92-98% employment rate in the labor force which involves 42-47% of the total population.

During the 1970s, foreign loans were necessary as well as available with the idea of modernizing the economy and with the result of subsidizing it. Beginning with the 1980s, it appears, all of those additional resources ran out, resulting in new decreases in Hungary's economy.

Administration

After the 1960s and during the early 1970s, a mass decentralization took place in public administration. In contrast with the 1950s, when public administration was both called and used as state power, the 1960s and 1970s stressed that administration would focus on public services. Since educational administration was closely integrated into county and local administration, the feeling was that it should also be decentralized.

The Ministry of Education is responsible for the content of public education. Although syllabi are not called (at least not officially) the law of the state, civil servants of the Ministry took care of the textbooks, curricula, and (in a restricted way) methods. They are responsible for what is going on in our schools, and their responsibilities are seen as valid before the government, the public, and the party itself. In other words they are responsible for any false practices due to textbook contents, lazy pupils or stupid teachers. However, they have no legal access to schools, since schools do not belong to the Ministry of Education nor does it pay the teachers' salaries. They are paid by the Ministry of Finance via county and local authorities. The Ministry of Finance decides upon ongoing educational budgets, including teachers' salaries. The Ministry of Education has the right and duty to consult them to put the "needs of education" (as planners usually call them) into the budgeting plans.

Schools are financed directly by county and local authorities (local: general schools, counties: secondary schools). It means that they receive money from one Ministry while incentives from the other; however, they should decide upon them. There is only one area where they have no access and it is the on-going teaching-learning process of their schools together with textbooks and curricula. It is precisely this area in which the Ministry of Education holds responsibilities. Teachers are hired by the school principals who, in turn, are nominated by local authorities (county authorities). However, their salary scales are fixed and their work is supervised (more correctly, counseled) by supervisor-advisors coming from the county capitals. The system is not truly centralized, but not yet decentralized. It is something in between.

The new Hungarian government introduced its program of stabilization and development in the summer of 1990. It adopted, as a means for stabilization, a policy of financial restriction. There are good arguments for financial restriction, even if such a policy compromises earlier welfare promises. However, in the state educational services, a restrictive policy results in serious problems.

First, overcrowded school buildings and deteriorated physical conditions exist. The school network was originally damaged during the war. Statistics show that in the years 1944-1945 when Hungarian territories were turned into war operations fields, as much as 53% of the school buildings were ruined. Destroyed as they were, an increase in compulsory schooling has occurred in the same network which practically duplicated the number of children. Instead of earlier day school services, several schools had to organize two shifts (morning as well as afternoon lessons) to teach children of the same age in two groups. Especially serious are the years 1986-1992 when a demography wave crest will reach the secondary schools with around 15-25% more pupils than before.

Second, a shortage in school facilities is also the result of the modernization of educational services during the last one and a half decades. It is unfair to compare school facilities, libraries, and laboratories to pre-war situations at the lower secondary level. (The upper level of the general school is obligatory everywhere in the country.) The lower secondary level also includes places for recreation and sports, games, and children's social events. They should possess facilities for child care, food supply, and kinds of boarding. It is one of the top priorities of the educational administration since boarding is closely connected with social policy and as such is a constant part of the state political aims. (That is, welfare state services should balance economic downtrend.)

Third, since the war, an increasing educational service-paid by the state-employed growing numbers of teachers. Hungary had as many as 15,600 teachers (1930 diploma holders only) before the war. Their numbers grew to 51,000 in 1960; 97,000 in 1970; and to 177,000 in 1980. (Part of the statistics reflects the fact that several teachers had only secondary school graduation, while these figures show only the numbers of higher education graduates.) In any event, it was an extremely rapid growth of the Hungarian teacher corps. (Today, every third graduate holds a teacher's diploma.) Since their salaries are guaranteed by the state, they account for nearly 70% of the yearly educational budget. An economic decrease means a steady decrease of teachers' salaries.

Fourth, parents and their children today have much higher requirements for school facilities and educational services. For example, they suffer shortages in school health care, infrastructures (like showers, lavatories, or restaurants) and even the heating system which is being adopted this year. Several argue that if parents are heavily taxed they should have the right to require better services for their children (not to mention other arguments against local taxation versus central curricula and teaching obligations).

Even if teachers, parents and the local educational administration accept the new government policy restriction in general, those facts and realities make them nearly impossible to accept cuts in the educational budget. This is the very reason why school finance has become a key issue today.

The Structure of Schooling

Before World War II, Hungary had a German-like schooling system-not by chance, since the system had been inherited from the Austro-Hungarian Empire. The same is true of other new-born countries in the region such as Czechoslovakia, Austria, and parts of Yugoslavia. Elementary and secondary education were financed mainly by the state but partly also by local authorities and the churches. Elementary education was free-since it was obligatory-while several secondary schools required high tuition fees. The system involved the following stages: An elementary education, in principle equal for all, was obligatory for the 6-12 year olds. Three choices were offered (or even forced) for the 10-year-olds:

1) To remain in the elementary school for two more years repeating the 3 R's. This led practically nowhere, except into skilled work or semi-skilled jobs.

2)   To follow their studies in the so called citizens' schools. They offered four-graded subject-matter teaching into the main school subjects with a school leaving certificate that was necessary for further studies in commercial or trade upper secondary schools.

3)   The 10-year-olds might turn to the "royal mile" in education, that is, the Gymnasium. It was a classical-type grammar school which contained a four-graded lower level as well as a four-graded upper level. After successful studies in subjects like math, physics, linguistics (Latin and Greek) and the like, the Gymnasium provided its pupils with the most respectable Abitur (secondary school graduation).

Since World War II, this system has been fully reformed. The top priority of the reform was the General School (altalanos iskola).

General School (classes 1-8)

The general schools were created on the basis of the elementary schools. A common curriculum has been introduced with compulsory textbooks all over the country. In 1948, all of the schools were nationalized. The general schools were not only comprehensive but also compulsory for ages 6-14 and free of charge. (Hungary, at present, has tuition-free general schools with a school obligation for the 6-16 year olds offered since 1961. It secures, at least in theory, an opportunity for all to accomplish their general education.)

Secondary Education (classes 9-12)

Besides the comprehensive General School, the upper secondary educational system remained selective. Today, pupils after 14 have three options. One is the four year grammar school (gymnasium). Grammar schools have even today a kind of social respect. They offer academic subject-matter teaching with the promise of the traditional Abitur and the illusion of easy access to universities. The second option is vocational training. Apprenticeship as it is, vocational training is officially called vocational education (that is, declared as a part of the state educational system).   Third, students may choose upper secondaries of a comprehensive kind (szakkozepiskola). They aim to combine Abitur preparation with skilled work training. All options are state financed. In other words, education after 14 is also free in Hungary, although it is obligatory only before age 16.

Higher Education

Access to higher education is not easy. Before 1956, it was politically controlled, and today, it is controlled by the serious shortages of free places for full time students. That is to say, only 10-15% of an age cohort has a realistic chance of admission. It is within the higher education system today where hierarchy and selectivity of a pre-war kind are still alive. Well-known features are: long queuing for entrance, competitive exams, entrance examinations controlled by the state bureaucracy and sometimes penetrated by corruption, segregation according to sexes and social backgrounds, femalized professions, etc. The teaching staffs are underpaid, although still respected. Students remain traditional in their compositions: mainly full-timers, usually youngsters between 18-24. (The reason is, among others, that higher education is free for all.) All these are features of a growing isolation of the university from Hungarian life-as the asylum for socially respected while economically devaluated intellectuals.

The 1985 Education Act

From 1985 on, an education act has been adopted upon which democratization of the entire administration system was initiated. It is under debate right now and a new education act is likely in the near future. Although the framework of the administration has remained, some of its features have been totally changed. As yet, the results are mixed. The advocates call the changes democratization. Critics, however, use the term of deconcentration for several reasons.

First, according to the new taxation system, individuals (including parents) are taxed and a growing part of their taxes remains on the local authorities' bank account. However, neither the local authorities nor the taxpayers received clear rights to participate in school issues. Advocates point out the dangers of local influence on schools. Teachers, however, feel central bureaucracy is more dangerous.

Second, according to the 1985 Education Act, school principals can only be nominated for two terms. (Earlier, it was a life-time nomination.) It sounds a bit democratic in theory. However, it is not necessarily democratic in practice. It gives the local authorities the chance to change the principalship of the institute if the person does not fit his role (which was the original intention). However, it also gives local powers the opportunity to expel persons-even if they would fit in their role-in cases where principals would not accept local power systems. In this case, a strong central authority would better fit democratization than strong local elites with weak central powers.

Finally, according to the 1985 Education Act, the teaching staff of a given school has its veto right when voting for the new principal. A veto means that the staff can stop nomination of the person it wants for its principal. In other words, the veto right is only a half step. And, as on-going research clearly shows, the results are, as yet, more than ambiguous. After decades of nomination from the top, several teaching staffs use their veto rights as an exercise in power regardless of the fact that their schools could go on (sometimes during the whole school year) without a legal principalship.

Teachers

Teachers' attitudes toward present educational debates is also worth analysis. Their attitudes are reflections of an earlier bureaucratic centralization in the sphere of education (together with other spheres in the economy and political life). Namely, these attitudes stem from a nationalized school system which had:

1) A highly centralized curriculum. Sometimes it was interpreted not only as the content of the education but also as state law. Although the curriculum was not law, it was sanctioned by the highest level of state administration (namely, the Ministry of Education).

2) Obligatory textbooks together with officially required methods of teaching and learning. Curricula ideas have been incorporated into the state textbooks which had only one official interpretation, and that was the official method of teaching. If teachers did not follow the required method, they were accused of not interpreting the right book in the right way and, as a result, not accepting The Law (i.e., the curriculum in the sense of a traditional syllabus).

3) An institution to control teachers which was the state supervisorship. It was built in the county and local authorities, inasmuch as the supervisors appeared in the schools as the state authorities. They controlled whether the teachers would follow syllabi, textbooks, and methods.

4) An ideology called socialist pedagogy was manifested in politically influenced compositions of philosophical beliefs about individuals and their communities (the collective), moral judgments about youth, as well as in initiations of very practical skills called the generalized practices of the leading teacher personalities. Some debates about instructional techniques like teaching to read or using educational measurements were clearly fights against the bourgeoisie.

Although the symptoms mentioned above are from the past, training makes features of them come alive. For example, supervisors are called advisers today and have no legitimate authority to give the teachers "orders." Teachers are trained to accept those advisers' word as the authentic way of interpreting state laws (as they sometimes call the curricula). Every change in the system of those controls-which might weaken the power of administration- reminds the teaching staff of those early days in the 1950s.

Contradictions

From the arguments mentioned above, a series of further issues for present educational policy debates has developed.

Contradictions exist between smaller state educational budgets and growing state requirements for quality education. Every innovation in education suggests better facilities as well as sophisticated teaching. If there is not a growing budget to accompany growing demands, only ideology and rhetoric remain as the means and tools for such innovations.

Disparities among schools in different areas are growing. If the state budget is not adequate for a quality education, local forces must pay for it. They do so in some parts of the country, while in other parts, local authorities and parents are not able to pay or they do not want to finance quality teaching. Disparity is not a local issue because it seriously hurts the policy of equalizing the society through educational equalities. State bureaucracy tries to stop some local efforts in order to keep educational services throughout Hungary on the same level of development. However, it is hard to argue against local improvements if the central authority cannot finance them.

Contradictions between academic education and vocational training are manifested. Once, it was a state policy to prefer vocational training over academic education. As a state policy it has its own philosophy of vocational training as the most socialist way to develop the proletariat (while academic lines were considered as politically ambiguous). Today, vocational training is clearly much more expensive than academic education, besides the fact that most of the traditional vocations are closely connected to unproductive spheres of industry.

Although the educational boom of the 1970s was part of the boasted welfare state of that time, there is reason now to question its practicality, not only because of labor market realities but also because of the high costs a universal upper secondary schooling might incur if it was entirely state financed. To answer such a question is much more complicated than the contradiction mentioned above. It not only hurts welfare state ideology, but also it would hurt the very motivation of large groups of the society who gave up alternative life careers in order to get easier and cheaper access to upper secondary schooling. These groups, even today, believe that state education offers better chances for their children than the market economy and reprivatization of goods and services.

Future Challenges

While elementary schooling has no alternatives, secondary education offers options and thus creates a kind of voting situation among individuals. It is precisely this situation-the choice of secondary schooling possibilities--where individual attitudes toward state schooling can be monitored. They show general distinct features.

First, overcrowding of upper secondary education has taken place. While schooling obligation finishes at the age of 16, there is a steady growth in the proportions of those following their studies till 17-18. The result is a mass upper secondary schooling (or, we might also say, universal schooling) with more than 95% of general school leavers following their career in upper secondaries, which also means 86-92% of students in each age cohort. The process of overcrowding started as early as 1961 when the education act broadened school obligation from the age of 14 to 16. Similar processes took place in the First World countries from the 1930s, and in Central Europe between 1940-1960. However, upper secondary schooling has universally been accepted among the Hungarian population regardless of state pressures or economic reasons.

Second, there has been a growing demand for academic studies. The proportion of students choosing a grammar school option is less than 20% among general school leavers while vocational training is officially offered for more than 40% of them. The remaining 35-40% of the upper secondary students choose technical secondaries. Politicians from the 1950s and 1960s always preferred vocational training, arguing the need for economic development and for an ideology of supplying a traditional working class. However, statistics of applications-not those of access because entrance is controlled by the number of free places-clearly show a growing demand for academic studies and a decrease in applications for vocational training. It is not only the ambiguous promise of higher education which motivates parents and youth toward academic studies, but also, an effort to be saved from the early rudeness of life.

Third, a manifest decrease of apprenticeship applications is apparent. Apprenticeship-rhetorically called "vocational education"-leads as quickly as possible to concrete jobs. They are job possibilities which have not been modernized as yet, and where more manual labor is needed instead of new technologies.

Fourth, jobs and professions have been "femalized." Sometimes even types of schools have been femalized, although there is no official school segregation of that kind from the 1961 Education Act. Grammar schools-except for the most efficient-are nearly femalized and so are some of the technical secondaries (nursery teacher training, medical training, commercial secondary schools and the like). There are also professions at the level of university graduation that are becoming femalized (judges, teachers, chemists, dentists, etc.). The process again shows that the individual uses the state schooling services not only for education and training, but also-and in a growing amount-for social securities and for equalizing opportunities.

Finally, high drop-out rates are occurring. While universalized at the entry level, upper secondary education reflects Third World statistics at its exit. That is, of 90% or more following their studies at upper secondary level only 36% of an age cohort receive their secondary school graduation (Abitur). There are two reasons for this. First, apprenticeship and vocational training do not mean preparation for the Abitur. That is, vocational school leavers do not accomplish a full course in upper secondary education. Calling them a part of the educational system is, thus, misleading. Second, there is an unusually high drop-out rate for some educational options, like vocational training (15-25%) or technical secondary schools (10-15%), with the lowest drop-out rates in the grammar schools (less than 10%).

SPECIAL EDUCATION

The Disabled Population: Concepts and Criteria

In order to create a theoretical framework for further inquiry, we begin the analysis of the disabled population with a short etiology of disability. Following the suggestions of the World Health Organization all over the world, as well as in Hungary today, we distinguish three levels of manifestation of the deficient human existence: impairments, disabilities, and handicaps. "*Impairments* are concerned with abnormalities of body structure and appearance and with organ or system function, resulting from any cause; in principle, impairments represent disturbances at the organ level. *Disabilities*, reflecting the consequences of impairment in terms of functional performance and activity by the individual; disabilities thus represent disturbances at the level of the person. *Handicaps* are concerned with the disadvantages experienced by the individual as a result of impairments and disabilities; handicaps thus reflect interaction with and adaption to the individual's surroundings." (WHO, 1980)

These three levels may be in causal relation. The disease can trigger impairments, which can cause disabilities thus leading to handicaps. The general connection needs to be completed with two further restrictions. Primarily, it is not every disease that leads to impairment nor does every impairment cause disability and every disability does not trigger a handicap. From this point of view the levels of manifestation can be transcribed as narrowing circles. The other important restriction is that biological causes (disease, impairment) are not the only ones which lead to disabilities and handicaps, but inappropriate external conditions of development may also lead to a disability or handicap. On the levels of disability and handicap, the inducing causes can be classified into three groups: biological causes, environmental causes, and biological and environmental causes acting together.

Concerning the three levels of manifestation, certain criteria are needed to make a distinction between the impaired and non-impaired, disabled and non-disabled, handicapped and non-handicapped conditions. On the level of the organism, distinguishing the impaired condition from the non-impaired one can be carried out by means of biological criteria. On the individual level, the distinction between the disabled and non-disabled conditions needs psychological criteria and cultural standards as well.

Expected levels of performance and activity differ in each culture and subculture. Healthy and normal conditions of ability, aptitude and attitude develop through socialization and learning. Therefore, the criteria which we apply to differentiate disabilities from non-disabilities and handicaps from non-handicaps have social origins and are dependent on social context as well. Cultural, subcultural and family diversities may lead to great differences in the abilities and performances of the individuals.

The same person may be disabled in a certain social group or in a certain social situation and non-disabled in another. Social criteria of disability and handicap are flexible criteria in everyday life. Human diversities may be interpreted either as normal conditions originating from natural human differences of the individuals or as abnormal conditions or deficiencies which are regarded as aberrations from a required social state. Traditions, actually preferred values and behavior patterns, and many other social factors determine whether a deficiency is considered a disability and handicap or a natural condition and individual difference which can be tolerated. In Western Europe and Hungary the new anthropological trends of the theory of special education would suggest that disabilities and handicaps are variations of human existence which should be tolerated in the same way as other differences.

Highly developed societies not only raise requirements for the individual in every sphere of social life but for those who cannot comply with the requirements, they provide help for compensation. Disabilities and handicaps have therefore two facets. On the one hand they segregate and exclude the person from certain life spheres. On the other hand, they set the person in a privileged status which affords access to services and institutions which compensate for the deficiencies.

Services and providers can offer compensatory advantages only if the person submits himself to reclassification and is removed from the group of the normal to the impaired, from the group of non-disabled to the group of disabled, from the group of non-handicapped to the group of handicapped. This reclassification always means stigmatization as well because the individual's inability to be independent and his need for other's assistance is proven by his new social state. Dependence and stigmatization induce the individual to keep aloof from this disadvantage. However, if undertaking this classification allowed the individual to get favorable services which are a benefit for him, the person himself will insist on his reclassification.

The dynamics of advantages and disadvantages will determine practically where the borderline is drawn between disability and non-disability, handicap and non-handicap, and what the person's attitude is to the border of classification. Disability and handicap are social categories and they are dependent on the services which the society can provide to compensate these conditions. The classificatory criteria are very complex issues in Hungary too and are not influenced by science only, but by the instrumental value, and the provided privileges of the classified state.

Classification and Prevalence of Disability Groups

The legislation, institutions, and services in Hungary do not use scientific constructs but the expressions of everyday language for identification of the groups of individuals with deficient conditions. None of the meanings in Hungarian expressions and constructs are equivalent to the special meanings of the English terms of impairment, disability and handicap. The most general Hungarian label is the "rokkant" and the "fogyatekos." The primary meaning of the word "rokkant" in English is invalid. The primary meaning of the word "fogyatekos" is deficient. In both Hungarian expressions the meaning of "impairment," arising from biological causes, is dominant. The application of the word "rokkant" covers a limited sphere. It is restricted to adults and implies that the person was not impaired earlier in life. In the official language of social welfare, the word "rokkant" occurs most frequently. In the expression of the "Decade of disabled" the word "disabled" was translated to "rokkant" officially. The word "fogyatekos" represents impairments-existing since birth or infancy-as well as disabilities and handicaps as a result of the impairment.

The difference between the words "rokkantsag" and "fogyatekossag" in English is expressed by the distinction of disability and developmental disability.   For the word "handicap," "akadalyozottsag," and "korlatozottsag" are the equal labels. The "akadalyozott" and "korlatozott" labels do not have such a stigmatizing influence as the "rokkant" or "fogyatekos" labels have in Hungarian. Therefore, the new organizations prefer using the words "korlatozott" or "akadalyozott" rather than the traditional expressions of "rokkant" or "fogyatekos."

It is very difficult to obtain exact figures for the incidence and prevalence of disability and handicap in Hungary as well as throughout the world. The reasons are that the categories of the three levels of manifestation are not separated clearly, the borders are vague, and the categories for classification used by institutions differ from one another.

Medical institutions set up their categories primarily according to the criteria of disease and impairment and their classification is based on these terms.   Educational institutions in Hungary follow the medical classification, including additional criteria. Institutions belonging to social welfare use the criteria of medical classification but they complete them with the criteria established on the other two levels of manifestation. The category of mental retardation, for example, is used by the medical classification as well as the educational and social classification, but the meanings are not completely identical. Therefore, the figures of the incidence and prevalence statistics differ from each other in the three different types of institutions.

Today in Hungary there are 18,200 adult members in the National Federation of the Blind and Partially Sighted; 11,000 adult members in the National Federation of the Hearing Impaired, and 27,000 adult members in the Federation of the Associations of the Physically Handicapped. These traditional federations received 35 million, 24 million, and 13 million forints from the state in 1991.

According to the statistics of social welfare in 1989 there were 33,000 physically handicapped and almost the same number of blind persons supported financially by the state. For mentally retarded adults the state maintained 31 daycare homes with 810 patients. In 1989 the state institute for blind adults had cared for 300 patients. The number of the state institutes for moderately mentally retarded adults is 12 with about 10,000 patients.

Special Education: Historical Developments

The institutional education of impaired children began in the nineteenth century. A school for the deaf was established in 1802, and the first school for the blind opened in 1825. The first institute for idiotic and imbecile children was founded in 1875 and the institute for children with speech defects was established in 1891.

The institutional education provided by the state was developed after the Public Education Act was passed in 1868. This Act excluded the deaf, blind, idiots, and imbeciles from elementary school education. In the beginning, children excluded from the public educational system went to charity institutes. Compulsory elementary education was finally expanded to the blind, deaf, mentally retarded, neurotic, retarded, and maladapted children in 1922.

At the present time, in Hungary, the public education of disabled children is regulated by the 1985 Education Act. This Act gives the right for learning and completing compulsory education to every child. The Act ordains that the state has to maintain kindergartens for deaf, blind, motoric impaired, and mentally retarded children and for children with speech disorders. For the non-disabled, the age of compulsory education is 6-16; for the disabled it can be 6-18. According to the regulations of the Act, disabled children at the pre-school level needing special preparation should be attended to. This Act intended to reduce the stigmatizing influence of the official labels. Therefore, it gave the same official names to the schools of the disabled as for the schools of the non-disabled and it put a halt to the use of discriminative names. Previously there had been names like "The Auxiliary School for the Mentally Retarded" or "The Primary Boarding School for the Blind," etc.

Despite this progressive effort, the Act also prolonged many previous traditional solutions. The school system of the disabled, now as well as earlier, operates apart from the elementary school system of the non-disabled. The schools for the disabled remained segregated, isolated schools and the disabled children could only attend their own schools which were designated on the basis of the type of their disabled condition.

Special Schools and Services

Today in Hungary there are separate schools for children with particular disabilities, e.g. the educable mentally retarded, the trainable mentally retarded, the deaf, the hard of hearing, the blind, the partially sighted, the motoric disordered, and the speech disordered (see Tables 1 and 2). The schools are maintained by the state. Special schools receive more financial support than the schools for the non-disabled. These classes usually contain 20 children. The education takes place in the morning and early afternoon. Children may have lunch at school, and in the afternoon they either go home or do their homework in the school. The majority of the schools for the disabled are boarding schools because school-bus systems are nonexistent and parents are unable to transport children daily from a great distance. For the educable mentally retarded children there are auxiliary classes operating in mainstream primary schools. However this is only a temporary solution and does not help the implementation of integration.

The education of disabled pupils and the legislation in Hungary do not use the concept of "special educational needs." Education still builds on the traditional concepts of the medical model. Accordingly, our educational system determines which groups should be segregated on the level of impairment, using biological criteria. Therefore, in Hungary today, there are three groups of pupils who do not have special schools, as is common in the highly developed Western-European countries.

The behaviorally disordered, emotionally disordered and maladapted children belong to the first group. These children do not receive special educational services. They learn in mainstream primary schools. The mild disorders are treated with therapy by psychologists working in counseling centers. Children with severe disorders are put into boarding schools.

In the second group there are various forms of learning disabilities: dyslexia, Minimal Cerebral Damage (MCD), and attentional deficits. The special educational needs of these children have recently been recognized by the primary schools. Normal primary school teachers are being prepared for the meeting of the special needs of these children.

The third group includes socially disadvantaged pupils. The number of children belonging to this group is rather large. About 10-15% of each age cohort belongs to this group. The majority of socially disadvantaged pupils cannot comply with the requirements of compulsory education and therefore drop out of school before they are 16. The 10-15% drop out rate cannot be reduced easily by the primary school. To achieve the reduction, the disadvantaged families should be supported by social-political services. Unfortunately the state cannot afford the necessary financial support.

In the third group there are also many Gypsy pupils. The subculture of Gypsies does not prepare these children for compliance with the requirements of primary school. Therefore, many of these children cannot finish primary school. They drop out, and even more move to schools for the educable mentally retarded. The rate of Gypsy pupils enrolled in mainstream elementary schools is less than 5%, but in the special schools for educable mentally retarded, there are between 30-40%. This high rate indicates that mainstream elementary schools cannot meet the special educational needs of children from the Gypsy ethnic subculture. Gypsy pupils are only educationally handicapped. But when they move to the schools for educable mentally retarded children, they simultaneously move to the group of disabled pupils. This reclassification is not appropriate for their educational state and it violates social justice.

Admission and Training

The 1985 Act of Education ordains the examination by a State committee of those children who cannot learn in the primary schools successfully or of children who are suspected of learning disabilities prior to schooling. This State Committee is charged with making decisions concerning a child's admission into schools for non-disabled children or schools for the disabled. The committees are similar to the outpatient clinics. They carry out medical, psychological and pedagogical examinations and evaluate the child's elementary teacher's written records. These data, with the parents' consent, are used to prepare a proposal in regard to admission. The decision of the Committee is binding on the parents who can appeal against it, but these cases are rather rare. Theoretically, the Committees regulate not only the admission to the schools for the disabled, but the replacement in regular primary schools as well. However, the replacement procedure is rather infrequent.

The curricula of the special schools are reduced variations of the mainstream primary schools, adjusted to the disabled condition, and completed by special elements. Special education in Hungary is called "remedial education," which originates from the German term "Heilpaedagogik." The first Hungarian Special schools followed the German models and adopted the term, "remedial education." From this, the characteristics of therapy have received a stronger emphasis in the Hungarian special education than in the special education of other countries. The effort of remedial education is not only to prepare children for an independent life and general socialization, but to reduce the handicap and, if possible, the disability as well.

This kind of therapy is mostly concerned with the motoric disordered children's conductive education. The conductive education elaborated by Andras Peto is a sovereign education system separated from special schools.

In the last decades, special education services have begun to extend to fields other than schools. The importance of early intervention has been recognized by experts in all fields of special education. Therefore, the intention of these schools is to develop children as early as possible, mainly before kindergarten age. This can only be carried out if the schools encourage the parents to take part in early intervention. There are significant attempts at guided support for the families in the field of special education for the hearing impaired, visually impaired, motoric disordered and speech disordered.

The vocational training system of the disabled, in Hungary, is less developed than the compulsory primary education system. The blind and the deaf are trained in traditional jobs such as brush maker, broom maker, basket weaver, masseur, piano tuner and upholsterer (for the blind); and (for the deaf) carpenter, upholsterer, weaving, sewing, carpet weaving, locksmith trades, and mechanics. There is a special vocational school for motoric disordered youngsters. The blind, with good academic ability, attend high schools, then colleges or universities. There are attempts at secondary education of the deaf.

The 1985 Act of Education organized special vocational schools for the educable mentally retarded pupils to learn simple professions or jobs. These vocational schools are experimental. The experiences show that there are not only educable mentally retarded pupils but children with social disadvantages in these schools. The future existence of these schools depends on the labor market and the opportunity for employment of the disabled. Earlier there were laws providing priorities to those employers who hired disabled people. These laws should be changed because of the new economic situation in Hungary and in the free market. New regulations are needed for employing the disabled.

In the schools for the disabled there are special teachers who are called "remedial teachers" in Hungary. They have been trained in an independent Training College begun in the first decade of this century. Students can attend Teacher Training College after high school graduation at the age of 18. The training takes four years. Special teachers are qualified for two special fields of education. Every student is qualified for teaching educable and trainable mentally retarded children. This faculty is compulsory. The other field or faculty of special education is optional. The majors are the theory and practice of special education, philosophy, sociology, human biology and pathology, psychology and the arts. The advantage of this kind of training is that the students get more detailed knowledge about human biology and psychology than do those who attend normal teacher training colleges. The disadvantages of this training are that the students are not adequately prepared in the field of normal education and their diploma does not give them the competencies to teach in normal elementary schools. The segregation of pupils, schools and teachers raises significant difficulties in the implementation of the integration of the disabled.

New Trends

The system change (the change of the regime in 1989-1990) basically transformed the philosophy of education, and it will modify the legislation and school system. It is expected that this system change will have a great influence on special education of the disabled. Some of the changes and the signs which can be seen today include:

1)   Free access to compulsory primary school for disabled pupils. The 1985 Education Act makes it possible today for parents with disabled children to enroll their children not only in schools for the disabled but also in mainstream local primary schools. The number of pupils in elementary schools is gradually decreasing so parents are urged to acknowledge this concept. Hereby, the situation of special schools becomes uncertain since the number of enrolled pupils are falling remarkably. The integrated education of disabled pupils is a reasonable solution from a professional point of view. Still, if the disabled child does not receive additional services in mainstream elementary schools suitable to his special educational needs, the integrated education concept does not fulfill its purpose.

2)   More non-state providers in the educational service. The state monopoly for opening schools has come to an end. Parents of disabled children, foundations, the church and entrepreneurs have the right to establish special schools. These initiatives presently meet with financial difficulties, but we may expect that with prosperity there will be more private schools for disabled children.

3)   Pluralism in the goals and content of special education. The curricula of special schools had been bound by the state until now. Today, every school, as well as special schools, is free to decide the purposes, the content, and the best methods of education. Schools have begun to form their own identities. This process has already begun, but it is slow because the teachers' preparation and grounding in creative, independent education is not thorough enough; the infrastructural condition of schools is not appropriate; and the poor

supply of books and equipment cannot support the establishment of alternative educational systems.

4)   Weakening state control and stronger consumer control. During the party regime, schools performed functions of the state as an organic part of state institutes. The prospect for the future is that schools will become service institutes and their main task will be to meet the demands and needs of children and families who intend to use these services. Primary schools will belong to the supervision of local authorities. Parents can participate actively in forming educational goals through local authorities or directly through the schools.

This will get primary emphasis in the case of special schools. Parents and the representatives of the federations, protecting the interests of the disabled, sometimes disagree with the opinions of the professionals and experts working in schools. Until now, they were not able to enforce their opinions because the state had central and uniform guidance and suggested only professional concepts. With a stronger participation by parents, the outdated professional traditions will be reduced. The control by parents will probably force some solutions which may be professionally questionable but they will assist in reforming procedures in the system of special schools.

Table 1

1978/79

	Number of institutions	Pupils	Percentage of pupils		Teachers	
			Related to pupils in special schools	Related to the whole population in compulsory education	Number	% with gradua-tion in remedial education
Primary schools with special classes for EMR pupils	415	12788	35.0	1.10	1109	36.2
Schools of EMR	84	12584	34.4	1.40	1714	71.5
Schools of MR	56	8847	24.2	0.75	1423	60.5
Boarding schools for deaf	7	1144	3.1	0.10	280	74.6
Boarding schools for deaf and MR pupils	1	100	0.3	0.01	23	73.9
Boarding schools for hard of hearing	1	274	0.7	0.02	57	87.7
Boarding schools for blind	1	268	0.7	0.02	66	68.2
Boarding schools for partially sighted	2	201	0.5	0.02	53	45.3
Boarding schools motoric impaired	2	271	0.7	0.02	59	64.4
Boarding schools speech disordered	1	63	0.2	0.005	13	?
All together	640	42253	100.0	3.1	4825	60.0

Table 2

1988/89

| | Number of institutions | Pupils | Percentage of pupils | | Teachers | |
			Related to pupils in special schools	Related to the whole population in compulsory education***	Number	% with graduation in remedial education
Primary schools with special classes for EMR* pupils	461	13674	32.36	1.01	1351	40.26
Schools of EMR	95	15827	37.45	1.10	2612	67.38
Schools of MR**	68	10274***	24.31	0.72	2134	53.93
Boarding schools for deaf	7	966	2.28	0.05	354	73.72
Boarding schools for deaf and MR pupils	1	100	0.23	0.007	29	68.96
Boarding schools for hard of hearing	1	390	0.92	0.02	106	80.18
Boarding schools for blind	1	287	0.67	0.01	75	78.66
Boarding schools for partially sighted	2	315	0.74	0.02	74	66.21
Boarding schools motoric impaired	2	338	0.79	0.02	93	51.61
Boarding schools speech disordered	2	82	0.19	0.006	38	76.31
All together	640	42253	100.0	3.01	6866	58.34

*EMR: Educable mentally retarded
        TMR: Trainable mentally retarded
**MR: Mentally retarded (educable+trainable)
***   from this 3844 pupils are TMR
****   100% = 1341866 (the whole population in compulsory education from the ages 6-15 years)

References

Bachman, W., Gordos, Sz. A., Lányi, E. A.: Biographien ungarischer Heilpädagogen. Rheinstetten 1977.

Csányi, Y.: Hörgeschädigtenpädagogik in Ungarn. Hörgeschädigte Kinder. 1981. 3. 127-134.

Freiburg, G.: Das ungarische Sonderschulwesen - Entwicklung, Stand, Probleme. Teil 1. Sonderpädagogik 1983. 13. 2. 80-87, Teil 2. Sonderpädagogik 1983. 13. 3. 133-137.

Gordos, Sz. A.: Über einige Grundfragen der allgemeinen Theorie der Heilpädagogik. Wissenschaftliche Zeitschrift der Humboldt - Universität zu Berlin. Ges. - Sprachw. R. XXVI. 1977. 3. 307-311.

Illyés, S.: Die Ausbildung der Heilpädagogen in Ungarn. In: Asperger, H. (Hrsg.): 4. Internationaler Kongress für Heilpädagogik. Wien 1970. 500-502.

Illyés, S.: Über die heilpädagogische Situation in Ungarn. In: Asperger, H. (Hrsg.): 4. Internationaler Kongress für Heilpädagogik. Wien 1970. 564-568.

Illyés, S., Meixner, I.: Learning and reading disabilities in Hungary. In: Tarnopol, L., Tarnopol, M. (Eds.): Reading Disabilities an International Perspective. Baltimore: University Park Press 1976. 209-227.

Illyés, S.: Ungarn. In: Klauer, K.J., Mitter, W. (Hrsg.): Vergleichende Sonderpädagogik. Berlin 1987. Carl Marhold Verlagsbuchhandlung. 381-391.

Illyés, S.: Deviance and socialization in Hungary. In: Münnich, I. Kolozsi, B. (Eds.): The Complex Analysis of Deviant Behaviour in Hungary. Research Review on Hungarian Social Sciences Granted by the Government. 1989. Project No. 4. 113-129.

92   Education and Disability in Cross-Cultural Perspective

Illyés, S.: Die Schulintegration für behinderte Kinder in Ungarn. In: Innerhofer, P., Klicpera, Ch. (Hrsg.): Schule und Integration. Bozen 1990. 126-134. (Herausgeber: Landesassessorat für Sozial-und Gesundheitswessen. Bozen.)

Illyés, S.: Kontinuität und Diskontinuität in der Theorienbildung der Heilpädagogik. In: Bachmann, W., Mesterházi, Zs. (Hrsg.): Trends und Perspectiven der gegenwartigen ungarischen Heilpädagogik. Heil - und Sonderpädogogik. Band 11. Institut für Heil - und Sonderpädagogik. Justus-Liebig-Universität Giessen 1990. 13-43.

Illyés, S. Socialization and deviancy. Theoretical aspects and empirical findings in Hungary. In: Münnich, I., Kolozsi, B. (Eds.): Studies in deviant behaviours in Hungary. Research Review on Hungarian Social Sciences Granted by the Government. 1991/1. Project No. 4. 181-197.

Lányi, E.A.: Budapest Study on Mental Retardation. Psychological Aspects: In: Primrose, D.A.A. (Ed.): Proc. of the third Congress of the Int. Assoc. for the Scientific Study of Ment. Def. Warsaw 1975. 276-280.

Pálhegyi, F.: Die Ausbildung der Heilpádagogen in Ungarn. Vierteljahresschrift für Heilpädagogik und ihre Nachbargebiete. 1974. 3. 299-301.

CHAPTER 5

EDUCATION AND SPECIAL EDUCATION IN CROSS-CULTURAL PERSPECTIVE: THE ISLAMIC REPUBLIC OF IRAN

by G. Ali Afrooz

DEMOGRAPHIC BACKGROUND

Iran,[1] a Muslim country in the Middle East, covering an area of 1,648,195 square kilometers in south western Asia, is the sixteenth largest country in the world. It is bounded on the north by Azerbaijan and the Caspian Sea (the largest land-locked body of water in the world), on the east by Afghanistan and Pakistan, on the west by Iraq and Turkey, and on the south by the Persian Gulf and the sea of Oman. The land of Iran is characterized by mountain ranges surrounding interior plateaus, and the country can therefore be considered mountainous. More than 50% of Iranian soil is covered by mountains, about 25% by deserts and less than 25% is suitable for agriculture. Iran's geographic position has made it the bridge for communication by land between Far Eastern Asia and Europe.

The climate in Iran ranges from as high as 55°C in the summer in the southern part of the country to as low as -20°C in some areas in the northeast and northwest during the winter. Annual average rainfall is about 12 inches. The lowlands of central and eastern Iran are extensive desert regions and the southeastern corner of the country receives less than six inches of rain a year. The northwest corner of the country often benefits from 15-36 inches.

The northern part (Caspian coast) presents a very different picture. The annual rainfall is from 40 to 60 inches and rain usually falls throughout the year.

According to the latest statistics, from October, 1986, the population was 48,089,597. As is now very common in many developing countries, improved health facilities have brought about a decline in death rates and a large increase in population. The growth rate in recent years has been 3.2% annually, compared to a world average of 1.9% (Iranian Statistical Center, 1987). This high rate of growth creates considerable problems in providing adequate public health services and appropriate education for all.

The population density was reported to be 29.2% per square kilometer (Iranian Statistical Center, 1987). About 50% of the total population are farmers and craftsmen who live in rural areas in about 66,000 villages. The rest of the population resides in towns and cities, nearly 14% of the total population. The majority of the population is extremely young. The statistical age breakdown demonstrates that 43% are below 14 years of age, 52% are between 15 and 59, and only 4.4% are above 60 years of age. The average age for the male population is 55.1 years and 56.3 years for the female. The birth rate per thousand is 42.1 while the death rate per thousand is 11.3.

The average age of marriage for men is 25 years and for women nearly 19 years. In both urban and rural areas, the average family has five members. The divorce rate is about 10% in large populated cities and less than 4% in small towns and villages.

About 66% of the Iranian people are of Farsi origin, 25% of Turkish. Kurdish, Arabic, Lori, Guilak and Baluch are spoken in various parts of the country.

Most of the population (98.8%) are Muslim and 91% of these belong to the Shiite school of thought. There are 1.7% Christian, 0.3% Jewish, 0.1% Zoroastrians, and 0.1% belong to other faiths.

Political Ideology and Stability

After a long revolutionary movement led by the late Imam Khomeini, Iran was transformed from a monarchy--that lasted centuries--to an Islamic republic in 1979. This historic event brought great changes in the life patterns of the Iranian people. Because of the Islamic revolution of Iran, its history reflects fourteen hundred years of religious leadership and Islamic government. Soon after the victory of the Islamic revolution, through which Iran became a center of social, cultural and political dynamism in the region, Iraq invaded the southeastern part of Iran, and imposed a war that lasted about eight years. As a result, hundreds of thousands of houses, schools, hospitals, and medical centers were destroyed. Through air bombardment, missiles, and chemical attacks, many thousands of civilians were martyred and several hundred thousand were seriously injured. Most of the survivors became physically disabled. Under such a long lasting and stressful situation, an enormous number of pregnant mothers gave birth to premature babies; now most of those children who are still alive are suffering from some kind of handicap.

The Islamic Republic of Iran, Its Goals and Objectives

Understanding the nature, the ideological and philosophical foundation and value system of the government, and its attitude toward its people in general, and toward the disabled and culturally disadvantaged individuals in particular, is very important. A realistic criterion for its people's level of expectation derives from an accurate comprehension of the ultimate goals, objectives, and social commitments of the government. The Islamic government is different from the customary modern concept of constitutional democracy, and it is more accurate to call it Islamic government than democracy or theocracy. From the Islamic view, the government does not derive from the interests of certain classes, nor does it dominate an individual or a group. It represents rather an organized crystallization of the political ideal of a people who profess a common faith and have a common outlook in order to aid the process of intellectual and ideological evolution toward a final goal.

The Islamic Republic is a system of government based on faith: the unity of God is Allah, the divine revelation and its fundamental role in the expounding of the laws, the resurrection and its constructive role in man's perfection towards God, the justice of God in the creation and legislation, the uninterrupted Imamat and leadership and its role in the continuity of the Islamic Revolution, and the sublime value of man and his freedom, together with responsibility before God.

The principles of equality and social justice are the main goals of Islam. Therefore, the present government of the Islamic Republic of Iran is responsible for improving and raising the standard of living of its citizens, and for seeing that all the material and spiritual needs of its people are fulfilled. All its resources are applied to the realization of the following:

1)   Create a favorable environment for the growth of spiritual virtues based on faith and piety, and to struggle against all forms of vice and corruption.

2)   Raise the level of public awareness in all areas, using the public press and the mass media, and any other means for the diffusion of ideals according to Islamic principles.

3)   Provide free education and physical training for everyone at all levels, and to facilitate and expand higher education.

4)   Provide a just and independent economic foundation according to the Islamic principles, in order to bring about the welfare of all citizens, eradicating poverty and eliminating deprivation in food, housing, health, and jobs, and providing social insurance.

5)   Secure self-sufficiency in all areas, asserting the comprehensive rights of the individual, and strengthening Islamic fraternity and public cooperation among all the people.

6)   Eliminate all inequitable discrimination in order to bring about reasonable possibilities for everyone to obtain satisfaction in all material and spiritual areas.

7)   Create a sound administrative system in order to offer better social services to the people of Iran.

The ruling powers in the Islamic Republic of Iran relying on the above-mentioned goals and objectives are the executive branch, the legislature, and the judiciary. All three operate under the direction and guidance of the Supreme Leader of the Republic (Vali-e-Faghie).

SOCIO-ECONOMIC CONDITIONS

The management of the economy in the Islamic Republic of Iran is subject to Islamic law. The economic theory of Islam is rooted in its principles of social justice, moral elevation, and general prosperity. The Constitution of 1979 establishes specific guidelines for the administration of the nation's economic and financial affairs. The ultimate objectives are to ensure economic independence, eradicate poverty and deprivation, create a comfortable standard of living, provide essential needs such as housing, food, health, therapeutic services, education, and all necessities for family formation, and full employment opportunities for all people.

Iran's involvement in the imposed war with Iraq has caused considerable disruption in its economy. The economy is divided into three sectors: public, which includes major industries, banks, insurance companies, utilities, communication, foreign trade, large mines, and mass transportation; cooperatives--including the production and distribution of goods and services; and private, which consists of all activities and services that supplement the cooperative and public sectors.

In addition to mandatory government taxes, religious alms are given on a voluntary basis by devoted Muslims. These religious alms (or taxes) are collected by highly respected religious leaders to be used for charitable causes, public welfare, education and rehabilitation. Many non-profit organizations which care for the handicapped have been financed and supported by these voluntary, religious, and obligatory taxes.

Iran's most important natural resources are oil, natural gas, and other mineral resources like magnesite, uranium, etc. Oil is produced for export and domestic consumption. Iran has been one of the world's major exporters of oil, and the economy is still significantly tied to the income from the oil industry.

Public Health and Welfare

Although the health conditions and standard of living have improved in recent years, public health facilities are still far from adequate. There is a considerable shortage of medical doctors, nurses, and medical supplies, especially in rural areas. In certain parts of the country, such as the Hormoz Island in the Persian Gulf, and in some rural areas in the southeast, there is a significant percentage of people suffering from a variety of health problems due to the lack of sanitary waters and unhealthy conditions. The incidence of visual impairment is particularly high, mostly due to infectious diseases such as trachoma. Infant mortality is higher in the villages than in the urbanized cities. In 1976 infant mortality was 112 out of every 1000 babies. This rate was reduced to 70 per thousand in 1985 (Ministry of Health Report, 1985). On the other hand, the flow of population to the larger cities has created urban housing and health problems. In the cities purified water is piped into the houses, while most of the villages rely on wells, springs, or rivers. In some cases widespread disease and illness are related to the low sanitary standards and to malnutrition.

There is, however, increasing concern for the problems of public health. Public hospitals provide free treatment for all citizens. These are supplemented by private institutions, but all are inadequate. All health services are supervised by the Ministry of Health. All government employees, and industrial and commercial workers receive free medical services, disability benefits, and retirement benefits.

CULTURAL NORMS AND VALUES

Religion has always played a significant part in the cultural life of Iran. Despite the conceptual distinction, culture and religion are mixed and very much interrelated in Iran. Nevertheless, Iranians do have a very rich and ancient culture among other nations. Much of Iranian cultural life has been strongly influenced by Islamic culture and heritage. Religion has always been central to Iranian history and politics. Attempts by the old monarchy to separate religion from politics in the twentieth century met with very little success.

Islamic values and teachings pervade an Iranian Moslem's daily life, and include teachings on prevention of handicapping conditions. According to Islamic ideology, whatever is physically, psychologically, mentally, and sociologically harmful to human beings is prohibited. Consequently, Islamic laws explicitly forbid the consumption of alcohol, pork, narcotics; and the practice of gambling, usury, homosexuality, adultery, sex out-of-wedlock, and fraud. On the contrary, whatever is good and beneficial for man's secular and spiritual life, such as cleanliness and purity, prayer, fasting (one consecutive month a year from the break of dawn till sunset), patience, endurance, charity, honesty, devotion, sacrifice, justice, forgiveness, fraternity, helping others, and protecting the handicapped, are strongly advised.

Family ties and loyalty are very significant in Iran. Iranians pay great attention and respect to family solidarity and woman's position in the family and the society. Family solidarity also means that every one in the extended family supports and respectfully obeys an influential individual (usually a family elder) throughout his or her entire lifetime.

The Iranian family at its best gives its members the combined services of protection and family counseling. This gives Iranians a valuable social support structure. Iranian men feel obligated to protect the honor of the family's women and children. It is the duty of men to support economically, socially and psychologically all family members. Family strength and formation is emphasized in the tenth principle of the Iranian Constitution, that says: "Whereas the family is a fundamental unit of Islamic society, all pertinent laws and regulations, and planning shall aim at facilitating family formation, safeguarding the sanctity of the family institution and strengthening family relationships on the basis of Islamic laws and ethics."

Mothers have a special place in Islamic culture. The prophet Muhammad has declared: "Paradise lies underneath the feet of the mothers." This means that mothers, through compassion, love, and concern for their children's growth and development, and appropriate education and training, provide them with the Islamic path of prosperity and promised Paradise. A majority of mothers who are physically capable of breast-feeding their children do this for up to 24 months. Breast-feeding is highly advised by Islamic teachings. As the holy Koran declares:

"Mothers shall give suck to their offspring for two whole years[2], if the father desires to complete the term. But he shall bear the cost of their food and clothing on equitable terms. No one shall have a burden laid on him/her greater than he/she can bear. No mother shall be treated unfairly on account of her child, nor the father on account of his child, and an heir shall be chargeable in the same way. If they both decide on weaning, by mutual consent, and after due consultation, there is no blame on them. If they decide on a foster mother for the offspring, there is no blame, provided they pay (the mother) what is offered, on equitable terms. But fear God and know that God sees well what you do." (Chapters 2-234.)

Iranian women carry out a wide variety of jobs besides childbearing and homemaking. In rural areas they weave most of Iran's famous carpets and perform a variety of agricultural tasks. In cities, they hold professional jobs working as teachers, doctors, nurses, and clerks. They also are employed in different types of factories. In support of women's rights, especially the protection of mothers, government has great responsibility. The twenty-first principle of the Constitution states:

"The government must assure the rights of women according to the Islamic criteria in all respects and accomplish the following goals:

1) To create a favorable environment for the development of woman's personality and the restoration of her material and spiritual rights;

2) To protect mothers, especially during pregnancy and childbearing, and also to protect orphan children;

3) To establish a competent court for the protection of the existence and the continuation of the family;

4) To provide a special insurance for widows, the elderly, and those without family;

5) To grant guardianship of children to worthy mothers for the benefit of children where there is no legal guardian."

Concerning marriage, although the marriage between first parallel cousins is not forbidden in Islam, by no means is it recommended or encouraged. However, in Iran, as in many other Middle East countries, this type of marriage has often taken place. Many Iranians view this kind of marriage as an honorable and strong family foundation, without considering the risk of genetically transmitted handicaps. In reality, and in most cases, because of the socio-geographic nature of the country, distribution of the population, and extended family structure, especially in rural areas with small towns and villages, the number of inhabitants is very low,[3] and approximately all the families are somehow blood related. Under these socio-geographic conditions, the occurrence of marriages with cross-cousins is not an unusual matter and it may not be fair to blame. As a result of this type of blood related marriage, particularly first-cousin marriages, there is a relatively high percentage of genetically transmitted disabilities.

In a comparative research study conducted by the author in special and regular schools in Tehran (1988) it was found that parents of 71% of deaf students (in day and residential schools), and about 40% of mentally retarded students were somehow blood related. These findings were presented to the public during a nationwide live weekly radio program which was broadcasted for three years by the author (1986-1989). The main objective was to give families some psychological and educational information on child rearing and to promote awareness as to the main causes of disabilities.[4] However, because of the natural, social and cultural structure of the society (where about half of the population live in 66,000 villages), and the limited possibilities for non-related marriages, there cannot be many alternatives for young men and women who wish to get married within the community to which they belong and to start their own families, especially in rural areas. However, extended marriage counseling and genetic consultation in screening clinics needs to be planned and established all over the country, with special attention to the rural areas.

As part of its cultural heritage, Iranian creativity is exemplified in its architecture, poetry, painting, carpet weaving, miniature, and music. Carpet weaving and miniature painting are only the best known Iranian art forms. Almost every city in Iran produces some kind of special handicraft. In most cases, in small towns and villages handicapped individuals are involved with this artistic handwork. There are many mentally handicapped individuals who are trained to weave coarse kinds of carpets. It is not unusual to see a blind person weaving an intricate carpet.

Iranian language and literature are very rich, with poetry being the greatest Iranian artistic achievement. There have been many famous blind poets and writers in Iranian literature.

Religious people have positive and protective attitudes toward handicapped individuals. Although there are still some misunderstandings and misconceptions about mentally retarded persons in the society as a whole, usually as soon as people become aware of the nature of mental retardation and the characteristics of retarded persons, they develop a sympathetic attitude toward them. Yet there has always been positive and protective feelings among religious people toward the physically handicapped, especially the blind (Afrooz, 1978). They have a feeling of responsibility to help and support them. The holy Koran and the sayings of prophet Muhammad call for much sympathy, affection, and social and individual recognition and treatment of disabled individuals. As prophet Muhammad has said, "Serving handicapped people is like being in the service of the prophets of God." For religious people in Iran it is a great honor and blessing of God to be in the service of the handicapped and to be actively involved in charitable organizations working for the causes of handicapped individuals.

EDUCATION: HISTORY AND ORGANIZATION

In order to gain an understanding of the development of education in Iran, the religious, cultural, linguistic and historic considerations discussed in the previous section must be kept in mind. In particular the religious influence in Iranian education has been especially strong. For centuries, the mosque has been the chief center of schooling outside the home. Affiliated with most mosques were religious schools (maktabs) supported by individual philanthropy or by religious foundations. The curriculum consisted of Koranic study, ethics, Arabic language, literature, logic, mathematics. This traditional system of education was gradually, although never completely, replaced by a system of state education.

In the nineteenth century, Iran began to adopt a modern educational system. In 1851 Darol-Funun, a polytechnic college, was founded. In the 1920s, this college became a typical secondary school Elementary education in modern Iran began in the late nineteenth century after higher education had been started. By the early twentieth century, several modern secondary schools were developed.

Following the 1979 Islamic revolution, the Islamic Republic of Iran initiated reforms in the entire educational system. Moral training and curriculum development have received much attention over the last ten years in order to make the teaching-learning process more effective and to respond to Islamic social and cultural objectives. The guidelines for schools were based on the principles and teachings of Islam. Particular importance was attached to the relationship between education and work. Secondary school students were to be equipped with academic and scientific techniques and work skills in order to make them aware of the need for industrial and agricultural production (Ministry of Education, 1989).

According to the Constitution, the ultimate goal of the Ministry of Education is to furnish universal and free schooling for the school age population (ages 6 to 18). Principle Thirty of the Constitution of the Islamic Republic of Iran clearly states the government's responsibility in this important matter: "The government must provide the means for free education (including special education) for all people until the completion of secondary schooling. With respect to higher studies, they shall be provided gratis to the extent that the self-sufficiency of the country is met." In general, the main goals and objectives of the Ministry of Education are: physical growth and hygiene, moral and ethical development, intellectual development, creative thinking, social responsibility, and artistic development of all regular and exceptional pupils (Ministry of Education, 1989).

Educational System

Iran has a 5-3-4 system of primary, guidance, and secondary levels of education. Twelve years of schooling will lead to a high school diploma. The structure of the formal education cycle is presented in Figure 1.

Pre-schooling is not compulsory, therefore it is not adequately available for all pre-school age children, except in some school districts and cases like special schools, and the provision of some educational facilities for mothers working in government organizations. Most day care takes place in private government-supervised institutions. The overall aim is to prepare children for formal school education. In the academic year of 1989-90 there were 2,547 preschools (including 504 in rural areas) in the country sponsored by the Ministry of Education (statistic bureau of the Ministry of Education, 1989).

FIGURE 1

**Structure of General Education
Systems in Iran-1989**

Higher Education in Vocational and Technical			Higher Education in Universities	
Technical	4		4	Physics-Math
and	3	Secondary	3	Experimental Sci.
Vocational	2	Education	2	Humanities and
Education	1		1	The Arts

	3
Guidance Education	2
	1

	5
	4
Elementary Education	3
	2
	1

	1
Pre-Elementary Education	Flexible and Non-compulsory

Primary school begins at the end of age six and lasts five years. This leads to a guidance or orientation course lasting three years. Following that, students are expected to pass the final examination for secondary education. Based on their scores and interests they must decide upon their future occupations or academic pursuits.

Secondary education lasts four years and is divided into two major tracks: The older and larger of these is the academic track which is subdivided into two main branches, science (experimental sciences and physics-mathematics) and humanities (culture and literature: economic, public service and arts). The secondary technical and vocational field is relatively less well developed and includes industrial and agricultural branches.

The public school system is controlled by the Ministry of Education. Official and centrally published textbooks are provided for all students and in each level throughout the country. There is a centralized form of examinations in the final stage of each level of education conducted by authorities in the Ministry of Education. All schools are either government-run or government-supervised. Boys and girls, starting from primary school, are totally separated. Christian, Zoroastrian, and Jewish religious minorities are permitted to maintain their own schools, but implementation of the content of the general academic curriculum is required. Very recently (1989) the parliament (mujlis) passed a law authorizing the Ministry of Education to give non-private and non-profit school establishments privileges to eligible individuals, groups, or institutions.

Education in Iran is financed predominantly by the government. According to the *UNESCO Statistical Yearbook* (1989), in 1984-85 (while Iran was involved in the imposed war with Iraq) 16.9% of the total government expenditure was for education (programs for educable exceptional children included). In the scholastic year of 1987-88, 12, 011, 106 pupils were enrolled in 74,039 schools, and according to the latest report in the academic year of 1988-89 the number of pupils was increased to 13,046,358 (7,433,708 boys and 5,612,660 girls were enrolled in 77,659 schools, attending 422,129 different classes with 613,515 teachers and staff members all over the country). These figures demonstrate an 8.6% increase in the school population and nearly 5% additional school units. The ratio of one personnel member for every 21 students is also indicated (Statistic Bureau of Ministry of Education, July 1989). Such an extraordinary and very unusual increase in the school population within one year created real problems for the government of the country with the youngest population in the world! This large increase in school age children is due to the lack of systematic approaches for controlling the very high rate of population growth, and the increasing demands from families for schooling for their children, specially in rural areas.

Literacy

A relatively high rate of illiteracy has been a matter of concern for the Iranian education authorities. According to the *UNESCO Statistical Yearbook* (1985), in 1977 the total percentage of illiterate persons in Iran was 52.5. Very soon after the Islamic revolution (1979), religious commands highlighted the necessity of literacy for all Muslim men and women. The late Imam Khomeini appointed a well-known clergy as head of the Iranian Literacy Movement, and invited everyone to feel responsible in this important social dilemma. He started a new movement that has had remarkable success in this vital matter. Since the creation of the Iran Literacy Movement, Iran has been very successful in developing schemes for reducing adult illiteracy. After a few years of hard work, pursuant to the census taken in October, 1986, the illiteracy rate was reduced to 38% (Statistic Center of Iran, 1987). Of course, the illiteracy rate in rural areas is much higher than in urban ones.

Problems and Plans

The educational situation in developing populated countries like Iran has some problems. The high growth rate creates a major problem in providing an adequate place for every child of school age. Although a considerable number of schools have been built since the revolution, the general opinion is that in most cases quantity has been increased at the price of quality. In some major cities, classes are too large and overcrowded. The supply of trained teachers is too small. The system of education produces more graduates than can be absorbed into the government services, and too few with vocational or technical training (less than 1.5% of secondary school students are in vocational and technical schools).

Currently some attempts are being made to make fundamental changes in the educational system of Iran. The government's plan is to pay more attention to preschool education and the vocational and technical training of students. At the present time, in almost every major city in Iran, there is a center for teacher training. These pre-service two-year teacher training centers are within the responsibility of the Ministry of Education and are primarily organized for the preparation of elementary and guidance teachers. There were 358 teacher training centers with 64,948 students in 1988-89 (Statistical Bureau of the Ministry of Education).

It is expected that the national universities, whose numbers have increased very rapidly, will train teachers for the secondary level. A separate Ministry of Higher Education is responsible for the universities. In 1989, the Council for Cultural Revolution required all colleges and universities to allocate 80% of their capacity, in the areas needed by the Ministry of Education, for teacher training purposes.

In reaching the main objective of universalization of general education, in recent years Iran has adopted a comprehensive program for the further improvement and expansion of school building. Government, local communities, religious organizations, individual philanthropy, and clergy, have played a very important role in providing school facilities and in eradicating illiteracy. According to the Principle 147 of the Constitution, in peace time the government must employ military personnel and technical facilities to aid educational and productive work.

SERVICES FOR SPECIAL NEEDS CHILDREN

Concern for handicapped children has a long and distinguished history in Iran. Traditionally, religious orders and charitable organizations have given comprehensive help to handicapped individuals. In Islamic societies like Iran, religious people have very positive and protective attitudes toward handicapped people. Caring for the handicapped and supporting them in any way is considered a blessing of God. The holy Koran declares: " . . . if any one saved [revived] a life, it would be as if he/she saved the life of the whole people" (Chapter 5-32).

As was mentioned before, active involvement in a voluntary organization with the aim of helping handicapped children or adults is believed to be a social honor. It is very important to understand that in Islamic teachings disabled individuals, especially those with multi-handicaps, are somehow viewed as innately oppressed (Tabata-baie, 1959) and it is an obligatory religious duty for every Muslim to do his or her best in meeting the needs of the disabled person.

Of course, one of the main responsibilities of the Islamic government is to protect and provide comprehensive help and facilities for the handicapped. War-wounded disabled (blind, deaf, and physically handicapped) individuals in a religious country such as the Islamic republic of Iran hold very high prestige and have a great respect and honor in society. They are named "the living martyrs."[5] Their honorable position in society has had considerable effect on the thinking and life style of other disabled individuals and people's attitudes toward them.

In recent years, in such a warm and enthusiastic atmosphere, the majority of handicapped individuals (both war victims and others) have been socially very active and taking part in different aspects of the society and participating in various special national and international sports and tournaments and championship games for the disabled. The Iranian Association of the Physically Disabled has held numerous local and national meetings in regard to educational, rehabilitational, social and political issues and problems related to handicapped people.

Definition and Prevalence

In theory, all logical criteria and definitions given by experts or scientific associations widely used in the United States and some European countries in regard to exceptional children are accepted in Iran by educational authorities. The following examples of handicapping conditions are being considered:

The accepted definition of mental retardation is that of the American Association on Mental Deficiency (AAMD), which states: "Mental retardation refers to significantly subaverage general intellectual functioning existing concurrently with deficits in adaptive behavior and manifested during the developmental period" (Grossman, 1983).

A distance of 20 feet is used as a base measure of visual activity for legal and clinical definitions of partial sight and blindness, with a 20/20 vision designated as normal; a person with a visual activity measure of 20/200 or worse in the better corrected eye is classified as blind, and an activity of between 20/70 and 20/200 will classify a person as partially blind.

An individual is classified deaf or hard of hearing when his hearing loss in both ears is at least 50 decibels. Finally, those children and youth who are not able to behave normally in normal circumstances, or who are unable to maintain acceptable interpersonal relationships with peers, family and teachers (i.e. hyperactive, autistic, aggressive, or very depressed, etc.) are viewed as emotionally disturbed.

In practice, handicapping conditions among children in Iran are influenced by the general definition of handicap, as being in serious need of attending special schools. Up to the present, because of the shortage of expert personnel, insufficient facilities and inappropriate screening systems, it has not been possible to provide relevant and accurate data on incidence of some handicapping conditions, especially in rural areas of

Iran. Nevertheless, based on different reports on the handicapped population by the Statistical Center of Iran (1988), the Department of Special Education (1989), and the Welfare Organization (1989), the prevalence of noticeable handicapped children could be estimated as nearly 10% of the school age population (Table 1). This figure does not include learning disabled and speech impaired children.

TABLE 1

Estimated Prevalence of Handicapped Children in Iran

Handicap	% of School Age Children
Mentally retarded	2.3
Blind and visually impaired	1.5
Deaf and hard of hearing	1.5
Physically handicapped	1.2
Emotionally disturbed	2.0
Multihandicapped and other health impaired	1.0
TOTAL	9.5

High incidence of deafness and blindness are associated mostly with poor environmental conditions, inadequate preventive health care, and genetic problems, mainly resulting from blood-related intermarriages. Since there is no compulsory testing and special education programs, and considering the specific socioeconomic condition of the country with respect to cultural retardation resulting from environmental deprivation in rural areas, by the AAMD definition of mental retardation (1983), the prevalence of mental retardation may be higher than estimated.

SPECIAL EDUCATION ESTABLISHMENT

Long before the official establishment of the Department of Special Education in the 1920s, the first school for the deaf was founded by Jabbar Baghcheban (1889-1966) in Tehran and the first school for the blind, with the help of the German priest Ernest Christofel, was established in Tabriz, northwest of Iran. In 1958 the Center for the Protection and Rehabilitation of the Mentally Retarded, under the supervision of the Ministry of Health, was established for mentally retarded children and adults. Following these very important and historic events, many other special schools and residential provisions and facilities founded by religious and conscientious individuals were established in other cities. The first residential school for the blind was inaugurated in Tehran in September, 1955.

In 1968 the Department of Special Education within the Ministry of Education was created. The main objective of this new department was to discern, select, and place educable exceptional children in special classes or schools. These children included those who were mentally retarded, blind, deaf, and emotionally disturbed. In order to accomplish these objectives many new special schools were founded in various parts of the country, along with the allocation of numbers of special classes within the regular school setting for exceptional children.

This department, until 1978, was able to give special education services to a limited number of students. In the academic year of 1978-79 about 8,000 exceptional students attended special schools or classes within the department's responsibility. In this ten year period, in 1976-77, a one year pre-service special education teacher training center with about 80 students was formed. Lack of proper public awareness about the effectiveness of special education, insufficient facilities, and the shortage of trained special education teachers were the main problems. After 1979, following the Islamic revolution, some significant changes took place in special education programs. The author was the first Iranian holding a Ph.D. in special education in 1978. Within a few years some other colleagues with special education backgrounds returned home from abroad. In the spring of 1979, I was asked by the Minister of Education to serve as a new director of the Special Education Department. Since my main goal was to stay at the College of Education and develop a four-year special education program, I accepted work there for a short time. Meanwhile a few aware and responsible colleagues joined the department in order to continue the work. Consequently many new special schools in different parts of the country were founded. Important steps in special education teacher training were taken as special schools and parent-teacher associations were formed.

Parents of exceptional children with some degree of awareness were demanding more special education facilities from the Educational authorities. According to the latest statistical reports, in the academic year 1978-79 a total of 29,127 exceptional students (18,157 boys and 10,970 girls) were enrolled in 449 special schools and attending 3,408 classes with 4,625 teachers and staff, all over the country (Statistical Bureau of the Ministry of Education, July, 1989). These figures indicate that there is an average 8.5 students in a single class and the ratio of special education personnel (teachers and staffs) to students was 1 to 6. Only 62 special schools out of 449 (about 14%) were active in rural areas with 1,210 students (849 boys and 361 girls).

Although this statistical report of activities of a relatively new (in comparison with the western countries) formal educational program for handicapped children in Iran demonstrates remarkable progress, it is far from being desirable. At present, less than 1% of the school population receives special education services from the Department of Special Education, and approximately the same number benefit from rehabilitational services within the responsibility of the Welfare Organization.

Besides the Department of Special Education, different types of services are provided through the Iranian Welfare Organization, which is affiliated with the Ministry of Health. The Welfare Organization is responsible for providing adoption and foster care for handicapped and nonhandicapped orphans, aid to families with severely handicapped dependent children, protective and rehabilitational services for those handicapped individuals who, because of the age limit or severity of the handicapping condition, are not covered by the Department of Special Education. Pursuant to the latest report, nearly 30,000 handicapped (deaf, blind, mentally and physically disabled) children and adults are receiving protective and rehabilitative services in more than 300 rehabilitation centers (including residential units) throughout the country (The Welfare Organization special report, 1989).

CURRENT PRACTICE OF SPECIAL EDUCATION

The Department of Special Education headquarters is located in Tehran and it has branches in each province and major city. Throughout the country, parents of deaf and blind children will usually look for special education opportunities before the children reach school age. If they find a suitable one, they will go for enrollment. Otherwise, they will seek special classes within the regular schools or will ask for tutorial help from the Special Education offices. In some cases, if there is not any type of special education provision available within the local community, they may try to take advantage of local regular schools or residential special schools in larger cities.

The major problem in special education lies in the identification, assessment, and provision of services for mentally impaired individuals, the severely or profoundly retarded, or those with obvious physical handicaps. Identified as requiring special education and rehabilitation programs before they reach the school age, either by their own parents or through examination by a physician, these children are more likely to receive some type of special program or rehabilitation services from the Welfare Organization *prior* to entering school. Some parents of trainable mentally retarded children will try to place them in one of the special education schools, if possible, before going to the Welfare Organization.

In most cases, students with mild sensory problems or mental retardation are not identified until they are already in regular schools and after a period of time when they start to demonstrate continuous academic failure and in some way significant differences from the average peers. In these situations, the teacher and the principal will inform the student's parents about the problem and the child will be referred to the Department of Special Education in Tehran, or to one of its bureaus in major cities. In these cases anyone can recommend or refer the identified exceptional student for a special education program, but is is usually the regular school and parents' responsibilities. Since there is no nationwide formal medical or psychological school entrance screening, it is not surprising that a considerable number of mildly mentally retarded students in special schools have already spent almost a year in a regular school before being identified as exceptional.

Most parents of mildly retarded children are very reluctant to send them to special schools, because of insufficient information about their children's mental capacity and the academic demands in regular schools. In some instances, unfortunately, due to referral based on false perceptions, there are a number of unidentified learning disabled, hard of hearing, and partially sighted students in the first grade, who, because of their continuous failure in one or more school subjects (i.e. reading, writing, or dictation) have been labeled as mentally retarded and have been referred and placed in special education programs for periods of time.

Identification and Eligibility

When a child with a mild problem is identified by parents (usually well-educated and aware) as requiring special education, either before she/he starts school or after attending regular school for some time, the child is referred to the Department of Special Education or one of its bureaus, where certain eligibility criteria will be considered. In order to place a child in a special education school or classes, she/he has to meet special qualification criteria. To be eligible for a special education program a child must be classified as 1) educable mentally retarded (if trainable and severely retarded she/he will be referred to rehabilitation services at the Welfare Organization); 2) visually handicapped; 3) hard of hearing or deaf; 4) deaf-blind; 5) emotionally disturbed; and 6) multihandicapped. This classification is based on given definitions and within normal school age ranges. The partially sighted and hard of hearing children must provide a medical examination certificate from one of the authorized medical centers or doctors. Unfortunately, at the present time, there is no practical definition, identification or official system of special education for learning disabilities, although in some cases students are identified and receive some tutorial help. Despite the fact that intelligence tests are used to determine the child's IQ, in order to find out whether or not his/her intelligence lies on the range of the educable mentally retarded. The Raven Standard Progressive Matrics and the Colored Progressive Matrics, and the Leiter International Performance Scale (LIPS), which were field tested in Iran, and the Stanford-Binet Intelligence Scale which is in a systematic standardization process for Iran,[6] are the most widely used intelligence tests by the Department of Special Education and other referral sources.

Mainstreaming

The idea of mainstreaming as a choice of educational preference because of the quality of interaction for handicapped students when they are placed in regular classroom with nonhandicapped students and regular teachers has been in Iran in most cases the only alternative to provide access to education for handicapped children, and it is widely practiced. Long before introducing the new concept of special education programs and even now when the new idea of special education programs is widely accepted, many blind, deaf and physically handicapped children in small cities and villages where special schools or classes do not exist have been incorporated in local regular schools and have been able to take advantage of educational opportunities. In these small cities and villages, where life patterns are not complicated, social demands are few, most jobs are routine and simple, and minimum knowledge and skills in daily living may be sufficient to survive without any problem, mildly mentally retarded individuals have been getting along quite well. In other words, the mentally handicapped are being mainstreamed in the communities and in most cases, they become socially responsible and economically productive.

SPECIAL SCHOOLS

All special educational services are free of charge. In nearly every special school students receive free snacks and in some larger schools which have classes from 8:00 in the morning to 2:00 in the afternoon, hot lunch is served through the Parents-Teachers Association (PTA).

Usual school hours are 8:00-12:00, six days a week. Transportation is also supported partially by the PTA, and the financial contributions of some philanthropic individuals and religious organizations. There are also a few private non-profit special schools and rehabilitation centers. These types of private special institutions are being encouraged by the Ministry of Education and the Welfare Organization to be expanded and to serve more handicapped people. A few special schools in larger cities offer special services like physical therapy, speech therapy, and family counseling. Most of the special schools have less than 100 students. Usually, there are about seven to nine students in each special class. A class size of nine is typical, and the classroom is about five by six meters, with one or two windows that are decorated with some instructional materials. Electricity and running drinkable water are provided in each school. Almost every special school has a library, recreation and sport spaces, and playground. Girls and boys are completely separated. In special education schools for the mentally retarded, students are grouped according to their mental and chronological ages.

Unlike regular schools, the Department of Special Education in most cases has made preschool programs available to the blind, deaf, and mentally retarded. Therefore, special schools are composed of preschool (flexible, one or two years), elementary level (five years), guidance (three years), and secondary level (four years). In preschool the main objective is to develop children's skills in the areas of sensory-motor, emotional skills, grooming, social adjustment, verbal communication, and aesthetics and creativity. Although some special books and teaching material are available for preschool children, this largely depends on the extent of the teacher's knowledge, experience, and abilities. The curriculum in formal special schools is book oriented. Reading, mathematics, moral and religious education, art, physical education, and vocational training have an important place in the daily schedule. With few exceptions, subject curricula for special schools correspond to those of regular schools. A few specially designed textbooks are provided for educable mentally retarded students.

Vocational education is mainly provided at the secondary level and in the case of the mentally retarded, when their chronological age coincides with secondary education age (15-18). Its subject content varies for boys and girls and type of school. The aim is to develop the habit of working and to give the opportunity to every handicapped student to acquire general and some specific vocational skills. Some special schools in larger cities have sheltered workshops for their students, especially for the mentally retarded.

In schools for the blind, students are encouraged, besides using Braille, to become acquainted with the regular typewriters, and usually all blind students at the secondary level are able to type very skillfully. Each year a relatively large number of physically disabled, blind, and deaf high school graduates, after participating and passing the national and very competitive university placement examination (Conquer) are able to enter any university and continue their education in different fields, especially in human sciences, and vocational and technological areas.

Unemployment among handicapped individuals graduated from special schools is very rare. In fact, in some instances many governmental institutions and private companies offer jobs for the disabled people with special privileges.

Legal provisions for the advancement, welfare, and the rights of the disabled are derived from the constitution of the Islamic Republic (1979, articles 20, 29, 30) and from various laws established under the Education, Welfare, and Labor divisions of the government.

Special Teacher Training

As noted previously, one area in which both the Ministries of Education and of Higher Education are very much concerned is Teacher Preparation programs, both in regular and special education. In fact, the shortage of special education trained teachers is the main problem in serving the educational needs of handicapped children in Iran. One of the principal goals of the Department of Education is to increase the number of trained teachers, special schools, and consequently the number of exceptional students served. A more realistic estimate of the number of school age handicapped children is based on the ratio of 10% of the total number of the school population (more than 13,000,000) or well over one million.

At the present time special teacher training programs are being implemented in different ways. There are two main residential special education teacher training centers (one for men and one for women) under the control and supervision of the Ministry of Education. High school graduated students enter these centers through taking part in national entrance examinations for teacher training centers. In those residential centers students live for two years and attend classes six to seven hours a day, five days a week. There are 200 students in each center and 30-40 students in different classes, being trained in four major areas: mental retardation, visual impairment, deafness, and emotional disturbance. It is the students' choice to decide the area of specialization provided that there will be a desired minimum number of students in each category. After successfully passing at least 90 credit hours of study in both general and specialized courses, including practicum teaching hours, students receive an associate degree. Graduates from these centers are eligible to teach at elementary and guidance levels in special schools for the deaf, blind, and emotionally disturbed, and at all levels in schools for mentally retarded children. Of course, these teachers are able, under some conditions, to continue their higher education in colleges.

Besides this program, the Ministry of Education every year offers in-service teacher training programs in different levels and areas. A large number of today's special school personnel are those regular teachers who have attended special education in-service training. Regular teachers holding a high school diploma, associate degree, bachelor's or master's degree receive certificates to teach in special schools from elementary through secondary levels--based on their educational backgrounds--after they attended intensive courses of special education programs (20 hours a week for 8-16 weeks). In addition, special school teachers are eligible to receive 20% more salary than the regular teachers.

In 1983, the author proposed a four-year special education program with emphasis in mental retardation, at the College of Education of the University of Tehran. Similar programs are now being offered in several other universities throughout the country. At present, a total of 350-450 special education teachers have graduated from this college with a bachelor's degree in special education. After the first group of undergraduate students in special education graduated in 1987, the master's program in special education was inaugurated in the University of Tehran. In fact, at this time, the University of Tehran is the only university in the Middle East that offers a master's program in special education. It is intended that a Ph.D. program in special education will be offered by the early 1990s.

The main objective of the present graduate program is to prepare students to fill teaching positions in special education teacher training centers and in some colleges which are short of special education faculty members. Concerning the textbooks used in these program, within the last ten years more than fifty books in different areas of psychology and education of exceptional children have been written or translated into Farsi for use in these programs. The major textbooks and journals in special education published in America or Europe have been made available to faculty members and graduate students through college libraries.

FUTURE PLANS AND PRIORITIES

There is no doubt that the religious government of the Islamic Republic of Iran feels a great responsibility in providing appropriate educational opportunities for all handicapped Iranian children and youth. Two primary objectives for the immediate future include: 1) reorganizing the special education system in order to provide more effective services to exceptional children, and 2) allocating a higher percentage of the national budget for special education. In fact, during the time in which this chapter was prepared (December 1989), the Iranian parliament, in response to the suggestion made by the Ministry of Education on the establishment of a new administration system of special education, approved changing the present Department of Special Education to the Organization of Special Education, with more comprehensive and greater powers and responsibilities, under the supervision of the Ministry of Education. The head of this new organization will be serving as a deputy minister of education. These encouraging actions by the Iranian government are a good sign of future development in the education of exceptional children.

In 1988 the Iranian chapter of the Council for Exceptional Children (CEC)[7] held an international seminar. This seminar was inaugurated with the remarkable and historic message of President Khamenei[8] emphasizing the identification and education of all handicapped children, which was broadcasted via radio and television throughout the country. During the seminar, the problems and future plans of special education services were discussed in the presence of the ministers of Education, Health, and other special education and rehabilitation authorities.

The main suggestions for future plans and developments in special education and rehabilitation of disabled individuals, which were approved by Education and Health authorities, are as follows:

1) Reorganizing existing insufficient rehabilitation and special education systems, and establishing a comprehensive organization to be responsible for the identification, assessment, rehabilitation, education, welfare, and employment opportunities of all disabled individuals, from birth through their lifetime.[9]

2) Improving special education personnel preparation in all needed areas.

3) Establishing genetics counseling centers and special health care clinics all over the country in order to prevent or minimize the possible genetic origin and other causes of handicapping conditions, especially in rural areas where the health situation is poor and many cousin marriages are taking place.

4) Preparing means and methods for early identification of handicapped children, and implementing screening tests for all regular school first grade children and special school entry children.

5) Enhancing cooperative relations between regular and special schools for mutual understanding, integration, and mainstreaming purposes.

6) Utilizing all public mass media in the most effective and best way possible for public awareness on handicapping conditions, capabilities of handicapped individuals, and preventive strategies.

Notes

1. The official name is "The Islamic Republic of Iran."

2. Recently there have been several researched articles published on the influence of breast-feeding duration on children's physical, psychological, and mental development (i.e. Filho, Antonia, et al. 1984. Influence of breast-feeding duration on children's growth. *Journal of Early Childhood Development and Care*, V15, pp. 69-83; Dipietro, Janet A., et al. 1987. Behavioral and heart rate pattern differences between breast-fed and bottle-fed neonates. *Journal of Developmental Psychology*, V23, pp. 467-477).

3. There are many villages in Iran that contain less than 500 inhabitants.

4. During and after such nationwide radio programs, considerable numbers of cousins and their parents were asking for more details and seeking genetic consultation.

5. Martyrdom in holy defense and for the sake of believing in God's words has the highest value in Islamic faith.

6. *The Development of the Individual Intelligence Scale, Tehran Stanford-Binet (T.S.B.).* The need for preparation of a culture-free comprehensive intelligence test to be used in the intellectual assessment and identification of mentally retarded (or gifted) Iranian children has been recognized for a long time. In 1979, the author proposed a long-term research project in the College of Education and invited a number of highly qualified expert colleagues to choose an internationally-known intelligence scale to be field tested and adopted for the Iranian setting, in the Persian language. The working committee chose the most commonly used individual intelligence test, the Stanford-Binet Test (1973 version) for standardization in Iran. The recent 1985 edition of the Stanford-Binet Test and its differences with the edition chosen in Iran has also been considered. The project was planned in three main stages. Up to the present time, two stages of the plan (translating and selecting sample groups, experimental implementation of translated and adapted test, statistical analysis of the findings, choosing appropriate test items, and administering the test with sample groups (age 18 months to 18

years) have successfully been completed. It is predicted that the test and its findings will be published in the early 1990s.

7. The Iranian chapter of the Council for Exceptional Children, as an international member of the CEC, was formed during 1985-86.

8. Ayatollah Kahmenei was supreme leader of the Islamic revolution.

9. The mentioned very recent change of the special education system of administration is a noticeable step toward this ultimate objective.

References

Afrooz, G.A. (1987). *Attitude assessment of Iranian regular school teachers toward handicapped individuals.* Doctoral dissertation, College of Education, Michigan State University.

Focuses on attitudes of regular school teachers in Iran toward blind, deaf, and mentally retarded children from cultural perspective.

Afrooz, G.A. (1988). *Introduction to Psychology and Education of Exceptional Children* (Farsi), 10th Ed. Tehran: University Press.

An introductory text about Psychological characteristics and Educational provisions of Mentally retarded, Deaf, Blind, Emotionally Disturbed, Learning Disabled, and Gifted children.

Algar, H. (1969). *Religion and the State in Iran.* Berkeley: University of California Press.

Focuses on the role of the religion on different aspects of Iranian society.

Algar, H. (1980). *Constitution of the Islamic Republic.* Berkeley: Mizan Press.

A complete English version of the constitution of the Islamic Republic of Iran.

Ali, Y. (1983). *Translation of the Holy Quran.* Maryland: Amana Corp.

English translation and commentary of the Holy Quran.

Bureau of Statistics. (1989). *Statistical Report of the Ministry of Education.* Tehran, Iran: Ministry of Education.

The latest official report of Ministry of Education on total number of students and teachers in different levels, percentage of exceptional children enrolled in special schools, number of students attending teacher education colleges, and the rate of illiteracy.

Grossman, H. J. (1983). *Classification in Mental Retardation.* Washington, D.C.: American Association of Mental Deficiency.

Presenting a new revision of the definition of mental retardation with respect to current status of scientific knowledge in this field.

Jafari, M. T. (1989). Islam and Mentally Retarded Children (Persian). *Journal of Exceptional Children*, Vol. 1: 19-28. Tehran: Iranian Chapter of the Council for Exceptional Children.
Explaining the status and the rights of mentally handicapped individuals in Islamic teaching.

Jalal, A. H. (1985). *An Outline of the Islamic Countries*. Chicago: The Open School.
A study of the goals and objectives of education in the Islamic countries.

Kauffman, M. J. and D. Hallahan (1981). *Handbook of Special Education*. New Jersey: Prentice Hall.
A basic text on philosophy, history and current practice of special education in United States and European countries.

Ministry of Health. (1987). *Special Report on Health and Infant Mortality*. Tehran, Iran: Ministry of Health.
An official statistical report on the situation of health, availability of medical services to the public, and the latest infant mortality rate in Iran.

Mirkhani, M. (1987). Activities of the Welfare Organization. *Journal of Exceptional Children*, Vol. 1: 32-35. Tehran: Iranian Chapter of the Council for Exceptional Children.
An official annual report of activities and achievements of Iranian Welfare organization.

Mohseenpour, B. (1988). Philosophy of Education in Postrevolutionary Iran. *Journal of Comparative Education Review*, Vol. 32: 76-86.
A comparative study of philosophy of education in Iran, before and after the Islamic revolution (1979).

Motahhari, M. (1981). *The Human Being in the Quran*. Tehran, Iran: Islamic Guidance.
Focuses on status and psychological characteristics of "Man" from Quranic view-points.

Motahhari, M. (1981). *Sexual Ethics in Islam and in the Western World*. Albany, California: MSA, Box 6322.
A comparative study of sexual ethics, value of women, and moral philosophy in Islam and Western world.

124   Education and Disability in Cross-Cultural Perspective

Motahhari, M. (1985). *Iran and Islam*. Tehran: Anjoman Eslami
    Mohandesin.
    Elaborates the important factors that Islam is based on how Iranians
embraced Islam, and their significant contribution to Islamic Arts and
literature.

Noori, Y. (1985). *Islamic Government and Revolution in Iran*.
    England: Royston.
    Consists of three chapters on the Islamic concept of state, the nature
of Islamic revolution in Iran, and the Islamic political and judicial
system.

Pollak, S. (1982). *Traditional Islamic Education*. Cambridge, MA:
    Harvard University Press.
    Explaining the historical trends of Islamic education, the role of the
mosques as a chief center of schooling outside the home, and the religious
schools (Maktabs) for general education of children.

Posttlethwaite, T., and Thomas, R. (1980). *Schooling in the Asian
    Region*. New York: Pergamon Press.
    A comparative and comprehensive study of educational systems in
some of the Asian countries, such as Thailand, Singapore, Malasia,
Philippines.

Shariati, A. (1979). *On the Sociology of Islam*. Berkeley: Mizan
    Press.
    Analysis of important factors in Islamic society of the concept of
equality and brotherhood amongst Moslem nations.

Singh, R. R. (1986). *Education in Asia and the Pacific*. Bangkok:
    UNESCO.
    Looking at the educational systems, objectives, universalization of
education, literacy movement in the Pacific and Asian countries.

Statistic Center of Iran (1987). *Statistical Report on the Iranian
    Population*. Tehran, Iran: Statistic Center of Iran.
    Statistical report on population distribution in the cities and villages,
the age breakdown of the population and the birth and the death rate.

Tabatabaie, S. M. H. (1968). *Almiza, Interpretation of the Holy Quran*.
    Iran: Dar-el-elm Qum.

The most comprehensive existing interpretation of Holy Quran, written in 40 volumes.

Tabatabaie, S. (1982). Woman in Islam. In *Iran, Essays on Revolution in the Making*. 105-119. Robert Olson and Ahmad Jabbari (eds.). Lexington: Mazda Publishers.
Elaborating the status, duties, and rights of women in Islam and also the woman's role as a wife and a mother in the family, and an active member of the society in professional, social and political scenes.

Tabatabaie, S. M. H. (1982). *The Spiritual Life*. Tehran, Iran: Bethat Foundation.
Explaining the moral and spiritual life of "Man," while taking active part in secular life.

United Nations (1988). *Statistical Yearbook, 1985/1986*. New York: United Nations.
Presenting demographic, socio-economic, and educational details of member countries.

Wilberr, N. D. (1981). *Iran. Past and Present: From monarchy to Islamic Republic, 9th Edition*. New Jersey: Princeton University Press.
A relatively comprehensive book, describing demographic characteristics, influence of religion in Iranian culture, and socio-economic, and political situations before and after the Islamic Revolution (1979).

CHAPTER 6

CURRENT DEVELOPMENTS AND THE PROBLEMS OF CULTURE AND SPECIAL EDUCATION IN JAPAN

by Yoko Itagaki and Kunihiko Toki

GENERAL UNDERSTANDING OF CULTURE AND DISABILITY IN JAPAN

Land and Population

Japan is an island country stretching along the northeast coast of the Asian continent. It consists of four main islands: Hokkaido, Honshu, Shikoku and Kyushu from north to south with an additional 6,900 smaller islands. The total land area is 377,719 square kilometers, or 0.3% of the total land mass of the world. Japan is divided into 47 administrative regions; 43 prefectures and four special divisions.

The population of Japan as of October 1989 was 123,255,000, making it the seventh most populated country in the world with about 2.4% of the world's population. In 1989 the population density was 331 people per square kilometer. This makes it the fourth most densely populated country among the countries with a population of more than five million. As Japan has a limited area of flat land, its population density in terms of habitable land is far higher in real terms. (See Figure 1.) There has been a slight decrease in the last couple of years resulting in a population of 122,745,000.

Figure   1

Population   Density   (1989)

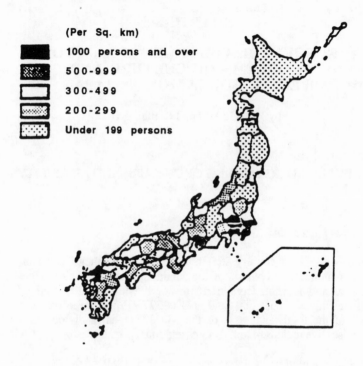

Life expectancy among Japanese has shown a remarkable improvement and has come to be the highest in the world. In 1989 it was 81.77 years for women and 75.91 years for men. The reason for this is that the mortality rate of infants and aged people has been decreasing. On the other hand, the birth rate has declined to 1.57 per female of child-bearing age, in 1990.

A moderate increase in the future population of Japan is predicted, reaching a peak of 136,000,000 by the year 2013. Therefore, the national rate of increase will decline owing to the aged population, which will account for a high percentage of the population. The problem of an aging society is one of the most serious socio-political questions confronting Japan today. (See Figure 2.)

Figure 2

Changes in the Population Pyramid

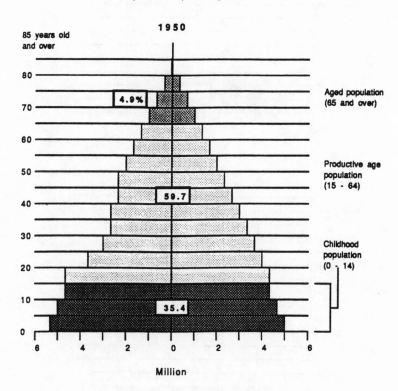

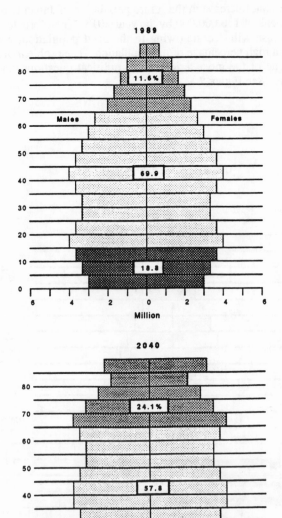

Education

The school system of Japan is illustrated in Figure 3. The levels of
education are divided into elementary school (six years), lower secondary
school (three years), and higher secondary school (three years).
Elementary and lower secondary schools are compulsory.

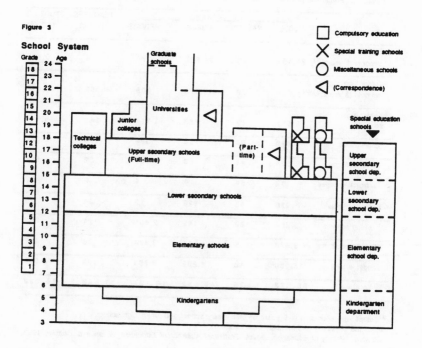

There are also kindergartens for pre-school children and special education schools for physically and mentally retarded children. Moreover, there are special training schools and miscellaneous other schools for vocational and practical training. As for tertiary education, there are three types of institutions; universities, junior colleges and technical colleges. Public and private schools are found at all levels. Table 1 shows the number of schools, teachers and students in 1989.

TABLE 1. Public and private schools in Japan: Number and enrollment (as of May 1, 1989)

	SCHOOLS				TEACHERS	STUDENTS
	TOTAL	NATIONAL	PUBLIC	PRIVATE	(1,000)	(1,000)
Elementary schools (6 years)[a]	24,851	73	24,608	170	454	9,607
Junior high schools (3 years)[a]	11,264	78	10,578	608	302	5,619
Senior high schools	5,511	17	4,183	1,311	343	5,644
Universities	499	96	39	364	208	2,067
Junior colleges	584	41	53	490	52	462
Technical colleges	62	54	4	4	6	52
Special schools[b]	938	45	876	17	44	95
Training schools	3,254	169	182	2,903	121	742
Miscellaneous	3,570	5	91	3,474	46	442
Kindergartens	15,080	48	6,239	8,793	109	2,038
Total	65,613	626	46,853	18,134	1,688	26,768

[a]Compulsory education is 9 years of elementary school and junior high school.
[b]For the physically and mentally handicapped.
Source: Ministry of Education, Japan, *Statistical Abstract of Education, Science & Culture*, 1990.

According to the 1990 Education White Paper, 95.1% of lower secondary school graduates entered upper secondary schools or technical colleges (boys, 94.0%; girls, 96.2%). The number of graduates advancing to higher education from upper secondary schools was 36.3% (boys, 35.2%; girls, 37.4%). The ratio of advancing students to universities totals 24.6% (boys, 33.4%; girls, 15.2%).

In the stages of compulsory education only the curriculum set by the Board of Education is taught. The class size limit for elementary schools is 40. It is hoped that the present limit will be reduced. The budget for education for fiscal 1990 was 5,113 trillion Yen, or 7.7% of the total fiscal budget. Only 2.4% of that education budget went to special education, or about 121 billion Yen.

Number of Special Needs Children

Table 2 shows the number of special needs children enrolled in public special schools over the last few decades.

TABLE 2.   Changing the number of students in special education source; School Basic Survey by Ministry of Education

YEAR	BLIND	DEAF	SPECIAL CARE STUDENTS
1950	5,155	11,600	110
1955	9,090	18,694	358
1960	10,261	20,773	4,794
1965	9,933	19,684	14,699
1970	9,510	16,586	24,700
1975	9,015	13,897	40,636
1980	8,113	11,577	72,122
1985	6,780	9,404	79,217
1990	5,599	8,169	79,729

There were 170,000 students enrolled in special schools and classes including public and a few private institutions in May of 1990. The number of compulsory education students is 131,000 (1% of the total number of students at the same level).

The Japanese government has been improving the special education program whereby students will be able to get a satisfactory education in order to develop their own capability and skills for a future independent life. Nevertheless the projects are still inadequate. The class quota in special education is 15 students. Two teachers undertake teaching responsibility in each class. Neither teacher, however, is required to be a specialist (licensed in special education). Sometimes one of the teachers is less experienced in special education.

THE SOCIO-ECONOMIC AND POLITICAL SITUATION:
A BACKGROUND OF SPECIAL EDUCATION

Socio-Economic Stability

Japan has influenced world economics by its evolutionary development of the GNP since the mid-1970s. The rate of economic growth since 1990 was 3% more than the previous year. Stability in the cost of living depends on successful development of technology, effective management strategies, and rationalization of enterprises. Low inflation has been maintained over the past two decades. Recently however, a shortage in the labor force has become a problem. An increasing number of foreign workers has supported the labor market of Japan. It is reported that about 150,000 foreign laborers (including illegal workers) are now working in Japan.

In spite of the stability in the cost of living, land and house prices have risen drastically. In 1986 land and real estate prices suddenly soared to triple those of the previous year. For most Japanese workers it has become difficult, if not impossible, to buy their own home in a city or urban area. It can be said to be an exceptionally ironic phenomenon in such a stable economic situation as in Japan. On the other hand, as people's awareness of the environment increases, the recycling movement is actively growing. People are not satisfied with a superficial sense of wealth with overwhelming consumer power.

Standard of Living

In a survey on living conducted by the General Affairs Agency of the Prime Minister's Office, men and women over 20 years of age were interviewed. 10.6% of the people evaluated expressed an increase in the standard of living compared to the preceding year. This rate increased 2.9% from the previous survey. On the other hand 13.7% responded that there was a drop in the standard of living from before, a 6.2% decrease from the previous time period. Japanese household accounts compared to the USA are shown in Table 3. Further, class perception by Japanese householders is as follows: middle-middle class 53.1%, lower-middle class 27.7% and upper-middle class 8.2%.

TABLE 3.

Japanese Household Accounts (1989)[a]

	Amount per Month	
	(YEN)	(US$)[c]
Income	**495,849**	**3,594**
Regular[d]	318,898	2,312
Temporary & bonuses[c]	91,219	661
Disposable Income	**421,435**	**3,055**
Living expenditure	316,489	2,294
Food	76,794	557
Housing,[b] fuel & light	54,231	393
Clothing & Footwear	22,577	164
Medical care	8,092	59
Education	15,349	111
Reading & recreation	29,585	214
Propensity to consume	**75.1%**	

a) For salaried worker households. b) Includes payments of debts for houses & land. c) US $1.00 = Y137.96 (annual average). d) Household heads only. Source: Management and Coordination Agency, Japan.

Overall, 89% of the people perceived themselves as being middle class. This rate is somewhat lower than in 1989. (See Figure 4.)

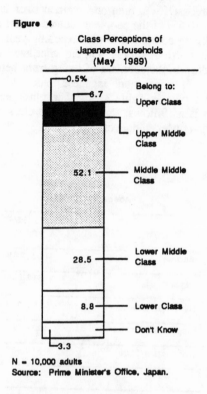

Figure 4

Class Perceptions of
Japanese Households
(May 1989)

0.5%

6.7

Belong to:

Upper Class

Upper Middle
Class

52.1 — Middle Middle
Class

28.5 — Lower Middle
Class

8.8 — Lower Class

Don't Know

3.3

N = 10,000 adults
Source: Prime Minister's Office, Japan.

Sixty-six percent of respondents expressed total satisfaction with their standard of living. However, a contradictory tendency is apparent. Despite the high frequency of middle class perception, half the Japanese feel dissatisfied with their standard of living because they do not have enough free time after work hours, and/or feel over-burdened in relation to their job. Over half the Japanese preferred to live with peace of mind rather than acquire expensive material goods. The government has now been required to develop a new policy on economic life whereby people are able to choose a lifestyle with more free time and adequate social welfare as opposed to receiving a set amount of income for the hard work they perform.

The Unchanging Political Situation of the Leadership by the Liberal Democratic Party

The Liberal Democratic Party (LDP) has taken the initiative in the politics of Japan since World War II except for a very short period of leadership by the Japan Socialist Party from 1947-1948. The political climate has been maintained in a conservative and stable manner because there is no balance in power of diet resolutions through active debate by several powerful parties. Although political criticism of the LDP has been increasing since the Lockheed Grafe scandal, increasing opposition is not strong enough to overthrow the government through Diet elections. The Upper House elections in July 1989 resulted in a slight shift from the government to non-government parties boosted by a challenging voting trend by women. In the following election in February 1990, however, the LDP maintained a majority in the House. It was returned to power again in a conservative political climate. (See Table 4.)

TABLE 4. Results of the 39th Election for the House of Representatives and Current Diet Party Memberships

	39th H.R. Election Results[a] Votes Polled			Diet Membership (As of March 31, 1990)	
	No. (1,000)	Share (%)	Persons Elected	House of Represen- tatives	House of Coun- cillors
Liberal Democratic Party (LDP)	30,315	46.14	275	286	109
Japan Socialist (JSP)	16,025	24.39	136	139	73
Komeito, National Council	5,243	7.98	45	46	21
Japan Communist Party	5,227	7.96	16	16	14
Democratic Socialist Party	3,179	4.84	14	14	10
Socialist Democratic Federation	567	0.86	4	4	0
Other	340	0.52	1	1	19
Independent	4,808	7.32	21	6	5
Vacancies	- -	- -	- -	0	1
Total	65,704	100.00	512	512	252

a) Eligible voters as of the election day (Feb. 18, 1990) were 90,322,908 people. The voting rate in the election was 73.31%.
Source: Secretariats, House of Representatives and House of Councillors, Japan.

Changing the Japanese political situation through independent voter trends is an interesting and complex key point. It is regrettable that today's Japanese educational policies put forth by the leadership of the LDP have not been serious in support for the individual growth of children. As a result, the program of education does not take individuals into consideration but is designed for the group, in each class and grade. Expectations that the government would think more carefully and provide more enthusiastic support for educational services for special needs children have not been met.

CULTURAL NORMS AND ATTITUDES TO DISABILITY

Homogeneous Society and Strong Group Identity

How people accept disabled persons differs in each cultural climate and norm. In the first half of the twentieth century, Japanese society had a strong tendency to regard these people with great aversion and hide them within the family, because there was no established sense of human rights. This feeling has still not been completely eradicated.

It is generally said that Japan is a homogeneous country because it consists of a unitary race. But this is a misconception. Japan includes the Ainu and Ryukuy (Okinawa) races too. Despite this fact, the Meiji Government ignored these races in order to accomplish a unified modern policy of militarization. This governmental strategy aimed to strengthen people's loyalty to the nation and was reinforced by the emperor's worship system. By inspiring people with the idea that Japan is a country with a unitary race, cultural uniformity in Japan is conceived as a political device, not a cultural reality.

After the Second World War, the uniform trend of consciousness has been converted into contributions to a fast-developing economy by hard work.

There have been few chances historically for people to be able to challenge an irrational society with their own value and identity. Of course there is a problem of individual difference too--independent Japanese are now increasing. Such people are trying to cope with modern society beyond the pressures of uncomfortable compulsive norms.

The Japanese Constitution specifies that sovereignty rests with the people. The Japanese Emperor is considered a human being, not a god as people were forced to believe during the Second World War. The attitudes and consciousness of most Japanese are, however, problematically influenced by the emperor worship system. When the former Emperor Hirohito passed away, his death was shrouded in a sombre mood in all facets of Japanese life. Most people were apt to exercise self-restraint in public discussion irrespective of their feelings.

On the other hand, a few anti-emperor worship movements sprang up while Hirohito was ill in the latter part of 1988. Women in Tokyo held a meeting to "Reconsider the Emperor System" with over one and a half thousand people participating. At this meeting, a female novelist, Sue Sumii, gave a stimulating speech in which she stated: "It shall be difficult to abolish all sorts of discrimination in Japan unless people reject the high personage of Emperor." She stressed that the Emperor is not a mere symbolic person of the nation, but on top of the hierarchical status structure of Japan. As long as the above mentioned feelings permeate modern Japan, disabled and special needs people will be situated in the lower rank of society. Of course most people are not aware of the emperor system. If ever a major problem in the nation occurs, however, it could be said that emperor worship will work as an initiator to control the minds of the people. It is still dangerous because the norm of the emperor system has remained and has been allowed to take advantage of national affairs.

Furthermore, Buraku-discrimination remains as one of the difficult social problems in Japan. Buraku is a political and social standing system established in the Edo (Tokugawa) period. Despite the emancipating policy of the Meiji government, it has remained in some people's discriminative view to the present day. The word Buraku was done away with officially when the government took on a modern and improved emancipation policy again in 1969. It is now called Dowa-district. Although there have been efforts to eradicate discriminative thinking toward Dowa-people, severe discrimination still exists in the job market and in marriage. This is the most problematic discrimination in Japanese society as an extension of the emperor worship system.

Thus, Japanese society has forced a difficult life on minority people. There is a need to develop a philosophy of equality which liberates Japanese people from the social ranking. A new social climate is needed where each person is esteemed as an individual. This climate would contribute to the future of special education.

Stability-Oriented Social Climate

In the eyes of the world, the uniform community of Japan is said to "stick together." Generally Japanese actually prefer to conform to the majority opinion rather than to confront or be an assertive minority. Kenichi Yoshida, a literary critic, has described this preference as follows. "We have an expression, which literally translated means 'to pull one's leg'; however, its true meaning has nothing whatsoever to do with ragging. Our expression actually means pulling the leg of anyone seen to be climbing up, in the sense of achievement, so as to prevent the person from climbing any further. And with luck, by implication, the pull will bring the individual toppling down." [1]

This feeling is related to an others-oriented attitude of people because it has been internalized in individuals through early child rearing and education. It could be said that our social climate is supported by group-identity rather than individual-identity, coupled with a submissive attitude rather than an assertive one. Although it is contradictory, this spiritual climate has been influential in closing the circle of disabled people. It is difficult to develop an interdependent relation between disabled and non-disabled people. For two decades, the social welfare system and services have evolved for special needs people. It has become necessary to improve the grass-roots movement for disabled people without further delay. It is regrettable that although concerns for disabled people are increasing, a natural inclination for helping has still not manifested itself as acceptable or natural. Of course people think that by no means are disabled people outsiders to the homogeneous community. Nevertheless, an others-oriented adaption is standing in the way of a global movement to live with handicapped people.

As mentioned in the previous section, 90% of Japanese perceive themselves as middle class. It is hoped that we won't remain conservative for life in order to hold on to the stability of middle class existence, but will share enriched feelings with disabled people or other minorities. On the one hand, young Japanese are developing a sense of freedom. On the other hand they are bound to the illusional prestige of upper level schools and companies, and exhausted by exam-hell. This is ironic in a stability-oriented society.

Strictly speaking, to be handicapped or disabled is in opposition to the illusion of upward-orientation. It might be said that the wealth of Japanese has remained an exclusive commodity. It must be stressed that cultural innovation which will allow the acceptance of others who are different is long overdue in today's Japan.

General View and Policy toward Disabled People

The Japanese government's policy for handicapped people has developed in response to the objectives of The International Year of Handicapped People in 1981, whose aims are their complete participation and equality in society. In 1982, the government did not waste any time in considering the long term perspectives of a counterplan and established a General Office for the Handicapped. Then in 1988, the policy for ensuring a life of independence for the handicapped was incorporated into the National Welfare Visions.

Policy for Physically Handicapped. In 1984 a partial amendment was made to The Welfare Code for those with physical handicaps. The amendment specifies that all physically handicapped people should be given a chance to participate in social, economical, cultural and all kinds of activities in the life of their communities. Deaf people, for example, are offered the conveniences of a sign-language-translated and subtitled video library, and for blind people a service is now available for obtaining public information in braille from each local administration branch. The number of government-aided sheltered factories near the homes of the physically handicapped where they can work is also increasing. There are approximately 20 workers in each factory. For seriously handicapped people who need special care at home, helper service is available. Recently, gymnastic facilities for sports therapy or athletic activity have been gradually expanded.

Policy for Psycho-Physically Handicapped and Mentally Retarded. To keep pace with the expansion of early education and therapy systems, a positive social environment should be developed in order to enable handicapped people to grow and live comfortably in each community. For mentally handicapped youth over 18 years of age, day care homes and sheltered factories for future job training have been established. Through these policies, the most important factor is that social conditions which have enforced an inconvenient lifestyle for the handicapped should be changed. It should not be considered as only a problem of changing awareness. It is necessary that emphasis changes toward living with handicapped people rather than just giving them a helping hand. A related issue of importance is preference for a personal life of co-operation, rather than hard work to maintain a life of material wealth. A new culture in which handicapped people can make a meaningful and beneficial contribution to society would be of benefit to all people.

CURRENT IMPROVEMENTS

Increasing Experiences with Handicapped People

Investment in Each District. The Group House System, started in 1989, has produced excellent results in helping handicapped people to live an independent life to the extent possible. Several mentally retarded persons live together in an apartment or house in each community. They are provided with a food service or consultation service for self-management of health and financial affairs if required. This new idea attempts to deal with only the difficult tasks. This policy is one of the steps taken toward normalizing the relationship between the general public and handicapped people. The 1990 edition of the White Paper of Health and Welfare reported that many social and cultural events and exchanges have been taking place, allowing handicapped people in each administration district to participate.

Example 1: In 1983, the farmer parents of a handicapped person living in Nagareyama City (Chiba prefecture) held a barbecue party inviting many people in the community. After five years, this party began to be sponsored by the City, and developed into a wider annual exchange festivity drawing over ten thousand citizens in the municipal sports-ground. The participants of the festivity enjoy singing and listening to songs together. Ordinary people experience being in a wheel chair and try walking with a white cane, as the blind do.

Example 2: Chiba City founded the Therapeutic Education Center in 1981 as a commemorative project for the International Year of the

Handicapped, including a rehabilitation center for the psycho-physically handicapped, a job training center for the mentally retarded, and a welfare service center and factory for the seriously handicapped. In each facility, volunteers have offered a reading service for the blind, sign language translation for the deaf, and many exchange events.

These improvements are, however, not necessarily sufficient. The amount of information available on the daily lives of the handicapped is rather little. For instance, in The White Paper referred to in this section,[2] the number of pages with articles on handicapped people's problems are few. In the case of The White Paper for Education, the pages regarding disability issues account for only 0.78% of the total number of pages and in The White Paper for Health and Welfare, it amounts to 2.27% of the total. The substantial information service is an index of adequate social concerns for special needs and handicapped people. However, it is still in an embryonic stage of development.

Students' and Women's Activities: Wheel Chair Experience. We see an increasing number of handicapped people on the streets who are going out and enjoying themselves. It is delightful to see that the discriminative feelings toward the various handicaps are gradually diminishing. This current magnanimous tendency is credited to volunteers' activities supported by students and women. There are many popular movements to take part in helping on weekends all over Japan.

A student told us a wonderful story involving his own wheel chair experience as follows. In the beginning when he belonged to a service group of students for "handicappers," he had an idea that he should help them because they are a weak minority. After initiating relationships with them, he still had to cope with his inner feelings of inequality. He felt that it was difficult to speak frankly with them. In attempting to deepen the personal relationship with these people, he decided to try using a wheel chair himself. He was the subject in this experiment and his handicapped friend followed in another wheel chair a little distance behind him as an observer.

He said that through his experience, he realized that all over the city, structures and facilities are very inconvenient for handicappers. Even a partial improvement was not sufficient. He understood that if handicappers want to cross a railroad track, they need an unexpected amount of power. The people around him at the railroad crossing seemed to hesitate to give him a hand. He became aware that their reaction had been the same as his had always been. It was particularly frustrating to go to public toilets and be helped by someone, which made him realize the harm to one's self-esteem. Although he had wanted to give up halfway through the experiment, he did manage to complete it. He admitted that he wanted to get out of the wheel chair and walk on foot, time and time again.

This experience was most valuable in opening up and understanding the world of the handicapped. This kind of experiment adds to a meaningful exchange with handicapped people.

Consciousness Raising toward Self-Esteem

The sense of self-esteem is the most important condition for moving toward normalization between handicapped and non-handicapped people. It has especially been ignored in the social climate of group-identification in Japan.

The concept of "consciousness raising" in order to be responsible for one's own life has been well known in our society since the modern women's liberation movements in the 1970s. Women and handicapped people have been living in the same situation as a psychological minority group to this day. Origins of oppression have forced handicapped people to live an allotted and confined lifestyle, just as in the case of women who have been assigned an inferior gender role historically. We have still not acquired a steady trend in living together with the handicapped with the sense of self-esteem for each other. However, minority groups have been able to develop an increasing number of co-operative movements toward future equality.

Virginia Satire wrote a simple but beautiful poem, quoted here in part.[3]

> I own everything about me;
>> my body, including everything it does;
>> my eyes, including the images of all they behold;
>> my feelings whatever they may be, anger, frustration, love,
>>> disappointment, excitement,
> I can live me and be friendly with me in all my parts.
> I can then make it possible for all of me to work in my best interest.

POLICY AND MOVEMENT TRANSITION OF SPECIAL EDUCATION AFTER WORLD WAR II

When considering the present conditions of special education in Japan, it is necessary to understand the following two trends since World War II: the policies of the Japanese government, and the movements of teachers and parents. An overlapping point of both clearly shows the fundamental problems in the system and the substance of special education in Japan.

Establishment of The Right to Education by The Constitution of Japan and Other Laws

In Japan before World War II, the right to education belonged not to the people but to the nation. The national authority with the Emperor as leader had the right to education, and people were obliged to accept it without any reservation. At that time Japan was invading other countries imperialistically. As a matter of course the government did not treat the handicapped well. Their needs were considered unrelated to education.

However, "The Constitution of Japan" and the "Fundamental Law of Education" (enforced in 1947) mandated that the right to education belonged to the people. The people were to have equal rights to education. It was especially important that all children become eligible to receive compulsory education for nine years. The School Education Law was enacted in the same year. Thus the blind schools, deaf schools, and protected schools were incorporated into the system of compulsory education. Nevertheless, the government decided to postpone executing compulsory education for these schools for handicapped children. The reason given was "the bad condition of national power."

Although education for handicapped children before World War II was not in good condition, blind and deaf education had been advanced to some degree. Therefore, the teachers in deaf and blind schools were against the postponement of compulsory education for handicapped children. As a result of their advocacy, the system of compulsory education for the deaf and blind began in 1948. In the case of protected schools (schools for children with mental retardation, motor disability, and physical weakness), the system of compulsory education was not soon realized. However, as a result of the efforts of parents and other advocates, the special classes in general schools and institutions increased step by step.

Standstill Period Under High Economic Development

Since the latter half of the 1960s, the Japanese economy has progressed rapidly. The top leaders of Japanese finance were required to advance "the man power policy" by the government. In answer to this requirement, the government advanced educational policy in order to contribute to economic development. Under this "ability-dominant policy," education had been organized with a view toward efficient training to produce excellent laborers.

This trend has also affected the education for handicapped children. They were viewed as end-laborers bearing high potential for economic development.

Although the government mandated a policy for the promotion of special education, it had nevertheless been undertaken only for mildly handicapped children. Education for severely handicapped children was neglected. The policy for the promotion of special education proposed the establishment of more special classes and protected schools. Though special classes in general schools for mildly handicapped children were established, the protected schools for severely handicapped children did not come into operation according to the plan. Thus differential treatment based on the degree of handicap was reinforced. As a result, severely handicapped children have been forced to stay at home or be institutionalized.

Subjective Power Beyond Political Obstacles

In earlier days, there were two remarkable civil rights movements. First, instructional practices in institutions for the severely handicapped proved that the most severely handicapped students could certainly benefit from education. These practices were developed through the co-operative work of teachers and psychologists, and have spread as "the theory of developmental security." This theory is critical of government policy, and has become the backbone of the civil rights movements.

Secondly, national organizations which try to advance the studies and programs for all handicapped people were established. Previously, every organization was separated by handicapping conditions. Supported by the theory of developmental security, "The Japanese Society for the Problem of Handicapped" and "The National Conference to Support the Life and Right of Disabled Persons" were organized in 1967.

At the same time, the movements for schooling of all handicapped children have been advanced in many places around Japan. These movements require the establishment of protected schools. The government enacted "The Law of Countermeasures for the Handicapped" in 1970. Although the government tried to improve special education, in fact, "the ability-dominant policy" was advanced more than ever. As before, the government had no intention of promoting education for the severely handicapped children.

Some changes, however, happened in a few local administrations. For example, the Metropolitan Assembly and the Assembly of Kyoto-prefecture extended a policy to secure the right to education for every handicapped child. The Metropolitan Assembly decided that schooling is the right of every handicapped child as of 1974. The government finally mandated compulsory education in protected schools beginning in 1979.

The realization of the system of compulsory education in protected schools is explained by the belief that severely handicapped children also have an equal right to education. Public opinion forced the government to grant it. Thirty-four years after World War II, the equal right to education (specified in Article 26 in the Constitution of Japan)[4] was at last realized.

The Conditions After 1979

The right to education for severely handicapped children was secured by the establishment of the system of compulsory education in protected schools. Consequently many children with profound and multiple handicaps entered not only the protected schools but also the blind schools and the deaf schools. Through this policy, new problems regarding the education of handicapped children arose.

After the oil crisis in 1973, the Japanese government had changed its social welfare policy by tightening its purse strings with the policy of "Social Welfare Reform." As the budget for social welfare was reduced, the policy was hardly an advancement. The government emphasized the importance of "self-help" in order to rationalize the budget-cut policy. As a result, this "worse" reform influenced the educational situation of

handicapped children. In other words, the government intended to lower
the cost for services to handicapped children because they were not
considered an important force in contributing to the future development of
economy in Japan. More details on this aspect of government policy are
explained in the next section.

SERVICES FOR SPECIAL NEEDS CHILDREN

Services for special needs children in Japan are prescribed by law, but
actually there are marked differences in each local government. Some
local governments have a better system of services than others. On the
other hand, there are local governments with an incomplete system of
services. On the whole, it is not an exaggeration to say that special needs
children do not have sufficient services. The policy of reducing social
welfare has influenced this tendency. The following sections describe the
present situation of services for special needs children from infancy to
adolescence.

Services for Infants (0-6 Years Old)

It is a problem at this stage that the system and substance of "the early
detection of disability and immediate contact" have been developing.
Most newly-born infants are subjected to mass-screening for congenital
abnormality. And in health examinations for infants, developmental
psychologists check on the developmental condition of children in some
local areas. Formerly, a health examination was an opportunity for
mothers and infants to get some medical advice and assistance. However,
this policy has become an opportunity for the authority to examine for
any developmental abnormality and impairment but not in the earlier
stages. When the findings of developmental psychology are made use of
in the examination, many cases of abnormality are found in earlier
infancy.

Through this early contact, the chances of caring for pre-school
handicapped needs are increasing. Formerly even if the parents noticed the
abnormality of their child, they didn't have any means for determining the
condition medically. Thus many pre-school handicapped children had
been forced to stay at home or be institutionalized. Now a chance has

been provided to attend an educational facility for pre-school, nursery school, or kindergartens.

The early detection of disability and immediate contact have surely brought positive results in the children's development. As stated above, however, most local governments don't have a sufficient system for health examinations. They cannot respond to the requests and anxieties of parents because there are few educational facilities for pre-school handicapped in most local areas. Therefore many children who need to attend some kind of educational facility are forced to stay at home.

Services for School Children: The Stage of Compulsory Education (6-15 Years Old)

Schools for the handicapped include the protected school (for the children with mental retardation, motor disability, and physical weakness), blind school, deaf school and special classes in general schools. In May 1990, there were 170,643 handicapped children in these schools and classes (Table-5a, 5b). There are 131,830 pupils in the system of compulsory education.

TABLE 5-a.   The number of students in each kind of special school

		number of schools	number of students				
			pre-s.	element-s.	jun-h-s.	sen-h-s.	total
blind school		70	193	946	768	3,692	5,599
deaf school		108	1,531	2,456	1,748	2,434	8,169
Protected School	ment. retar.	482	55	16,217	14,864	23,321	54,457
	motor disa.	188	106	8,183	4,640	6,319	19,024
	phys. weak.	99	3	2,822	2,240	1,159	6,024
	sub-total	769	164	27,022	21,744	30,799	79,729
	TOTAL	947	1,888	30,424	24,260	36,925	93,497

TABLE 5-b.   The number of special classrooms and students in general schools

	elementary school		junior h-school		total	
	n. of classes	n. of students	n. of classes	n. of students	n. of classes	n. of students
mental retar.	9.547	33.181	5.238	21.817	14.785	54.998
motor disab.	315	832	133	304	448	1.136
phys. weak.	430	1.583	116	325	546	1.908
weak eyesight	65	163	22	44	87	207
hearing impair.	351	1.038	123	450	474	1.488
verbal distur.	1.338	5.914	87	183	1.425	6.097
emotio. distur.	2.338	7.243	1.173	4.069	3.511	11.312
TOTAL	14.384	49.954	6.892	27.192	21.276	77.146

Source: School Basic Survey, by Ministry of Education, 1990

The number of handicapped pupils accounts for about 1% of all pupils in Japan. In addition, there are many handicapped pupils in general classrooms of elementary schools and junior high schools. The exact number of these children is, however, unknown. The mildly handicapped pupils (for example hearing impairment, verbal disturbance, emotional disturbance and so on) have enrolled in general classes as well.

Since 1979, many protected schools have been established in every prefecture. Thus, the right to education for handicapped children was officially secured. There are, however, still some substantially insufficient conditions. These conditions are described as follows:

Guidance to School Attendance for Handicapped Children . Currently, all of the local governments have a guidance committee for school attendance. The committee plays an important role in school attendance for handicapped children. Specifically, in the guidance for school attendance it is necessary to consider not only the degree and kind of abnormality of the child, but also to understand the actual living conditions of the family. It is, however, not necessarily easy to do this. Most committees still have a discriminatory view of the children based mechanically and unilaterally on the degree and the kind of abnormality. Therefore many parents could not agree with the proposed decisions. In some cases, if the parents could not agree, they proposed the postponement of schooling. There are also many cases where the parents let the child move to another school after entering school. These cases occurred because of insufficient guidance by the committee without thoughtful understanding of special requirements of both the child and parents. In order to secure a sufficient education service for all handicapped children, a complete guidance system and skills which can support the children needs to be established.

Visiting Education. Since 1970, teachers started visiting the homes of severely handicapped children who were not attending school. Sometimes this is called "visiting education." In 1979, the Ministry of Education stipulated visiting education as an official form of education at the protected school. Teachers' visits have been set at twice a week, for two hours, uniformly. It was also decided that the curriculum of the visiting education should include only "nursing and training." This project realized directly the benefit of formally securing the right to education for the handicapped. It is a most important point that teachers of protected schools have acquired educational freedom from organized school hours and curriculum in order to meet the needs of children. Specifically, visiting education is prepared for the sake of the children who cannot go to school because they are confined by their health and physical strength. There are many children who cannot go to school because there is no protected school in their neighborhood. No matter how keen, they are forced to have visiting education in this case. In addition, there is the problem of working conditions of visiting teachers. They are not full-time but part-time employees. Some of them perform their job as a retirement job or as a non-specialist. It can be said that visiting education is situated in the shadows of institutionalized education.

Appropriate School Disposition. Today's number of protected schools and pupils has tripled since 1979. Particularly in rural areas, however, the disposition of schools is not appropriate to the situation of handicapped children. Therefore, there are many handicapped pupils who are forced to have visiting education. There are also many children who have postponed schooling or are exempted from it. In 1989, this number was 1,243 in total. Ten years have passed and the situation of children who cannot attend school still exists. We hope that the right to education will be secured for every child. For their sake we hope that more schools for the handicapped will be established and be able to better facilitate their needs.

Insufficient Facilities and Equipment. Few schools for the handicapped have sufficient facilities and equipment. For example, school bus transportation is not properly organized. Therefore there are many children who take a bus for more than one hour every day. Since the bus must pick the children up at many places, it takes a long time. These conditions have an impact on the health of handicapped children. In the case where a child lives far away, the parent is responsible for sending the child to school. If a parent becomes ill, the child is not able to attend school. For these children, a school bus is a very important means of transportation. Further, many schools for the handicapped are not equipped with a swimming pool and a gymnasium. In the practice of special education, it is important to have experience and study not only in the classroom but also outside of the classroom as well. It is not an exaggeration to say that insufficient facilities and equipment have resulted in poor practices in daily activities.

There are many other problems in securing the right to education for all handicapped children in Japan. Needless to say, the responsibility rests with the government and the Ministry of Education. Because the government tries to advance "low cost education," the movements to secure the right to education involve many parents, teachers, and volunteer participants.

Current Problems at the Stage of Senior High School (15-18 Years Old)

After leaving the junior high school, 95% of pupils (without any handicaps) enter senior high school. However, the entrance rates of the pupils who graduated from the protected schools and the special classes in general schools are lower. The former is 66%, the latter is 54%. The reasons are thought to be as follows. First, there are many protected schools without senior high school courses. Second, even if the protected school has senior high school courses, the pupils must pass a selective examination in order to enter the courses. Therefore, the severely handicapped are excluded. The parents and teachers are demanding the security of longer educational terms for the children who are developing more slowly. In some local governments, for example Tokyo city, Kyoto Prefecture and so on, all applicants can enter the senior high school course of the protected school. In many local government areas, however, it is difficult. Thus many children are not granted an education above the compulsory education level. It should be noted that in the local government areas which grant entry to all applicants for the senior high school course, there is another problem of too many students enrolled in the senior high school course of the protected school, as there are few protected schools in each prefecture. In either case, the senior high school course needs to be established to cater to all prefectures. Currently in many prefectures the movements to secure a more sufficient senior high school education are developing. Since 1989 national meetings on this problem have been held annually.

CURRENT PRACTICE

Educational Practice in the "Ability-Dominant Policy"

In Japan, educational practices for the handicapped have been advanced under the educational view based on the "ability-dominant policy." Here especially the development of social adaptability has been enhanced. For example, the chief of the special education section in the Ministry of Education discussed the education of mentally retarded children as follows:

> The development of the mental faculties in the mentally retarded is retarded everlastingly, and they are lacking in social adaptability. So they cannot become members to form a better society. They must be able to stand on their own feet without giving any trouble to other people and society. For the sake of society and nation, we need to make them stand on their own feet.

It is important that they do not become the troublemakers in the community.[5] This statement was made twenty-five years ago. The views of the Ministry of Education have not essentially changed since. In 1989, the Ministry of Education presented a new "course of study" for the handicapped. There are many expressions which are filled with educational views centered on raising social adaptability. In order to accomplish educational goals, "the study about the units of life" and "the study about working" have been enforced, particularly in the educational practices for the mentally handicapped. These educational curricula are centered on the acquisition of useful techniques to live and work independently. The study of the subjects has, however, been mostly neglected.

CREATION OF THE NEW EDUCATIONAL CURRICULA

Many teachers who learned the theory of developmental psychology criticized the above mentioned educational views and created new educational curricula. The viewpoints of the development of the handicapped are as follows:

1. Human development is restricted generally by neither genetic effects nor environmental effects. It is regarded as realized through both the acquisition of human culture and the creation of new products. Here the activity of the child is regarded as very important.

2. The process of human development is a stage of qualitative change.

3. The developments of the various psychological functions must be grasped not separately but synthetically.

4. Everyone, including the handicapped, will pass through the same process of development. The handicapped have a hard time passing the stage of qualitative change. But if they are given sufficient educational support, they would pass the stage at some time.

Even if the handicapped would develop more slowly, they would surely continue developing. This view manifests the significance of sufficient educational security for all handicapped children.

Through the diffusion of new views of development for the handicapped, many teachers have begun to look at the educational views centered on raising social adaptability again. They have been creating a new practice for not only the mildly handicapped children but also the children with profound and multiple handicaps.

Today, many schools for the handicapped have created a new curriculum. The teachers try to educate the children conscientiously. They always discuss what sorts of instructional groups ought to be formed for all handicapped children. Currently, their thinking is as follows:

1. Grouping based on grade level. The children of the same chronological age are organized into one grade. In this group, daily life guidance (such as putting on and taking off clothes, toileting, taking a meal and so on) is the major activity. Also guidance in developing friendships is given.

2. Grouping based on the stage of development. The children who have the same developmental task are organized into one group. In this group they study some subjects to achieve intellectual development. Further, for the children who cannot study any subject, guidance is given through play appropriate to their developmental tasks.

3. Grouping of the entire school. All children in the school are regarded as one group. In this group, they execute the same tasks (the athletic meeting, the meeting of the whole school, the cultural festival and so on). Mainly, guidance at bringing up the volition of activity and recognition is given.

Thus the children are secured by the various groups in a school day or during term time. In each group assistance to realize the positive development of all children is devised. In addition to the above mentioned three groups, specialty groups and additional groups are formed taking into consideration the chronological ages of the children. That is to say each group is organized by the following four stages. These are the lower classes of elementary school, the upper classes, the junior high school, and the senior high school. The characteristics of each educational practice are as follows.

1) The Lower Classes of Elementary School (6-9 Years Old)
   At this stage, because the children have a tendency to behave passively, various tasks which they are eager to do actively are organized (mainly play).

2)   The Upper Classes of Elementary School (9-12 Years Old)
     As the consciousness of a member of the group is growing in the
     children at this stage, various activities in which they need to play
     parts and to keep rules are organized (mainly the play).

3)   The Junior High School (12-15 Years Old)
     Because of the stage in which physical maturity tends to precede
     mental development, activities worthy of physical maturity are
     organized. Even if the mental development of a student is that of a
     more childish stage, he will not play as joyfully as a young child.
     Thus thought must be given to the activities appropriate to the
     students' physical maturity and their corresponding mental
     development. Therefore, various tasks in which the pupils need to
     think independently and to fulfill their responsibility are organized
     (not only the play but also the chores).

4)   The Senior High School (15-18 Years Old)
     Because this is the stage in which the students grow up mentally,
     various social activities are organized (the chores, the student activity
     council, the study about peace and so on). Through these activities,
     the ability to decide their future by themselves is developed. The
     creation of such methods and theories depends on the accumulation of
     studies by democratic groups of teachers. Of course there are still
     many problems with educational methods for the handicapped. And
     now the "ability-dominant policy" has been intensified by the
     government and the Ministry of Education. However, many teachers
     hold firmly to their opinions and continue to work toward the
     development of all handicapped children.

PRACTICE FOR SOCIALLY HANDICAPPED CHILDREN IN THE
SLUM AREA OF TOKYO

In this section, an exceptional school education service is described. It
was run for socially handicapped children in Sanya, the biggest slum area
in Tokyo from 1962 to 1977 (the author taught there from 1965 to
1970). At that time, quite a number of children had been without
schooling because they didn't have birth registration or had a long absence
from school due to parents' circumstances. Specifically, they should have
been accepted in public school in the Sanya district. However, the school

and parents in this school district rejected them for fear that the children would disturb the order in school. So, this exceptional service was started as a result of administrative fiat. For the above reason, as the Ministry of Education didn't want the general public to have knowledge of this service, it has been left unrecorded. The problem of this exceptional practice is unsolved even to this day.

Educational Situation in Sanya

There are many narrow cabinet-like inns or apartments (called "Doya") in the Sanya district for seasonal and daily laborers. This community was started in the middle of the Edo period in order to keep them segregated from the lowest social class people (called "Hinin") and criminals. Just after the Second World War, refugee camps were built for the victims of war bombs. They have gradually been changed into daily laborers' reservations as a result of economic revival.

At the beginning of this exceptional schooling service there were single male daily laborers accounting for over 80% of all residents in Sanya. As their jobs were unskilled heavy physical labor, they could easily move in or out of Sanya depending on the labor market situation. Consequently, their financial life was so unstable, they were forced to live without any savings. There were several cases related to criminal activity or debt from gambling. Although the parents had temporal or egocentric affection for their children, it was difficult to bring them up through parental contact.

In the first five years of starting the service, half of the children had no schooling experience because they didn't have birth or residential registration, nor did their parents. Schooling service for the children was initiated in 1962, in response to an improved policy of the Council of the Metropolitan Social Welfare. At first, the class was started as a branch of the public elementary school in Sanya, although it included the children who were of junior secondary school age.

Seven years later in 1968, the class became independent from the branch as "Taiei Public School," including elementary and junior secondary classes through the enthusiastic effort of Mr. Minobe, Governor of Tokyo at that time. Interesting service activities developed for socially special needs children until the school closed in 1977. The number of students frequently changed. For example in 1968, nineteen students entered the school and fourteen students moved out to other districts. Only 12% of 47 students in 1968 had schooling experience before moving into Sanya and 17% of all students had complete birth and residential registrations.

TABLE 6.   Changing the number of students and teachers
(April, in each year)

YEAR	NUMBER OF STUDENTS	NUMBER OF TEACHERS
1963	7	2
1964	10	3
1965	27	4
1966	34	5
1967	44	6
1968	47	5
1969	53	12
1970	43	12

CREATIVE SERVICES FOR UNSCHOOLED CHILDREN

The principal, Mr. Tetsuro Kagaya, was a pioneer of music therapy in Japan for mentally retarded children. His creative ideas for special education were applied in this school and supported by other teachers. The children ranged from 6 to 15 years of age, with their own very different individual life histories. They needed training in either the intellectual or socio-personal areas. We had difficulty classifying them, because each class could not be grouped with the same aged children as is standard practice in Japan. For instance in 1968, 47 students were grouped into multi-graded classes as follows.

Class A: mentally retarded children (4)
Class B: children who were able to learn materials in 1st grade
           and 3rd grade, not necessarily dependent on chronological
           age (12)
Class C: children in 2nd grade and lower achievers in 5th grade (10)
Class D: children in 9th grade and average achievers in 5th grade (9)
Class E: children in 6th grade and over-eleven years old who were
           ranked in junior high school (12)

Teaching materials were reorganized from textbooks and other sources simply and clearly in order for special needs children to be able to learn basic necessities in each subject. Officially approved textbooks were of little use.

Children who previously had no schooling experience were not illiterate. However, a lot of effort was required to motivate them to learn even easy materials. We were careful not to cause them to lose their own self-respect. On the other hand, teachers prepared individual study programs in math and Japanese language suitable to their achievement level. Music, art, gymnastics and domestic science programs were conducted in multi-grade classes or sometimes all together in a class. We had a conference once a week, viewing the individual record of intellectual and personal development for each child in order to exchange impressions and considerations with each other. Small step programs were usually innovated, with repeated trials and errors.

An interesting reciprocal study method was adopted in 1966. It was a pair or small group study run by an older child who had taken the role of teacher's aid. Two aspects in efficient learning were expected: one was that advanced children could gain knowledge and learning skills through the new experience of having a teacher's role to younger or underachieving classmates; the other was for underachieving and retarded children to enjoy a new study experience with the aid of older classmates. This project seemed to satisfy both sets of children because it provided a different experience from studying with a regular teacher. Teachers encouraged teachers' aides by advising them how to teach and prepare the materials for younger children. The trial was continued twice a week in the afternoon.

Through this cultivated method for socially special needs children, we were able to revise the curriculum of the Ministry of Education. Nothing was applied in detail in this exceptional service although it achieved general objectives. The teachers who taught in this school were happy because they were involved in creative teaching free from standardized curriculum. They could develop their teaching ability without enforced institutional restrictions. The service seemed very effective within the school. However, we sometimes were faced with a difficult case which was beyond the teacher's capacity to deal with. We missed a few children who disappeared with their parents due to some personal incident. Special education in slum areas should have been provided with linkage to the welfare policy in order to alleviate some of these problems.

PROBLEMS IN RELATION TO SOCIAL WELFARE

The teachers were required to undertake many jobs outside of teaching; for example, consulting with parents on financial problems, helping to complete legal registrations as a citizen, and listening to their complaints about their life and jobs. Occasionally we had to raise children's public awareness because they had no parental role model in their family. It was very difficult to help parents who were in a terrible predicament as a result of an accident or disease, as well as solve their financial problems. We needed to work in co-operation with social welfare workers. The difficult living situation of the children's families is shown in Table 7.

TABLE 7. Living situation of the children's family (1968)

relatively easy	15%
unstable and difficult	63%
subsidized by government	58%
unemployed	22%

They spent almost 30% of their income on housing expenses. The living space was very small; in some cases, six members of the family lived in a two-meter square room. (In these cases, average housing expenses were 15 or 20% of total income.)

A hand-to-mouth existence did not make for any psychological reserve, the ability to enjoy life or to plan for the future. Their life was, however, in some ways easy and comfortable to them because it was linked with a sense of freedom for the moment without struggling to realize their dreams. As most daily laborers in Sanya lived in the same painful situation, they could share warm feelings and empathy with each other. They gave mutual help to each other in daily life, like living in an unsophisticated form of communism, although they were united by a strong feeling of resentment against the discriminative communities outside of Sanya. This feeling created a conflict of contradictions in the children. On the one hand, children could learn how one could live in warm personal relationships, and on the other hand they were apt to live in closed-mindedness. Nevertheless, most children were so strong in their belief in their own survival that they were not particularly worried about their poor living situation.

After a day of heavy physical labor, some parents would drink heavily. Quite a few children suffered from violence and battering in the family. I had an experience on one occasion when I visited the family in order to pick the absent student up for school. The drunken father shouted loudly, "Are you a kidnapper?" Of course it was an exceptional case. Many parents were warm hearted although they did not possess adequate ability in child rearing, and so delighted in whatever their children would study at the school without any discriminatory view. Street drunkards in Sanya also showed an understanding attitude toward school. Occasionally we welcomed them as an unexpected visitor to the classroom when they were not drunk. Moved by the first warm interaction in their school experience, some parents had tears in their eyes when studying in class with their children.

The most difficult thing was that the children grow up having a hopeful future model from parents as if they owed society some kind of debt because of their parents. In particular, children whose parents had escaped from some kind of past were afraid of being traced at the school. The school did not have any contact with police except major incidents because the priority of the school was to provide a stable and peaceful educational environment for those special needs children for as long as possible. How did our educational service help them? The answer is difficult because the school was closed down midway in its operation as a result of changing circumstances in education.

Closure of the School

The educational situation has changed since the school administration was moved into public administration by the Municipal Board of Education in 1968. The Board of Education no longer allowed the special curriculum to be used, insisting that this school was now a regular public school. Class activities soon fell into a regimented program and the increasing number of teachers being moved into the school did not possess the same kind of commitment and positive motivation in teaching such children but viewed teaching as more of a chance at "people management." Despite our protests against such an irrational policy, it was too difficult to continue sincere educational services.

The school was closed in 1977, after seven years when I resigned in protest against the injustice of the changing system. The surface reason given for the closure was because of the decreased number of special needs children. In the final year, only three children remained in the special class. The Housing Bureau of Tokyo accomplished its plan to build apartments for lower class people. It was almost near completion in 1976, so most daily laborers and their families who lived in Sanya were forced to move into collective apartments in other areas in Tokyo. Although the problem of educational services for socially handicapped children was not solved completely, its substance was hidden in the regimented public education system. Some families were returning to Sanya again as they could not adjust to the new community, but this fact was disregarded. One could say that the housing policy had suppressed a reliable special service for them. As a result, in reality nothing had been solved.

Unfortunately we don't have any exact data on the aftercare of the children. On collecting former teachers' information, it is supposed that half of the children are now living out of the Sanya area, earning a living independently. As for the other half, their whereabouts are unknown. Special education for the socially handicapped has regressed to its starting point without any future perspectives. One heartening fact is that nowadays the number of these children is eminently decreasing.

FUTURE PROBLEMS

In conclusion, ideally, everlasting peace in the world would secure a happy life for handicapped children. The actual situation of special education for the handicapped in Japan poses many difficult questions as have been described. Primarily, the most dominant question is how the national budget can be best allocated and utilized in special education.

However, it is a critical situation because the Japanese government makes a higher priority for defense funding than for education and welfare funding. Social welfare funds in 1990 were increased 3.6% over the previous year. On the other hand, the increase in the defense budget accounted for 6.1% increase over the preceding year. The situation is contradictory to the national attitude toward war, renouncing it under Article 9 of the Constitution.

Moreover, in The World Action Plan for the Handicapped which Japan has already ratified, it is specified that any war and violence should be averted because it would bring about a large number of handicapped people, and any international dispute should also be resolved in peace. We can say with confidence that to maintain world peace is the highest priority in order to develop future education, especially for the handicapped.

Since the view of world peace and handicapped children are related to one another, it is a matter of urgency to ratify The Treaty for Children's Rights, and we should be developing practical projects in detail. In Article 23 of the above treaty, it specifies handicapped children's rights to education, training, health control, rehabilitation, job preparation and recreation.

Nevertheless, we cannot find specifications for children's rights in any law of Japan, except as briefly described in the Children's Welfare Act and School Education Law. It reveals a fundamentally poor policy for special education in Japan. Since the ratification of the Treaty for Children's Rights, the Japanese government has been pressured to establish new laws or acts for handicapped children in line with the spirit of the treaty.

Now we are moving into the ninth year of The United Nations Decade for the Handicapped. We are anxious to support many more movements for the handicapped which are arising spontaneously from among the handicapped children's families, teachers, scholars, and other people of understanding.

Meanwhile, every person has his/her own developmental pace and stage. It has proven to be true even in seriously handicapped children through their clinical training. Today's education policy, however, has not learned from developmental theory in special education. Every revised curriculum by the Ministry of Education since the 1960s has increased administrative education without actual consideration for the handicapped. Most students are too busy with "exam hell" to examine their own value system. Consequently, it is very difficult for general students to have any chance to learn about an alternative way of life from handicapped students who have grown up in a gentle and slow-paced culture. This institutionalized separation between general and handicapped students has brought with it a senseless feeling of potential discrimination.

As long as the highly competitive education system exists, it cannot help ignoring handicapped children. It is hoped that the effects of the methods of special education will be exported to general school education. At the present stage in Japan, we need more educational services in protected schools, because esteem for handicapped students is difficult in the competitive school culture. Not until institutionalized competition is considerably eased, will handicapped children be able to share in normal activities with general children.

In conclusion, we need to reorient ourselves to a more gentle and spontaneous culture in school education which accommodates understanding of handicapped children. We also need to ask ourselves how we can share a meaningful world with all handicapped children.[6]

Notes

1. Yoshida, Kenichi (1981). *Japan Is a Circle*. Kodansha, p. 133.

2. The White Paper of Education, by Ministry of Education (1990) & The White Paper of Health and Welfare, by Ministry of Health and Welfare (1990).

3. Satire, Virginia (1975). *Self-Esteem*. Celestial Arts.

4. Article 26 in The Constitution of Japan: All people shall have the right to receive an equal education correspondent to their ability, as provided by law. All people shall be obligated to have all boys and girls under their protection receive ordinary education as provided for by law. Such compulsory education shall be free.

5. Meiji-Tosho (1966). No. 49. *The Research of School Management*.

6. Oe, Kenzaburo (1990). *A Quiet Life*. Kodansha.

CHAPTER 7

EDUCATION AND DISABILITY IN CROSS-CULTURAL PERSPECTIVE: PAKISTAN

by M. Miles and C. Miles

This chapter discusses some cultural factors in childhood disability and education, based on 12 years of resource development work at Peshawar, Pakistan, for children with disabilities (Miles, M., 1990). The format will be similar to that of other chapters, and will consider two further notions:

A) that child-rearing in Pakistan has not received the level of public and academic scrutiny now common in Europe and North America;

B) that special education concepts and practice imported from the West do not engage well with concepts of childhood and child-rearing common in Pakistan.

SOURCES AND VIEWPOINTS

The authors, being non-Muslim, Western professionals, acknowledge some risk of cultural, religious, urban and class bias, or of failing to reflect Pakistan-wide cultural differences. Much use is therefore made of material written by Pakistanis, with reference also to Indian experience. Admittedly, these writers are also from the educated, English-using elites of their countries. Furthermore, if notion A (above) is true, local

167

references may be inadequate to correct any expatriate bias. For example, of 540 annotated works in a bibliography of Pakistani social science research (Bhatti, 1986), only two concerned children. Of 88 M.Sc. theses accepted in Pakistan's sole university department of anthropology from 1977 to 1986 (Javed & Asghar, 1988, p. 17-53), only one concerned child-rearing. Psychology professor Hafeez Zaidi admitted in 1975 that "We know very little about our child-rearing practices." In the 1980s many studies of child-rearing were carried out (Pervez, 1989), but Tariq (1989) regrets that with a few exceptions they were "conducted by naive researchers - mostly university students," who "are expected to do research only to get a feel of what research is."

Relevant socio-cultural material is not easily accessible, regardless of its quality. Senior librarian Riaz (1988, p. 253-4), noting the discouraging state of bibliographical service in Pakistan and that "No institution in Pakistan has produced a regular, updated and comprehensive list of theses," pleads for a Social Science Documentation Centre. Anthropologist Akbar Ahmed, complains (1990, Foreword viii) that "The Pakistan Sociological Association and the Pakistan Institute of Anthropology are moribund institutions working in fits and starts. Not a single worthwhile journal of the social sciences is published in Pakistan." Shah (1989) alleges that most of the research in psychology in Pakistan in the past 15 years has been "sub-standard." Inayatullah (1989) is less dismissive of his fellow social scientists, but criticizes an over-dependence on Western paradigms and a lack of creative interpretation and applied relevance in research work.

The National Institute of Psychology, noting these flaws, has recently increased its publications and documentation services. Yet the research data, reference works and government publications that would underpin a chapter like this in the Western world, hardly exist in Pakistan. This dearth is not solely due to indolence among researchers. Sandgren and Asberg (1976, p.31), studying cognition and social change in Pakistani villages, noted "a tendency to faint among both the research assistants and the subjects tested" due to the excessive heat, followed shortly by heavy floods, when "we had to be careful that the roofs and walls did not fall on our small pieces of wood, pictures and coding forms. As many people, especially small children, died as their huts collapsed around them, we felt repeatedly that 'research' is a rather absurd activity in an absurd world."

A further point arises from Riaz's, Ahmed's, and Shah's complaints. Pakistanis writing on Pakistan often seem harshly critical or overly defensive. There is constant comparison either with idealized notions of well-functioning Western systems or with stereotypes of Western decadence. Converse stereotypes are, of course, found among Westerners comparing the ills or benefits of their countries with 'Third World poverty' or 'the wisdom of the East'. Most of the quotations used here on culture and childhood require critical appraisal. Few are based on formal research. Some are the reflections of experienced field specialists or senior journalists. Some report the deliberations of Government Commissions. Some are the views of academics with international standing, but who may be writing outside their field of competence or with defensive motives.

Akbar Ahmed (1988) exemplifies the pitfalls when, as *Muslim apologist*, he writes "Because of the emphasis on the group the Muslim family is still relatively cohesive and not broken down. Children are secure and sons pampered. Muslims can boast that their societies may need a RSPCA [Royal Society for Prevention of Cruelty to Animals] but not a society for the prevention of cruelty to children" (p. 220). Earlier, Ahmed *as father and anthropologist*, records widespread sexual and psycho-social abuse of girls in Egypt and Pakistan (pp. 185-195). Likewise Rauf (1975) states that, unlike in India, the Pakistani child's "culture and traditions do not impose any class restrictions or other artificial barriers whatsoever in social interaction" (p. 163). Yet he earlier describes how class differences separate Pakistani children at play (p. 157-9).

Literature review revealed no Pakistani source giving a detailed and quantified view of the realities of Pakistani childhood or a well-argued evaluation of the quality of education for disabled children. The present authors have formulated their own views, which mostly follow a middle line between positions quoted from Pakistani sources. These views evolved during work experience, in discussions with Pakistani colleagues, and from daily life amidst neighbors from the weakest socio-economic stratum. Politeness towards the country whose hospitality we enjoyed for so long might seem to rule out any strong criticism. However, the hospitality was often most warmly proferred by those for whom the government had clearly failed to make elementary provision of health, education and welfare services. For their children's sake we note shortcomings which more comfortable parts of the nation might prefer to conceal.

SOCIAL BACKGROUND

Demographic Information

Pakistan's 310,400 square miles now hold an estimated 115 million people (1991), compared with 33 million in 1951 (Pakistan Statistical, 1988). The people are 97% Muslims. The major home languages are Punjabi, Sindhi, Seraiki, Pushto and Hindko, while Urdu, the language of national unity, is the home language of only 10% of the people. English is generally used by government and educated people. The population is about 70% rural and the economy mostly agricultural, but there has been some progress toward industrialization and about 600% increase in Gross Domestic Product since Independence in 1947. The individual prosperity that might have resulted from economic development has largely been offset by population growth, exceeding 3% per annum (Johnson, 1979; Nabi, 1986). Per capita GNP is about US $380.

Pakistan has alternated martial law and "Eastern" democracy, reflecting what the Planning Commission (1988, p. 15) calls "difficulties in arriving at a consensual view of common objectives between a strong and wealthy modernizing elite and the relatively poorer, traditional mass of common people." This divergence is institutionalized by the two independent systems of education, the private English-medium school and the official Urdu-medium school (UNICEF, 1988a, ch. 5 sect. 7.4). Considering the political stresses, there has been reasonable stability within the country. Karachi and Peshawar experienced regular shooting and bomb blasts throughout the 1980s, connected with the trade in weapons and drugs and the presence of some 3 million Afghan refugees. Yet life for ordinary people was not seriously disrupted.

The Planning Commission (1988, p. 149) notes that "The policy making organs of the government and the statistical system at present interact only sporadically and in times of acute urgency." This is not surprising, since official data on Pakistan's child health, education and welfare is seriously unreliable, as illustrated by Zaidi (1988, p. 171-7) and by discrepancies in basic statistics from government and UNICEF:

		UNICEF 1982	Govt 1982/83	UNICEF 1986	Govt 1987/88	UNICEF 1988
Primary-age school enrollment	Boys	57%	68%	66%	79%	51%
	Girls	31%	35%	33%	45%	28%
Infant mortality per thousand		120	98	111	80	106
Life expectancy at birth (years)		50	58	52	61	57

(UNICEF, 1985, 1988b; 1991; Planning Commission, 1988)

The government initially classified disability according to a U.N. rule of thumb, as either blindness, deafness, physical disability or mental retardation, sometimes in combination, asserting that 10% are disabled, 2% severely, by category: physical 40%, mental 30%, blind 20%, deaf 10% (Handbook of Statistics, 1981). The 1981 Population Census reported a total of 371,420 disabled Pakistanis, representing 0.45% of the population, by category Blind (29.41), Deaf and Dumb (12.99), Crippled (17.61), Mentally Retarded (10.24%), Insane (6.41%), Other disabled (23.34%). The Federal Bureau of Statistics (1986) conducted a sample survey and, in a report of unusual obscurity, gave the following proportions of disabilities: Blind (22.53%), Deaf (4.16%), Dumb (7.54%), Deaf and Dumb (4.72%), Leper (0.76%), Retarded (12.35%), Handicapped (15.88%), Lame (18.66%), Others (13.41%). Absolute figures were not given.

The government next attempted a serious, scientific survey of a sample of 15,000 urban and rural households in Islamabad and Rawalpindi districts, which is said to have given an estimated prevalence rate (for informant-reported, professionally verified disability) of 2.6% in an all-age population of 2 million (Directorate General of Special Education, 1988). Classification was: physical 33%, mental 21%, multiple 19%, visual 15%, hearing 9%. Rehabilitation professionals have expressed skepticism about the validity of this survey. After several years, no published report is available.

Some local factors may increase the incidence of disability, e.g. the high rate of first cousin marriages (Shami, 1983), use of opium as a sedative for children (Kasi, Pervez et al., 1988), iodine deficiencies in mountain regions (Khan, 1985). Yet these are minor factors compared with the general poor health of mothers and children. There is widespread undernutrition which results in a low resistance to disabling diseases and reduces the effectiveness of immunization against polio, the main cause of childhood physical disability. A decade of immunization efforts has produced no significant drop in polio incidence (Miles, M., 1989a). Inadequate ante-, peri- and post-natal care gives children a bad start, which is exacerbated by the general poverty of health services whether preventive, ameliorative or curative. There would be a higher prevalence of disability were it not for a child mortality rate of 162 per 1,000, i.e. one in six Pakistanis dies before reaching five years (UNICEF, 1991).

Education, Health and Welfare

Rapid population growth, with investment of under 2% GNP in education, has seriously overloaded schools and produced a society where "we are becoming illiterate faster than we can educate the new generation" (*The Frontier Post*, 27 April 1990). The Planning Commission (1988, p. 243f.) noted that

> Primary education facilities are available to only 60% of the children five to nine years. Primary schools lack physical facilities; about 29,000 primary schools have no buildings and 16,000 schools have only one class room. . . . In rural areas, enrollment of girls is about one third of that of boys. Most of the teachers lack dedication, motivation and interest in their profession. . . . The curriculum is mostly urban-oriented and is not relevant to the daily life of the children.

This caustic view in 1988 reflects a situation unchanged from that in the National Education Policy 1979, p. 17: "[The] primary school programme is neither interesting and challenging to most of the students nor relevant to the needs and demands of the community. The net educational experience provided in a village primary school is perhaps far removed from the realities of life and skills needed by the community . . ." These are not the complaints of disgruntled exiles or youthful agitators, but the considered judgment of senior officials, financed and published by the Government.

Educational management professors Qaisrani & Khawaja (1989, p. 16-18) note that most of the admittedly meagre national expenditure goes not to primary schools where most of the students and teachers are, but to the higher levels. Yet secondary education presents no better picture. "A large majority of students graduating from classes VIII and X have acquired no marketable skills for absorption in the economy. Class room instructions focus on external examinations which encourage rote memorization." (Planning Commission, 1988, p. 243). Over 70% of adults are non-literate. Every year 4 million unschooled children and dropouts join the pool of non-literacy (*The Pakistan Times*, 4 and 6 Nov., 1989). [This may be a newspaper misprint for 1.4 million].

Central educational planners and editors of national dailies may be expected to pontificate on the basis of presumed omniscience, without descending to personal observation and verification. However, field researchers Jaffer, Welle-Strand & Jaffer (1990, p. 46-47) provide first-hand substantiation of the official view:

> Most teachers simply do not teach. . . . Often teachers stopped teaching as soon as the observer left the classroom. Many classes, especially the junior ones, were teacher-less. . . . The greatest amount of activity in schools was chanting and rote memorization. This was often done in a typical style, children shaking their heads in a rhythmic way as they chanted and memorized their lessons. . . . There was a great deal of verbal abuse and physical punishment . . . as teachers became used to our presence they unconsciously fell back to what appeared to be their natural methods and inclinations. . . . Some teachers appeared to lack basic knowledge about the subjects they taught.

National Institute of Psychology studies reveal massive incongruence between the cognitive developmental level of primary school children and the cognitive demands of prescribed textbooks at all levels. For example, Israr (1985) notes that "Thirteen out of sixteen concepts in the text of class one Mathematics were much beyond the cognitive levels of this class." Pupils have little choice but to parrot their textbooks (*The Pakistan Times*, 26 Jan., 1989). Having failed to grasp the first year's concepts, they are unlikely to grasp subsequent years' work. Eventually some basic concepts are learned through extra-curricular experience. By then many pupils have dropped out, most have been discouraged and all have apprehended a gulf between school and real life.

The Pakistan Commission on the Status of Women (1989) noted ". . . the dismal literacy rate among the female population [16% overall, 7% rural] and the disparities in the provision of opportunities and facilities for education of women at different levels which were particularly pronounced in the case of rural females (p. 17)." "The average rural woman of Pakistan is born in near slavery, leads a life of drudgery and dies invariably in oblivion. This grim condition is not fantasy but the stark reality of nearly 30 million Pakistani citizens, who happen to have been born female and dwell in the rural areas of the country (p. 31)." Johnson (1979, p. 23) outlines the 15-hour daily work routine of the rural woman.

Health and welfare services are chronically inadequate and under-funded. Institutions for curative medicine exist only in urban areas. Less than half the rural population has access to clean drinking water and electricity. Both modern and traditional health services rely heavily on injections and drugs, often of poor quality. Health economist Zaidi (1988) documents how formal health provisions serve the needs of only a small urban elite and cannot conceivably meet those of the masses. Medical researcher Mubarak (1990) notes that "the masses lack even the primitive health protection." Family planning and health education get little attention. Formal welfare services hardly exist. The 'extended family' system still provides some support but this informal network is breaking down in the cities and is faltering everywhere.

To improve rural mother and child services requires many more trained *female* teachers and health workers, since males are culturally inappropriate. To increase the supply is very difficult. Training colleges are mostly urban, with urban intake. Their graduates usually prefer urban unemployment to a rural job with either primitive accommodation in the village or a long, unsafe, daily journey (Klitgard, Siddiqui et al., 1986; Bhatti, Khalid et al., 1988). Teachers' and health workers' pay and status are low. With a few honorable exceptions, the land-owning classes have little interest in village uplift. Some try a little development, meet with suspicion and resistance, and stop. There is little political incentive to make any more than token gestures to the rural masses.

The Planning Commission (1988, p. 299) notes that "The social welfare sector committed to provide special schooling and a package of integrated and comprehensive rehabilitation services has yet to make a beginning. . . . Existing facilities for special education and rehabilitation services are few and inadequate." Journalists report the situation more harshly, e.g. "Here where the conditions of education for normal children are appalling those regarding the disabled don't even bear thinking about" (Haroon, 1989). Widespread child abuse, e.g. forced labour, kidnapping, beggary, physical, sexual and psychological violence, have begun to claim attention, without the planning, skills and budget needed to begin solutions (*The Pakistan Times*, 2 Oct., 1989).

The Educational Hidden Agenda

Education in Pakistan is in a mess not merely by chance. The British Raj and Hindu hegemony no doubt contributed to diverting Indian Muslim culture into unproductive channels. However, when these shackles were broken in 1947, the nation's founders did not think that 40 years would be too short for Pakistan to establish a viable, independent, educational system. That it has hardly done so arises from a combination of factors not anticipated by earlier optimists. Most traditional school systems are naturally conservative. They transmit to the rising generation those features of society that can be simplified and reduced to writing, a sort of cultural sludge at the bottom of the barrel. Whatever may be officially prescribed, the ordinary teacher tends to reproduce his own schooling from 30 or more years earlier.

Conflicts between Islamic modernizers, radicals and traditionalists have been bitter. There are some wild-eyed men on each side of this triangle, as well as some reasoned arguments. Aftab Kazi (1987, pp. 1-4, 72f) discusses Pakistan's deep divisions along ethnic lines, and the failure of the education system to remedy this problem. Conflicts have been sharpened by geo-political developments in the Middle East, by the advent of modern mass communication technology and by the early soundings of Quranic critical studies by Muslims, comparable to the Biblical criticism that shook European culture in earlier centuries. In the 1970s, Pakistan's modernizers made progress. In the 1980s, the traditionalists seemed to hold the field, securing a grip on the prescribed textbooks of the nation's schools. Yet in this decade, the school as a formative influence was being undermined by radio and television. Neither medium has much that would interest an experienced Western child audience, but Pakistani children find them scintillating compared with their school books. Other books for children are mostly "cheap imitations of the children's books published in foreign countries and are thus divorced from [this] country's environment" (Jafri, 1990).

Pakistan's educationists routinely denounce the British for schooling their grandfathers to be competent clerks. The current system fails to produce enough even of this commodity, let alone the technicians, skilled machinists and many other mid-level workers needed to strengthen the economy. There are skill shortages in every field, but also a shortage of posts funded for skilled people if they were available. Schools act as a series of filters, taking in roughly half the nation's children, discarding half of these by the end of the primary cycle, forwarding only one fifth of the survivors to secondary or vocational education, discarding many more along the way. From 1977 to 1987 the number of children in primary schools rose from 5.0 to 7.3 million (no mean achievement, yet barely above the rate of population increase) while those in secondary schools rose from 0.53 to 0.69 million (Pakistan Statistical, 1988, p. 9, 375f.). Kumar (1987/88) notes a similar drop-out rate from schools in India.

Among the survivors, some are clever, many are industrious, while others are well-connected and can buy the necessary exam success all the way to university graduation. The level of corruption led one leader-writer to complain that "our degrees [have] become so downgraded that a B.A. signifies nothing more than simple literacy" (*The Pakistan Times*, 13 Sept., 1981). A decade later, a World Bank report is quoted bemoaning that "By international standards, the Pakistani M.A./M.Sc. degrees could soon come to be the equivalent of the secondary school diploma elsewhere" (Alam, 1990). Lamentation over the falling standards of education is a universal pastime, but is seldom pursued with such detailed insider knowledge as that of Peshawar University's long-time registrar, Yousuf Ali Khan (1990, pp. 48-99).

Pakistan is making the long, hesitant trip from aristocracy to meritocracy: from privilege and leadership based on birth and class, to privilege and leadership based on technical competence. Those enjoying birth-privilege often agree that Pakistan needs more trained people in positions of responsibility, but only after their own job and those of their relatives have been secured by *safarish* (influence). *Safarish* permeates the education system. Klitgard, Siddiqui et al. (1986) found that neither teachers' academic qualification, nor their competence by any other measure, had significance in their obtaining employment. It was all done by influence and recommendation. As a result, Bude (1990) found a sample of 'trained' primary teachers to be substantially ignorant of the actual contents of the primary school curriculum, especially in Maths and Science. Bude's objective was to evaluate innovative methods of teacher training, but he notes that "If teachers do not know what they are teaching, they can involve children in as many activities as we can think of, and still the effect on the children's achievements will be negligible" (p. 6).

CULTURE AND THE CHILD

The official verdicts above make dismal reading. Fortunately, ordinary families of Pakistan still seem to measure their situation not by Western, 'official' or statistical yardsticks but by that of their immediate neighbors and by their old people's memories of earlier decades. The most urgent need is still to maintain *izzat* (face, honor, family pride) in the neighborhood, regardless of any progressive standards or attitudes in the outside world. (By the same disregard, it is unlikely that mass attitudes towards disabled people can quickly be changed by external manipulation through the mass media.)

These localized standards may change slowly as the mass media reveal the possibility of much higher consumption and the disparities of comfort between 'haves' and 'have-nots'. Quddus (1989, p. 137f.) claims already to see such change among the burgeoning middle classes, driven by imitations of Western culture. Quddus sees comparatively little change in the culture of the ruling elite, who "stepped into the shoes of their old colonial masters, as is abundantly clear from the arrogant manifestations of their culture." The culture of the poor also "remained unaffected except for some minor adjustments." Yet he admits that "Our social, cultural and moral values are in a state of flux. We have not yet settled down to what may be called a real and lasting Pakistani culture" (p. 141).

Hasan (1988) sees more continuity with the Indian past in "the cultural pattern of Pakistan, or to be more precise, the amalgam of her regional cultures." He considers the temporal and economic environment to be largely formative for the masses:

"It has been existing for centuries and is basically feudalistic with remnants of tribal tradition still strong. . . ." "If they are determinist in their outlook, if they believe in pre-destination i.e. in fate (taqdeer), they are so conditioned by their existence. . . ." "Obedience to authorities, both spiritual and temporal is another distinct characteristic of our feudal-oriented thought system. No questioning, no doubting, no denying what has been prescribed but total conformity with ancestral creed and belief."

The present consideration of cultural norms and values in Pakistan will focus on aspects pertinent to special education, i.e. children's lives and the concept of childhood, play and early learning, and attitudes towards disability.

The Child in the Family

Senior psychologist Rauf, celebrating the benefits of Islamic culture, paints a rosy picture of Pakistani childhood:

"An average home in Pakistan overflows with warmth and vigor. Children are attended to. Parental care and affection are lavishly showered. Majority of the parents are home-centred and the homes child-centred. Constant parental devotion to the multifarious needs and demands of children lends predominantly humane colouring to the entire atmosphere of an average Pakistani home." (1988, p. 100)

Rauf's earlier, Western-influenced, views were quite different (1975, p. 156-7). The lower class child's "diet is simple, unwholesome and insufficient. His environment is barren and unstimulating." His or her parents "don't get much time to pay adequate attention to the needs of their children. The home-life and hence the pattern of growth of such children is dictated by disorder, squalor and neglect." The middle-class child is better off, but may suffer by excessive parental ambition: "He is often expected to learn too much too soon. . . . He is usually pushed excessively . . . producing an anxious child." The upper-class child is "usually over-indulged . . . pampered by his parents . . . constantly protected by nurses and tutors. . . . Everybody is there to serve him."

Rauf's 1975 observations seem more realistic than those of 1988, yet the latter can by no means be ignored. Anyone observing Pakistani homes across the social spectrum will find many in which children are accorded great warmth, care and kindness by the many adults and siblings present. Whether these are, as Rauf claims, "average Pakistani homes," has not been the subject of any controlled study. It is also possible that some change has occurred during the 13 years between Rauf's comments, though the interval is unlikely to have produced so substantial a difference.

Khan (1972) gives a detailed and appalling picture of childhood in feudal and tribal areas, influenced by purdah and polygamy. Very largely a female task, "The techniques of child-training and character-building in the Purdah family and society are harsh, repressive and inhibitive. The most common technique is that of creating fear in the mind of the little child . . ." (p. 107). Beating and humiliations, fears, jealousies, frustrations and helplessness, producing docility mixed with sly deceit, indolence, slovenly habits, petty squabbling, mental rigidity etc, are only a few of the ills Khan sees in this system. Again, there is no controlled study to show whether this reflects the average purdah household. It is tempting to dismiss Khan as merely polemical, yet many of his points on child-rearing reappear in later studies not linked to purdah.

Child psychiatrist Tareen (1983, p. 18-9) notes the absence of fathers from the child-rearing process, and the lack of parental perceptiveness about children's problems. Tareen, Bashir and Nasar (1984, p. 76f.) found little attention being given even by mothers in Lahore slums, where "the family atmosphere was usually one of tension, worries, stress and strain," with physical punishment as a normal disciplinary method. Research psychologist Bano (1988) links "child rearing practices lacking training in self-mastery and independence" with the low achievement motivation in many areas of life. Psychotherapist Shahid (1987) blames overwhelmingly authoritarian and repressive child-rearing methods for the clinical anxiety, hysterical and obsessive-compulsive behavior he has to treat later on. In Minturn's (1963) description of child rearing in a rural north Indian purdah society, many of Khan's observations find parallels, though the American anthropologist presents them more sympathetically.

Pediatric researcher Akhtar (1989) states that "child neglect is rampant in the society" and reports abuses similar to those detailed by Khan and Rauf 17 and 14 years earlier. Ikram (1990), reporting on

runaway children, observes that some are trying to escape "the misery and
sordid reality of life at home and quarreling parents . . . after severe
beatings, social injustice, discrimination . . ." Research psychologist
Hassan (1979) reports chronic neglect by both parents and beatings by
fathers among the causes of psychopathology in urban primary school
children. Anwar & Naeem (1980, p. 139) report from a survey among
rural Punjabi mothers:

> "The data suggests that a majority of respondents did not have much
> leisure time which they could spend in recreation or playing with
> children. Even if they had some, very few of them thought of
> spending it playing with their children. . . . It also implies that the
> children on the whole, get less attention for general social interaction
> with their mothers."

The Girl Child

Massive prejudice against girls is reported. In a study of rural Punjabi
women, 97.2% preferred boy children, 2.2% were neutral and 0.6%
preferred girls (Anwar-ul-Haq, Ahmad, et al., 1989). Abortion data is
unavailable for Pakistan, where it is illegal, but Zafar (1987), reports a
study of 8,000 abortions following amniocentesis for sex determination at
Bombay, in which 7,999 cases involved a female fetus. Sachar, Verma et
al. (1990) confirm this phenomenon, which may be expected when
prenatal sexing becomes more widely available in Pakistan. "The attitude
towards women as inferior beings is visible from the birth of a girl,
which is greeted with guilt or despair on the part of the mother, shame or
anger on the part of the father, and the general concern and commiseration
of the entire circle of friends and family" (Mumtaz & Shaheed, 1987, p.
23). That this is not only a feminist viewpoint is confirmed by Akbar
Ahmed (1988, p. 186): "Problems for the girl begin at birth. From her
childhood she is made to feel unwanted, an accident, a poor substitute for
a boy." "Her very childhood's joy, jubilation, laughter and gaiety are
snatched away from her at an early age" (Isa, 1990). Pakistan's
demographic imbalance of 110 males to 100 females also suggests that
the female baby is liable to infanticide through neglect (Hisam, 1984;
Alam & Shah, 1986), though Johnson (1979, pp. 17-21) discusses under-
enumeration as a possible cause.

Discrimination has been condemned since the time of the Prophet Mohammad: "When any of them is told the news of the birth of a female, his face becometh black and he is deeply afflicted: he hideth himself from the people, because of the ill tidings which have been told him, considering within himself whether he shall keep it with disgrace or whether he shall bury it in the dust. Do they not make an ill judgement?" (The Koran, Ch. XVI, v. 57, Sale's tr.). Specific Islamic rules favoring females are also customarily ignored. "Islam has ordained a particular share for the female child in the law of inheritance, yet in most cases it is simply unthinkable for a sister to demand her due share in her deceased father's property from her brothers" (Roghani, 1989).

The young girl soon learns that her destiny is to be a good wife, housekeeper, and mother (Haque, 1987a). Studying children's personalities, Pervez (1984) found "significantly different apperceptions, which probably is a reflection of their early socialization, in which the parents generally have a different set of values and norms for the rearing of boys and girls." Hassan (1985) reports that "By the time a girl is fifteen years old she is expected to be completely subjugated to the wills of her parents and elders. Ideally she should be self sacrificing, hard working, obedient, nurturing towards males in the family and willing to give up her rights in favour of her brothers and later her husband." Even the cost of her food may be considered a burden, to be relieved by marrying her off quickly (Daniel, 1990; Khattak, 1990). The Pakistan Commission on the Status of Women (1989), after nationwide interviewing, wrote in 1985 a fierce indictment of the oppression of females from conception to burial. Despite the undoubted pressures and resulting damage, many Pakistani girls and women appear remarkably self-possessed and uncrushed.

The Child at Work

Most rural children, once beyond infancy, work in the capacity of small adults. Rafiq's observation (1979, p. 89) in a Punjabi village is typical:

By the time the children are seven or eight years old they also begin to contribute to the village economy, mainly by helping their parents. . . . Boys graze cattle, take them to the canal for drinking water, help in bringing green fodder to the barn and in cutting and putting the fodder before the cattle. They bring water and food to the fields during the harvest, protect the wet rice from the birds and deliver milk to nearby consumers. Girls help the mother in cooking, washing, bringing water, making dung cakes, cleaning the house and barn, and taking care of the younger children. The Meo girls also help their mothers in collecting wood and cowdung, and in making artificial jewelry.

Staley (1982, p. 116) and Singer (1982, pp. 36-7) give similar descriptions from other rural parts of Pakistan. Asberg (1973) and other studies have shown this work requirement to be a major cause of school drop-out, along with the irrelevance of the school curriculum to rural concerns.

Some urban forms of child labour are more clearly harmful, where children must do an adult's work for very low pay, without security and often in unsafe conditions (Khan, 1986; Ahmad, Jan & Nisar, 1989). Haq (1989) reports that "A large number of children are forced to do menial jobs in teashops, cafes, hotels, filling stations, factories, repair workshops etc. Although there are certain labour laws . . . the fact remains that a large number of children, working under miserable conditions, are unashamedly exploited by their employers. They toil day and night to get a bare pittance for their blood and sweat." Chaudhry (1979, p. 52f.), outlines an even more disturbing problem, "a huge one in quantitative terms," of children kidnapped and kept in forced labour camps in remote areas, or forced to beg in cities.

The Child Playing and Learning

These grim notes do not mean that Pakistanis always have a dismal childhood. At the very least, millions survive these years to become normal enough adults. The cheerful mien of pupils coming from school, the glee of kids flying kites in parks, the angry joy of teenagers in video game arcades, the song and shriek of children in playgrounds, the giggles of those watching TV cartoons, testify in millions of places that Pakistani childhood can be fun. Probably at least thirty million Pakistani kids are loved and well cared for by their families, plus several million who are not.

We do not know the true balance of care/neglect, and cannot dismiss the millions who suffer. There is a tendency to hope for the best and discount more disturbing views until the evidence is overwhelming. Cross-cultural sensitivity demands an openness to different ways of living and a recognition that there may be rather few ethical absolutes. Yet we cannot avoid the responsibility of "developing a practice that takes seriously the subjective realities of other cultural norms and values but that attempts at the same time to protect the interests of the children concerned" (Channer and Parton, 1990). There are certainly thousands of children seriously abused in every Western nation. The difference in Pakistan is that comparatively there are fewer instruments to prevent abuse and a greater official complacency, ignorance or fatalistic tolerance.

Staley (1982, p. 116) writes from one of the economically poorest parts of Pakistan, "Most of our friends remember their own childhood with affection but without sentimentality. They found it difficult to talk about those days. We were just children then and lived at home like any other children. What is there to talk about?" Staley describes some games played by these hill children such as 'sheep and wolf', horses and riders, board games with pebbles, hiding and finding games, scratch hockey. Singer (1982, pp. 36-45) provides a photographic record from the North West Frontier of similar "games that the world's children have played since time began."

Cambridge University Asian Expedition (1962, p. 14) report from the Punjab:

The children of ten to fifteen like to gamble with small shells for one paisa coins; however, the shells were often confiscated for this reason. Other games of elder children are a primeval and very rough form of hockey (kedu-tila), kabbadi [a physical contact team game of capturing territory], tug of war (rassa kashie), pitu-gurum, hop-scotch, and gulli-danda. Schoolboys have also learnt to play football and volleyball. . . . The younger children mainly play with their own brothers, sisters and cousins, though the rowdier and less conservative elements do combine to form a fairly heterogeneous group. The less noisy children tend to be dominated by elder sisters, who often lead games to the tune of various chants and nursery rhymes."

Rauf (1975, p. 158) finds children's play "deeply influenced by their respective cultural backgrounds." The upper class child develops a taste for "expensive mechanical toys, recreational instruments, guns, horses, bicycles, automobiles, pets etc.," as well as embracing the middle-class child's fascination for team games learned at school, such as "hockey, football, basketball, cricket, scouting, guiding, hiking etc." The poorer urban child meanwhile is occupied by the same low-cost games as his rural cousins. Maulana Thanvi, whose venerable rule-book is still presented to Muslim brides (English tr. 1981, p. 373), bans the giving of dolls to children. Yet even poor children do commonly play with rag-dolls, which have survived the Islamic ban on making of human figurines or effigies (Quddus, 1989, p. 194). Rauf records class differences in the way children play with dolls, assigning them duties appropriate to the home background of the child, though he expresses the hope that these class distinctions are on the wane.

There is little adult awareness of the significance of children's play in terms of learning and discovery. Chaudhary & Khan (1969, p. 176-9), in a still current sociology textbook, devote a chapter to "Play and Recreational Institution" without mentioning children at all. Ajmal (1978) records that

At the National Institute of Psychology, when we embarked upon a study of cognitive development of children, we discovered that most of the children were culturally mute. After a great deal of trial and error we decided to introduce play in this serious test. As soon as play intervened, the child opened up and solved the problems we set. Of course, there were individual differences, but we discovered that the child comes to know where he is only when serious work is associated with play. It was a great surprise for us and children gave responses which surprised both us and them.

Israr (1987) describes at length the "critical method" interview for conducting Piagetian task investigations, following the discovery of play recorded by Ajmal. The child and the child's viewpoint are central, which in the educational world of Pakistan is a sort of Copernican revolution. The dominant teacher/adult is replaced at the center by the learner/child. "The child's curiosity and exploratory behavior must be provided by [a] warm and permissive atmosphere" (Gul, 1979) in place of the educational system which is "based on repetition, conformity and rigidity."

If these notions amazed Pakistani psychologists as late as 1978, they are unlikely to be familiar to rural teachers or mothers--though mothers may know more about practical child-handling than the research psychologist. Ajmal later writes (1986, p. 27)

> Friendship with children is possible only for a dedicated teacher, especially when he is ready to cast off his 'persona' and become a playmate, at times, with a child or many children. Such a friendship is conspicuous by its absence in our cultural activities. In formal schools we do not find this kind of friendship, in classrooms we do not notice friendship-inspired discipline.

Ajmal is probably right, yet Henevald and Hasan (1989, p. 28) observed that teachers could quite quickly develop a more friendly attitude towards their pupils.

Jaffer, Welle-Strand & Jaffer (1990), reviewing a study of a new primary school textbook, comment that "most teachers neither understood the significance of allowing a child to play with lines, angles and circles nor its impact on future learning" (p. 7). They also state, among the cultural phenomena relevant to their educational study, that "*Few mothers, and still less fathers, play with their children.* It is commonly believed that if you play with your children they will not respect you when they grow up" (p. 21). Child psychiatrist Ali (1988) notes the skepticism of many doctors about whether children can have emotional and psychiatric disability and that "The concept of Play therapy is very far removed from the medical model and is not fully appreciated and utilized by patients and trainees alike." Ansari (1989a), reviewing childhood research at the National Institute of Psychology, notes that play is a neglected area.

There is no room for play in Pakistani schools. A child's first academic failure can take place at four years of age. When aspiring parents attempt to enroll him or her in Kindergarten, an admission test must be passed. If the child has not had adequate coaching to recite alphabets (both English and Urdu), numbers up to 100 and various other data, he may be rejected in favor of a more promising toddler (Parviz, 1988). Singh (1984), writing about the same system in Delhi, states that "This demoniac system of torturing little children was devised in the 1970s by school authorities when they discovered they had no hope of

accommodating the ever rising flood of applicants seeking admission."
Hutt (1979) comments that "Teachers consider themselves part of the
professional elite and scorn any manual exploit, even activities with mud,
sand or water, thus making a parody of pre-school education."

Concepts of Childhood and the Child

Much that is described above is identifiable in Western social history.
Some of the quotations echo those describing ordinary English families in
the 1880s (Adams, 1982) and in earlier centuries (Pollock 1983). Indeed,
elements of these experiences continue in some British Asian families
(Perkins & Powell, 1983, pp. 26-28), and in poorer English working
class communities. (Newson and Newson [1968, p. 23] found that "class
affiliations remain pervasively powerful even in the minutiae of the four-
year-old's daily life.") The fact that much of the material in preceding
sections is recognizable by Westerners can lead to an error, into which the
present authors fell. We failed to see, for our first seven or eight years,
that our Pakistani colleagues' *concept of childhood and the child* differed
substantially from ours. In some uneducated families it was hard to see
that they even had a "concept of childhood"--as Aries (1973, p. 125)
remarked of Western medieval society--though they might well be caring
and affectionate towards their children.

Every adult has been a child among children. In one's own country,
one seldom needs to formulate a 'concept of childhood'. We imagine we
'know what children are', within our own culture. Yet Pollock (1983),
reviewing the history of Western concepts of the child, indicates the
complexity of the subject and the risks of constructing grand theories on
inadequate or secondary data. Education professionals know that children
in different places are brought up differently and that other societies may
have quite different aims and objectives in educating their children. Yet
there is a persistent illusion that everyone must have similar ideas of
what a child is, even if they differ on what the child should become. The
more features we seem to recognize in people of another culture, the
harder it is to accept that they may still conceive some of those features
quite differently. A century of anthropological studies has hardly dented
the belief of otherwise educated people that they know what a child is.
Jahoda and Lewis (1988, Preface), remark on the dearth of systematic
ethnography of childhood even among anthropologists.

We entered Pakistan knowing that our Western methods of special education must be adapted and translated to suit the cultures and ideas of our Pakistani colleagues. This meant years of "unlearning the approach used in British schools; rethinking it all for Pakistan, in Urdu and Pukhto, in terms of family expectations and social context; relearning it in a fashion appropriate to these circumstances; and communicating it" (Miles, C., 1986, Preface). These were necessary stages, and we were reinforced by the appreciation expressed by our colleagues and by their application of what had been communicated. Yet we did not then see that both Western special education and our local adaptation of it *still were constructed on a concept of the child that was, and is, largely alien to Pakistan* and indeed to the Indian subcontinent.

Grotberg (1977, p. 405-8) points out that "There are no attitudes toward children which are or ever have been held by all members of the society at the same time. . . . However, there are dominant attitudes which may be identified over the centuries and which shaped many of the institutions or institutional changes over time." Among American views, Grotberg identifies (1) the colonial child as pilgrim, "treated as miniature adults, but also perceived to be full of sin or depravity"; (2) the docile child of the eighteenth century, derived from Locke and Pestalozzi, possessed of evil impulses but malleable and capable of being shaped towards the good; (3) the saintly child, a romantic nineteenth century notion from Rousseau and Froebel, innately good but corrupted by the bad adult world. Also of the nineteenth century were (4) the individualistic child, both good and bad and largely independent of adult direction, and (5) the alienated child, equally impervious to adult attempts to civilize or corrupt him; (6) the twentieth century child, subject of social engineering and in need of protection whether from an exploitative society or from the social engineers.

The twenty-first century may offer the 'designer child', ordered from a genetics laboratory with full specification of physique, intellect and temperament. Such a child might be strangely like the traditional child of South Asia, shaped and moulded in the image chosen by the parent of the same sex, though the Asian shaping and moulding takes place *after* birth. Genetic manipulation is involved only to the extent of selective breeding by Asian arranged marriages. Yet personality is assumed to be largely genetically determined; or derived from "'innate' psychic dispositions from its previous life" (Kakar, 1979, p. 450). Thus the middle and upper classes give their young children to illiterate servants, unconcerned that they might provide an 'unsuitable environment'. Whether or not this is logical, the intention exists to produce a closely specified child. A boy should grow up just like his father, to resemble him physically, to follow the same trade or profession, to have the same personality and characteristics, just as the father resembles his forebears. The destiny of the baby girl is to become a person closely resembling her mother and her grandmother.

Compared with North European / North American (NENA) childhood and parental expectation, Pakistani children, and indeed many South Asian children, start at a different place and are aimed in a different direction (cf. Suvannathat, 1985; Ghuman, 1975, pp. 61-68). Broadly speaking, while the baby is in its mother's arms no other attention is required for it. It is where it should be. There is nothing to be done. The Asian toddler is also much loved but hardly taken seriously - it is like a puppy, which staggers about, piddles on the floor, whines to be picked up and stroked. All this is expected. It occasions no comment and little interest. Parents are confident that they and the other adults and older children can meet all the toddler's needs. It is a highly permissive regime and there are few if any demands on the toddler.

The middle-class NENA parent, by contrast, has high demands, expectations and worries. Often the Western toddler undergoes a busy regime of feeding at set times, strict toilet training, being dressed and undressed in a variety of clothes, being laid down or sat up on a variety of furniture, sometimes with nobody present for long periods, while parents compare notes about her progress and set out to stimulate and interact with her according to the books they have read. In poorer families, the urban young mother must often travel about single-handed with one or two small children, on foot, waiting at bus stops, in streets with heavy traffic, to do shopping, to keep timed appointments with health, education, welfare or financial services. The conduct of these activities, which suit neither the rhythms nor the safety of small children, is largely dictated by urban time schedules and geography.

The small Pakistani, up to five or six years, gets plenty of close physical contact and petting, and is left to manage her own 'early development'. The child's world (mother, grandmother, older siblings), assumes that she will proceed in good time with the task of growing. In due course he will start to walk, talk, control his bowels (Kakar, 1981, p. 80-1), but "too much attention is not paid to toilet training. The attitude is even more relaxed in rural areas" (Kalwar & Ahmed, 1989). In many South Asian households there are plenty of people, often at close quarters, almost all of whom have been used to babies since their own childhood. Babies and small children are no problem, nor do they require much attention or earnest planning. Their world is also more likely to be rural, to move at a slower pace and to involve few external demands.

"Rajput mothers were puzzled by anthropologists' questions about the rearing of young children. There was nothing much to know about a young child. Early childhood was considered of little importance or interest" (Honig, 1982). Studying Pathan mothers and children, Currer (1983, p. 16) noted "the tendency was for children to fit in with adult lives rather than having special separate routines. This meant that children were paradoxically both more an integral part of the family and also given less special attention." (Compare the Nottingham working class mother's comment on her four-year-old: "Well--really--I never worry; I take him for granted just as he comes" (Newson & Newson, p. 478)). Such nonchalance contrasts with the middle-class NENA family with fewer children and where the one or two adults may have little experience of babies and child rearing. The NENA middle classes usually hope and expect that their children begin early to play constructively, interact with their environment, display personality and individuality. The small child has much to live up to.

NENA parents also have much to live up to in terms of society's predominantly middle-class demands. Their child is inspected by non-related professionals from the start: midwife, nurse in the gynecology ward, health visitor, social worker if there are problems in the family, and nursery school teacher. If the child is not doing well, more professionals appear. Even custody of the child may come into question. In Pakistan, by contrast, the child is a chattel, the possession of its family. Usually it has no independent legal existence, and effectively no individual legal rights. It is certainly not the business of any social worker, health visitor, or teacher to push her nose into the family's affairs and seek to advise them how to conduct themselves towards their child.

When their child reaches five or six years, Pakistani and Indian adults take more specific interest. The son enters the public (male) world, begins to be judged by adult standards and is expected quickly to conform to adult demands. Kakar (p. 126-133) describes the traumatic abruptness of the transition, reinforced with physical chastisement. The daughter does not enter the public world, but begins to be shaped towards her destiny as a wife and mother (Haque, 1987b). The parents expect and aim that the child will learn to obey their every wish and command, and automatically refer every decision to the parent. "Parents tend to be very strict with their children and do not allow them to do anything independently. Children must obey their parents, or else be severely punished" (Khan, S., 1987). By the time the child is 15, they will have a young person who is totally obedient to them because he or she will have, in effect, the same mind and personality as the parent. An Indian proverb is often quoted: 'Treat a son like a king for the first five years, like a slave for the next ten years, and as a friend thereafter'. The female equivalent might be 'Let a daughter play for five years, train her strictly for another ten, then give her away'.

In striking contrast, most (middle class) NENA parents expect that by the time their child is seven or eight, they will have nurtured an independent person, with his own program, tastes, timetable, interests, friends and ideas. They may hope to keep some direct influence until this individual is 12 or 13, but by then the child will have constructed a world of interests and influences largely independent of her parents, and often largely unknown to them. Parents retain some economic clout in the home, but otherwise their influence is confined to example and persuasion. This is considered normal, though parents complain about it to one another. They have supplied the technology and opportunities, whether bicycles, micro-computers, fishing rods, holiday camp fees, payment for washing the family car etc., which facilitate the creation of an independently functioning individual, who will go on to choose his or her own career, spouse and dwelling. The parents often doubt that their child has enough wisdom to choose well, but very few doubt that the child will choose anyway.

Cultural development is not a one-way street leading from 'traditional Asian' to 'modern Western', nor would there necessarily be any improvement in the human condition if it were. (Indeed, Hussain [1990] speculates that joint adult-child participation in television mass-culture is seriously eroding the status of childhood in the USA). Some Pakistani families with urban, educated parents can be seen making their own selection of 'modern' concepts and practices in child-rearing, without being noticeably 'Western'. One may find families in all stages of transition, some of which seem to work well as families while others are inharmonious. Grotberg and Badri (1989) report some success in persuading Muslim mothers in Sudan to adopt 'modern' child-rearing practices in preference to traditional methods similar to those of Pakistan, believing that this could enhance the children's intellectual development. They admit, however, that it is unclear whether the changes would permeate the culture. No audit is given of the possible side-effects of externally-induced cultural modifications.

The Child in Islam

Apologists like Shehab (1986) claim that Islam's teachings on children are "more comprehensive than those contained in the [United Nations] declaration on the rights of the children." Giladi (1989) refers to many Arabic sources on childhood in earlier Islamic times, reflecting devoted parent-child relations. Yet Islam, like the other monotheisms with which it shares its roots, is a religion run by adult males. In practice, in modern Pakistan, it is hardly eloquent on the realities of childhood. The child is important as a recipient of Islamic injunctions, starting with *Azan* intoned in the neonate's ear and the ceremony of *Bismillah* when the child first recites from the Quran (Kraan, 1984, p. 17). Rauf (1988, p. 99) happily asserts that "Many children commit the whole of the Holy Quran to memory during early years." This is in classical Arabic, hardly any of which is understood by the young Pakistanis who memorize it. The medium, remote and awe-inspiring, is the message.

Noting that earlier researchers in Morocco "contended that Quranic school has a negative effect on cognition and literacy," Ezzaki, Spratt & Wagner (1987, p. 163) found otherwise: "For the rural Moroccan child, whose parents are likely to be illiterate, the Quranic preschool may well be the richest print media and [Standard Arabic] language environment yet encountered." They suggest that the large, dispersed network of Quranic schools contributes much to socialization and pre-reading skills. This has positive implications for Pakistan, where the level of female illiteracy (around 70% urban, 93% rural) means that children's exposure to storybook reading is small.

Rizavi (1986, p. 99-108) outlines the views on education of notable Islamic philosophers of the past such as the Ikhwan al-Safa, Ibn Sina and Al-Ghazali, who approve an early start in forming and training children's minds. Rizavi believes there is great dependence in the Muslim educational world on the views of these earlier thinkers. Some of their ideas accord well enough with modern Western notions. Al-Ghazali, for example, advocated daily physical exercise and permitted the child to play after school. Ibn Sina favoured disciplinary methods that did not commence with a beating. Yet their educational universe remains confidently teacher-centred. The child is taken seriously only so far as he is quitting his essential childhood.

However, Ajmal, in a ruminative essay on psychotherapy and interiority (1986, p. 21-7), asserts that the "Child-archetype has been a persistent motif in the spiritual world of Islam. This motif played an important role in the creative aspect of Islamic culture." He instances the positive attitude of the prophet Mohammad towards children, and the child's ascribed ability to see angels, ultimate realities, and the nakedness of the emperor. Yet this has not led to any more positive view of Pakistan's children now. Ajmal warns that neglect of the positive sides of childhood may place adults at the mercy of a negative childishness in their own behavior. The warning may apply also to cultures where childhood is over-emphasized, its fun and nonsense carefully measured and documented, leaving little room for the child's natural spontaneity.

The Disabled Child

The child with a disability is first and foremost a child. Its parents and family know or fail to know the disabled child *in terms of their normal idea of children and childhood,* Western or Asian, Muslim, Christian or Hindu, upper, middle or lower class. In any of the concepts and systems generalized above, the disabled child is often seriously disadvantaged, but this takes different forms.

NENA parents may notice an impairment sooner and try energetically to correct it using available institutional resources. If it is not remediable, their disappointment may be the greater. The gap between their hopes and the child's achievement may widen rapidly, causing a grave loss of self-confidence in the child. The Pakistani impaired child is less likely either to benefit from positive early intervention or to suffer early by being labelled abnormal. Mother and grandmother, being familiar with babies and children, may notice that there is some difference in this particular baby, but are less likely to draw attention to it. There is always the hope that a child's weakness or deficit will simply disappear with time. If their men's attention is drawn to a possible problem with the child, it will certainly be deemed the women's fault. There may then follow some typically clumsy male intervention. In any case, there is often a resigned attitude and an acceptance of fate.

Eventually it may become clear that the Pakistani disabled child is unlikely to grow up as the image of father or mother. Even if character and disposition can be so moulded, the child may physically be unable to do the parent's bidding or learn their trade or craft. This sometimes proves incomprehensible to the parents. How can it be that a child of theirs does not turn out according to their image and determination? Especially with the problems of deafness or mental handicap, the child may be thought of simply as "stubborn" (Tareen, 1983, p. 19) and disobedient. Ishtiaq in her doctoral thesis survey (1977, p. 169-70) outlines the fate of such children: "It is further evident from the data pertaining to discipline that most of the moderately mentally retarded children (59%) are brutally treated." Paradoxically, this harsh treatment may be given by loving parents doing what they believe is their best to help their child, e.g. to 'beat the devil out of him'.

It is difficult to generalize. Some families clearly manage their disabled child with imagination and care. In others, the child may be beaten for his disability by one adult, comforted and overprotected by another, a third tries him with a local remedy of squashed ants in chalk dust, a sibling resents the extra adult attention and takes to pinching him steadily, the neighbors complain about excessive noise and damage to their fences, while the child becomes progressively malnourished simply through slow eating during the communal meal. Some disabled children suffer this sort of treatment for years. Their reaction, in maladjustment and problem behavior, provokes ever harsher retribution. Some die, some are kept heavily drugged, some are physically chained to beds or tables, some are handed over to custodial institutions. A small number have access to counselling services and special education.

Shanker (1976, Preface) notes that the plight of disabled animals occasions among the Indian public a greater outcry than the plight of disabled humans. The public in Pakistan seldom seems much moved by either. The secretary of Pakistan's Disabled People's Federation reports his experience that

> The parents and relatives consider the disabled as an economic liability and curse of God. Government functionaries take them to be nincompoop parasites. For the general public they are a nuisance. The disabled themselves are unaccepted by society, lose confidence in their faculties, lose self-respect and consider themselves fit for dependence upon others and beggary (Malik, 1988).

A survey of public attitudes towards disability and people with disabilities (Miles, M., 1983) confirms Malik's experience. Although the *range* of Pakistani self-reported attitudes is similar to that found among Western populations, the great majority of views were of the 'fear' or 'pity' variety.

SERVICES FOR SPECIAL CHILDREN

Families

We extended our review of Pakistani families and childhood in the belief that it is a major neglected cultural factor differentiating service needs in Pakistan from those in Western nations. As Honig (1982) notes, "Values held about young children permeate the social system in which children are reared and profoundly influence practices used." A list of current services in Pakistan might appear to be comparable with a list from 30 or 50 years ago in Italy or Canada, suggesting that Pakistan has merely to catch up on the same path. This idea is probably mistaken and may divert attention from more appropriate developments based on indigenous cultural and philosophical underpinning.

Most services for children with special needs are given informally by their families, who feed and clothe them, usually teach them basic communication skills and may involve them socially in family affairs. This may seem obvious, but in official inventories of knowledge and skills for disabled children it is normally overlooked. In Pakistan now over 95% of current useful experience with disabled children belongs to mothers and fathers, brothers and sisters. A further quantum of experience belongs with teachers in normal schools, where some 2% of the pupils have appreciable disabilities and are 'casually integrated' without appearing in any official statistics (Miles, M., 1985a).

Healing Professions

The first professional visited by parents whose child is impaired or 'different' is usually a local healer, or a doctor trained in Western medicine. In rural areas, the local healer may have some regular *unani* medical training, or may have picked up experience within a clan of healers, or may be a religious figure, or may be a complete quack. Some in each of these classes are acute observers and may have a therapeutic effect on both child and family. There are also bone-setters, masseurs, acupuncturists and operators of machines delivering electric currents, who earn their living among the rural populations and sometimes treat children with disabilities.

The emphasis among both local healers and Western-oriented doctors is on a 'cure'. There is little concept of the impairment that is not amenable to a cure but should be managed by a process of learning and adaptation on the part of the child, family and neighborhood. Western-oriented doctors are seldom better in this respect than the quacks. Paediatrics is a recent speciality, with modest status and remuneration. In city hospitals there is some orthopedic, ear and eye surgery, with modest success. (Criteria of success are decided by the adults. The disabled child is not expected to express any views on the question).

Special Schools

At Independence in 1947 (West) Pakistan had only a few urban schools for deaf and blind children. The first schools for mentally retarded pupils began in 1961. By 1970 only 268 pupils, 75 visually, 193 hearing handicapped, were officially receiving special education (UNESCO, 1974), though this is clearly an under-estimate. Abdullah in a 1981 survey found 10 schools for blind children, 24 for deaf children and 15 for mentally retarded pupils. Survey data by Akbar (1989) reflects the progress over 40 years:

	1947	1960	1970	1980	1988
Provincial Government Special Schools	2	5	10	35	62
Federal Government Special Schools					46
Non-Government Special Schools	1	5	18	31	50
Total	3	10	28	66	158

Akbar (p. 35-6) estimated that in September 1988, 10,373 pupils aged 5 to 14 years were in special schools, of whom 69% were boys, 54% were hearing impaired, 24% physically disabled, 13% mentally retarded, and 9% visually impaired. Enrollment per school averaged between 30 and 50 pupils, though a few were much bigger. Teacher/pupil ratio in federal, provincial, and non-government schools was reported as 1:14, 1:11, and 1:15. Teaching skills were limited, there was very little equipment in the schools and of that, much was in disrepair. From his mailed, self-administered questionnaire, Akbar states that pupils were 'severely disabled'. However, informal sources of information, and personal visits by the present authors, indicate that most of the pupils have mild to moderate levels of disability. Very few with multiple handicaps or behavioral problems were reported in Lari's mailed questionnaire survey (1987, p. 72, 74).

Provincial Government control of special schools varies between departments of education and social welfare. Each province has a different arrangement. In Punjab, special schools run under the education department but some residential institutions come under social welfare. In the North West Frontier, special schools were under education until the early 1980s, when they switched to social welfare. This trend-breaking move was made because the few special schools were smothered in red tape, lost in a corner of the large education department, and were seen as a career blocker for anyone working in them. Social welfare was a small, nascent department, keen to expand its responsibilities and with some freedom to move since nobody in the government paid much attention to it. In Baluchistan there was also some joint involvement of education and social welfare departments.

In Sind, Social Welfare ran a few special institutions, but the major emphasis was on integrating disabled children in ordinary schools. This was planned by an energetic and experienced educationist, M.H. Bhutto, who had studied Western trends of the 1970s and decided that mainstreaming was worth taking seriously. The extent and effectiveness of a decade's work in this direction awaits formal documentation and evaluation, but by 1988, some 20 special units were functioning in country towns in the interior of Sind, attached to ordinary schools and progressively integrating their special pupils with the ordinary school-children. Staff for the special units were given short bursts of inservice training. Coupe (1987) reports favorably on the commitment and professional standards of some of these personnel.

This Sindhi integration movement is one of the few educational initiatives that has been planned long-term and has kept a low profile in its early years. Politically, a disadvantage of integration is that, where successful, there may be little to see. Where children with disabilities are doing much the same as other pupils and are not marked out in any way, visitors often think that 'these children were not *really* disabled at all', and persevere in the belief that children with *real* disabilities (i.e. severe multiple disabilities without any rehabilitative help) cannot be integrated. The integration movement in Sind had no impressive new buildings to be opened by bigwigs. Federal officials were happy to tell foreign visitors that something to do with integration was happening in the interior of Pakistan, without knowing exactly what or committing themselves to believe in it.

Federal Government (cf p. 196 Provincial Govt.) involvement is recent. The National Education Policy (1979, p. 28) noted that "whatever progress has been made in the field of special education is the outcome of the efforts rendered by the philanthropic organizations." The Planning Commission (1986, p. 430) spoke of "integrated services for disability prevention and rehabilitation programmes" and intended to "provide full coverage to about 62,000 disabled children." Very little of this was achieved. From 1986, however, the newly created Federal Directorate General of Special Education (DGSE) began a program of expansion and founded 45 special schools in cities across Pakistan by renting buildings, buying vehicles and staffing the schools with ordinary teachers, doctors and psychologists. The main thrust of government efforts specifically in favor of disabled children has been in special schools, which is hardly surprising, since the only major child-targeted activity of the government is ordinary schooling. However, the DGSE was also responsible for coordinating cross-sectoral programming for disabled persons, supposedly covering "a full range of services including education, health, social welfare, rehabilitation and employment placement" (Farooqi, 1988).

Some 40 Western advisors visited Pakistan for periods from two weeks to several months between 1982 and 1988, giving a mixture of seminars and advice that ranged from marginally relevant to ludicrously inappropriate. At least one of them perceived that she was "asking the teachers to consider ideas which were not only new to them, but also extremely alien" (Emanuel, 1987). At a meeting of 20 of these advisors "the diversity of inputs into Special Education by different agencies putting forward different messages and the confusion this can cause was discussed at some length" (British Council, 1987, p. 10). Their confused hosts at the DGSE ranged from social welfare officers to Army Education Corps colonels, by way of Ear, Nose & Throat surgeons and civil servants borrowed from commerce and the navy. A group of these officials went on a multi-nation tour in 1986, returning with even more bright ideas for transforming special education in Pakistan (*Education & Care*, 1986).

Some Western oralist teachers of deaf children caused the government to adopt a strong oralist policy. In Federal schools for the hearing impaired, pupils sign to each other in the playground but must not sign in class, though there are two researched sign dictionaries published for northern and southern Pakistan and a regular television program signed for the deaf community. The teachers know the defects of the policy. Pupils' hearing aids seldom fit well, seldom work and are seldom used at home. The British Council consultants' meeting noted that "The education being promoted assumes a technical infrastructure that doesn't exist" (p. 4). These factors had already caused other Pakistanis with Western training in oralism to change their methods. The agency originally funding this supply of advice withdrew when it realized the inappropriateness of what it had supplied. The government persevered with Oralism until 1990, when it moved toward Total Communication.

On the basis of ideas collected from advisors and foreign visits, a short "National Policy for Special Education" was written one night in 1985 by three senior officials and was printed and bound the next morning in time to be presented to the President of Pakistan in the afternoon. At that time there was believed to be a substantial budget available for starting special education projects. The main problem was that nobody at a senior level had any clear idea of what constituted special education and how it could practically and speedily be implemented within government structures. President Zia-ul Haq, father of a disabled child, called loud and often for plans, action and results. He heard a lot of talk, but died in 1988 without seeing results.

Senior civil servants were frustrated by the vagueness of the field, wherever they tried to grasp it. Thinking that a child must either be deaf or not deaf, blind or not blind, they were told that it was not so simple. No two experts had the same definition of mental handicap, or gave a clear statement of the 'treatment' or equipment needed for this condition (Miles, M., 1985b). (A similar problem faced a Royal Commission investigating special education in Britain a century earlier [Pritchard, 1963 p. 105]). Even in 1990, a modernizing educationist could still confidently publish a detailed description of "mental deficiency" in terms of "idiocy, imbecility and feeblemindedness" (Quddus, N.J., 1990, p. 138f). At one stage it was decided that I.Q. tests were the "equipment" for mentally handicapped children. A consignment was ordered, only for the officials to learn that they could not have them as they were not qualified to administer them. They installed electro-encephalograph machines at vast expense in some special schools. The suggestion (Miles, M., 1982) that the most suitable basic 'equipment' would be a few dozen cheerful and intelligent young women who enjoyed playing with children, was not considered to be serious.

The bulk of current experience was with the government of the Punjab, running some 40 schools for deaf or blind pupils, and with 30 voluntary agencies running special schools. The Punjab schools were within government structures but failed to impress the foreign advisors and so were not a model for a Federal program. A few of the voluntary agency schools were doing useful work with mentally handicapped children, but their managers had little knowledge of government procedure and could give no convincing account of what they did in their schools, why they did it, what were their admission criteria and achievements and how these might widely be replicated by the government. Some of the cheerful and intelligent young women employed in these schools were getting good results with their pupils, by observation and constructive play with them using everyday 'equipment' bought in the local bazaar. Federal planners and educationists were unable to take these methods seriously, or to build a national plan around them.

The DGSE decided to plunge in and open new schools, i.e. some buildings with assorted equipment in which children with disabilities and adults with various medical, social work or educational training should interact for several hours daily. Unofficially, it was admitted that the results would be messy for several years, but it was hoped that gradually the staff would gain working experience and there could be short bursts of inservice training. Some staff could also be sent to obtain foreign qualifications while local training materials were developed. The planners knew that if they did not establish a regular institutional expenditure, they would lose both their capital and current budget. There was a rapid burst of expenditure, following which Fayyaz (1990) comments "These Centres have been furnished with costly furniture of the best quality and other unnecessary stores but the basic requirements are not provided. . . . More than half of the posts of the teaching and professional staff are lying vacant since 1987."

By 1989 the DGSE had 45 'special schools' with nearly 3,500 pupils enrolled (*Special Education*, 1990). It was gaining experience and was in the complex muddle anticipated. The National Policy had been revised with the help of another Westerner. This document (National Policy, 1988) veers between fine Western notions that are incongruous in Pakistan e.g. "All children should have access to the range of skills, experience, knowledge and attitudes which will *lead them to independence*" (p. 11, emphasis added); and Pakistani views that were advised against by most Western advisors, e.g. that residential institutions should be set up for disabled children (p. 10). The DGSE had settled down with the familiar gulf between official rhetoric and classroom reality.

Western visitors are baffled by the breadth and permanence of this gulf, a sentiment shared by Pakistanis viewing their country after many years abroad (e.g. Sheikh, 1990). Every country finds some gap between official plans and street reality, but those with a fair level of organizational experience act to reduce the more glaring inconsistencies, urged on by pressure groups and derisive noises from the mass media. Pakistan's press regularly slates the failings of ordinary schools, but has no norms by which to judge special education. The usual expectation is that nothing will be done for children with special needs, so any government action in their favor enjoys a long media honeymoon.

The DGSE estimated that there were 7,000 pupils in special schools in 1986. It aimed to increase this to 91,000 in 1992 by pumping resources into existing schools and by a double shift system, as well as opening its own schools. It hoped that 917,000 children with mild learning problems would be accommodated in 86,000 ordinary schools. However, by early 1988 the new Director General (one of four Directors General during four years) was grieving that "as a result of the economy cut, Rs.69 million have been provided in the current financial year as against the required budget of Rs.213 million" (Ahmed, S.N., 1988). The Seventh Five Year Plan in fact shows a steady decline of budget from 1988 to 1993 (Planning Commission, 1988, p. 462).

Activity in the new Federal schools initially was unrecognizable in terms of Western special education. Teachers from normal schools worked under doctors or social workers without previous special education experience or training. "The teaching in the special schools . . . relied heavily on the institutional practices of normal schools and the inclinations of the teachers. Little material was available in the form of teaching aids" (Malik, 1987). By 1990, more seasoned staff had been poached from voluntary agencies. Several hundred staff had orientation courses at a new National Institute of Special Education, hastily opened with minimal funds. The sole bombing in Islamabad during these years chanced to be near this NISE, causing much damage--an example of the trials undergone during the development of special education in Pakistan.

In 1989, Allama Iqbal Open University began special teacher training by distance-learning. At the same time, Karachi University started an M.A. course in special education and Punjab University will follow. However, a lack of hands-on work under qualified supervisors is a major drawback to most training courses in Pakistan, and it remains to be seen how practical these University courses will be. Efforts have been made to update the resources of Gung Mahal College, Lahore, for training teachers of hearing impaired children. Considerable input was made by Western lecturers, but Fraser (1987, p. 4) notes that "There was no evidence of any application of taught principles even though people in all schools remembered the courses with enthusiasm."

Enthusiasm for Western expertise sits incongruously with conventional denunciations of Western educational colonialism from 1835 onwards, said to have "resulted in the total disintegration of the country's existing educational and social structure. . . . Some of the evils in the present system of education in Pakistan are a residue of that period" (Lari, 1988, p. 110). Yet Lari then suggests two ways to train special education teachers: invite Western trainers to Pakistan, or send Pakistanis abroad (p. 111). True fundamentalists display no such ambivalence. The West was damnable before and is still damnable now. Western cultures with their seamless package of technology and scientific epistemology still threaten Pakistan, where in one corner children memorize the Quran and in another they use interactive computer games. To youthful minds, the computers tend to have a more immediate appeal.

It is a tribute to the resilience and determination of Pakistan's special educators, both government and voluntary, that they persevered through years of upsets, reverses and policy shifts and are still working to establish and improve special education. The voluntary agencies have long been used to tight budgets, bitter internal battles and personality politics. The DGSE has been in continuous revision and redirection since it began. The NISE was bombed and shifted about, limped from financial crisis to crisis, while being expected to develop thousands of expert teachers. These organizations' achievements are modest in quantity and quality, yet it is remarkable that they produced anything at all. If the above description lacks coherence, it reflects the realities of special educational provision in Pakistan. The present situation may be understood only by looking at the obstacles and reverses that are still current and by comparing the feebleness of normal education, health and welfare.

Pritchard's account (1963 p. 80-81) of early municipal education for deaf and blind children in England in the 1880s sounds remarkably similar. Nearer home, senior Indian disability planners Narasimhan and Mukherjee (1986, p. 55-61) describe a situation developmentally some 20 years ahead of Pakistan, which could serve as a warning:

[The] voluntary sector played a dominant role in the establishment of schools for disabled children. . . . The bulk of these schools is found in major cities. . . . They cater mostly to the elite group who can afford to pay for their services. . . . Most of the special schools are based on the western pattern, and even copy western books and other educational materials. . . . There is an exaggerated emphasis on academic education to all groups of handicapped children irrespective of the ability of the child to receive such education. Parent counselling does not find a place in the curriculum of most of these special schools. . . . One of the main reasons for this unsatisfactory quality of education in the special schools is a lack of professional manpower. . . . Teachers' training programmes have been ad hoc in character, without any professional guidance. . . . Special schools run by the government are equally poor in quality. They are rigid and far less flexible than the voluntary sector in their approach to understanding and tackling the growing needs of handicapped children. . . . The Central Government introduced a scheme called 'Integrated Education of Disabled Children' in normal schools. . . . Although 12 years have passed since the scheme was launched in 1974, it has not picked up satisfactorily. . . . In none of the experiments is there any real integration of handicapped children with normal children.

CULTURE AND SPECIAL EDUCATIONAL PRACTICE

Viewing the level of educational underdevelopment, it might be thought remarkable that Pakistan has any special needs provisions at all. In fact Pakistan, like many developing countries, has a 'modern sector', an ascendant, middle-class, westernized, urban population, who believe in organized solutions to social problems and who can seek modern know-how and technology. Arguments used in favor of special education are religious, humanitarian, economic, legal, and based on consumer demand and national pride. To open even one special school, however mediocre, enables the government to report to international bodies that "we have some services for handicapped children."

Influence of Islam

Within Pakistan's national ideology of Islam, there are both philosophical and historical resources to illuminate the development of services for people with disabilities. For example, in the Islamic legal schools in the eighth and ninth centuries A.D. there was detailed discussion of the civil rights of mentally disabled persons, differentiating various types of mental disability and their behavioral consequences a thousand years before the modern western debates on the same topic (cf The Hedaya). Equally striking is the notion of justice described by Wadud (1986) as being a fundamental principle and permanent value of Islam:

In the Quran, *Adl* [justice] and *Ehsan* come together. *Ehsan* is the next higher stage after *Adl* in the Quranic social order. *Ehsan* means a condition wherein an individual lagging behind in spite of his best efforts gets his deficiency made good by others to restore the disturbed balance of the society. This is not by way of charity but as a matter of right.

Ideas of 'deficiency' do not please disabled activists, yet Wadud's (possibly idiosyncratic) definition of *Ehsan* not only emphasizes the social dimension of disability but clearly sees *society* as being in need of restoration, rather than locating the 'problem' solely in the disabled individual. The emphasis on rights, rather than charity, is a necessary consequence.

Islam is an active, interventionist and basically optimistic religion, teaching that humankind is in a mess but the problems are soluble with the guidance of Allah. It also advocates getting knowledge, at least of the sort that promotes a just social order. Pakistanis vary greatly in the extent to which they practice what Islam teaches. There ought to be no drawback to 'making good the deficiency of an individual who lags behind'. Yet these philosophical resources are seldom used or quoted. "In practice, many who are unaware of the teachings of Islam, look upon the presence of a handicapped child as a sign of divine punishment" (Lari, 1987, p. 8). If not seen as a punishment, there is often a resigned belief that the child's disability is 'the will of Allah' and that to attempt remediation would be a form of rebellion. Parents do sometimes differentiate between congenital and adventitious disability: the former must be accepted while the latter can be given rehabilitative treatment.

Family Perceptions of Special Needs and Services

There is little tradition of birth registration or celebration of birthdays, so parents are often vague about their child's age and have no clear idea of the skills children normally develop by a certain age or of the sequence of skills. Some parents seem to guess their child's age roughly by major milestones, rather than by computing chronology. Lack of birth data is useful for the mildly retarded child: it removes the idea that he is '6 months behind the norm'. It is also impossible to standardize IQ and other age-related tests. However, if they are not judged by developmental norms, children with learning problems are liable to judgment against a norm of obedience: "He should be walking, but he won't obey me"; "He's stubborn, he won't write his alphabet"; "She's stubborn, she won't talk properly."

Parents expect their children to learn *to obey*. Other skills should be a natural product, developing automatically out of this obedience. Parents of young mentally retarded children usually regard walking and talking as important, but are less concerned about feeding, toilet management and dressing. There are always older female hands nearby to assist the latter tasks, whereas walking and talking cannot be done by proxy. Yet despite the importance attached to children's speech, the average Pakistani family is culturally unlikely to do the sort of Western language stimulation where ". . . adults intervene in actions to verbalize step-by-step features, ask children to recount what is already known to have been experienced by both adults and children, and elicit and reward accounts from children in which they assert themselves as primary actors or agents" (Heath, 1989, p. 346).

Through lack of adult awareness of the broad 'normal' range of ability, children of low/average intelligence with educated or ambitious parents may be labelled 'retarded', through their inability to fulfill parental requirements. Another way for parents to digest a child's 'stubbornness' and 'refusal to satisfy his father's wishes' might be to regard him as a juvenile delinquent. Where families expect a son to grow up like his father and a daughter like her mother, there is a greater sense of family shame and of parental failure when the child's disability stops expectations from being met. Normal childhood activities are often dismissed as being of little value--the child's art work or writing, for example, are likely to be judged only by adult standards.

These last two cultural features combined may cause mentally retarded people to be seen as a separate, different species, rather than as people who happen to be at one end of the spectrum of learning ability. Other prejudices may also be reinforced, disguised in a more sophisticated jargon of educational disadvantage. For example, journalist Parviz (1988) believes that "Children coming from less educated families have significantly slow learning ability. And in families where the parents are too busy to give any time to the child, the infants have a specific learning weakness which results in their functioning below their full intellectual potential."

Pakistani parents whose idea of child development does not include sequences of learned skills, do not easily accept child-centred, developmental methods of education, nor the value of educational toys. Indeed, the notorious question "When is [the pupil] going to do some real work?" is still asked by some British parents (Sedgwick, 1991) after decades of child-centred early education. Parents may regard preliminary skills as irrelevant, unless given a careful explanation of their purpose in constructing more complex skills. (Such a view may also be found among some Western behaviorists). Where parents seldom play with their children, mothers may not understand what is wanted when asked to 'play with', 'talk to', or 'stimulate' their developmentally retarded child. They may comply under professional sanction, but fail to do so at home. For most Pakistanis, 'learning' is either 'obeying' or 'memorizing', so they find it hard to grasp that children can be *taught*, by planned steps, the skills that they have not 'acquired automatically'.

Families usually resent intervention by outsiders, e.g. health visitors, community rehabilitation workers, special teachers. Parents may justify going outside the family for help only if they can 'hand over' the child to highly qualified professionals who will 'cure' it. This is particularly so in areas of Pakistan where the family is very private. Several of the above points may reinforce parents in perceiving the problem in medical terms. They may tour around doctors and shrines rather than seeking educational help. Helping parents to change their attitude or take in new ideas may also be harder in an extended family structure than in a nuclear family. The extended family makes it difficult for an outsider to influence individual members. As Rack (1982, p. 247) points out, "No individual member has a relationship with someone outside the family that is his or hers alone." A disabled child's parents may also have little authority within the extended family, even to do what they think best for their child. Decisions will often be made by senior family members (e.g. grandfather or senior uncle).

Teacher Perceptions of Special Education

Reports from observers and inservice trainers (e.g. Bude, 1990; Heneveld & Hassan, 1990; Jaffer, Welle-Strand & Jaffer, 1989; Israr, 1989) suggest that the average Pakistani teacher knows no more than the average parent about childhood, child development and learning, and would not care to know much more. He does not see it as part of his job to understand children, to befriend or play with them or stimulate them to ask questions or enter upon speculation and experiment. The teacher appears before the pupils, opens his mouth and gives forth knowledge, at least occasionally. It is the children's task to absorb the teacher's words. If, afterwards, they do not know their lesson, it is because they have failed to obey their teacher and commit his words to memory. There is a swift remedy: "In our education institutions the rod still reigns supreme and sometimes corporal punishment exceeds all the limits" (Shakil, 1990).

In 1976, Shah prefaced the national teacher training curricula with his belief that "With respect to the methodology of teaching, there is a movement away from a wholly didactic-reception learning situation to a more flexible interpretation of the teacher's role as a manager of appropriate learning experiences for the child and a resource person who operates in relation to the community. . ." After 13 years, no trace of this movement was found during a detailed study of classroom activity

(Jaffer, Welle-Strand & Jaffer, 1990). Some of the practical difficulties parallel those experienced a century earlier in the attempted export of Froebelian kindergarten methods from Germany to urban English schools: "For the practitioner, the kindergarten system posed enormous problems when translated from its erstwhile rural frame, a summery open-air environment with pupil-teacher ratios of about fifteen to one, into the circumstances of the large elementary school, with "preposterously large" classes of sixty to seventy children, and a need to follow the [Board of Education] Code in order to earn a grant" (Marsden, 1990).

Heneveld and Hasan (1989) are positive in their evaluation of modernizing moves in some schools in the Sind. They found teachers, after inservice training, advocating child-centred methods. Yet they suggest that "most of the teachers do not yet understand well the pedagogy they have embraced" (p. 14). "They lack the theoretical knowledge of the stages in a child's development of his/her critical thinking skills that is needed for effective child-centred instruction" (p. 39). Bude (1990, p. 125), evaluating attempts to introduce modern approaches in Northern Area schools, is less optimistic: "Some of the very important elements . . . like practical teaching, using teaching aids, children being the centre of attention, seem to vanish once the school is no longer under constant supervision and control." Kumar (1989) notes similar problems in attempts to introduce a child-centred curriculum in India.

Children with visual or physical impairment may be taught by the usual method, with moderate success. The problem, and also the strength, of the deaf or mentally handicapped pupil is that 'normal' pedagogy does not work. Their contribution to the educational systems of the world is to force the teacher to stop and ask herself: how can this child come to know the things that he should know? If she cannot hear my words, or tell their meaning, is it possible for her to learn some other way? If success cannot be achieved by beating him, what else could motivate the child? Here it is the child who is 'subversive', giving special education to her elders and betters by making them think laterally. Special education, worth the name, is a two-way process.

Some special teachers in Pakistan have been subverted--have separated themselves from a view of schooling as obedience and memorization reinforced by fear. A few have embraced a child-centred, developmentally sequenced, open-ended skill-targeting approach, with rewards rather than sanctions. This may happen without direct Western influence (cf. Jaffer & Jaffer, 1990). However, it goes against the grain. Visitors, seeing such activity, express surprise that the staff are relating to pupils in such a friendly way "as though they were their own children," but are disinclined to believe that such methods can produce beneficial results, i.e. examination success. Heads of 32 special schools surveyed by Lari (1987, p. 77) ranked "play activities" and "creative activities, music, drama etc." as seventh and ninth respectively out of ten choices on a scale of curricular importance. "Language and speech," "Vocational skills" and "Religious education" were ranked first, second and third.

Staff tend progressively to lower their expectations and require too little of their pupils (Jaffer & Jafri, 1989). Some feel that giving their time to the 'unfortunate disabled children' is a 'noble' occupation, which excuses them from any strenuous efforts to prepare work or stimulate their pupils. Where teachers wish to experiment and innovate there may be little encouragement, since most of them are women. Women in Pakistan are seldom expected to think for themselves or try out new ideas. [Here, the two authors diverge. C. Miles believes that 'seldom' should be replaced by 'never'].

POSSIBLE ALTERNATIVES?

Folie á Deux

The editor of the *British Journal of Special Education*, after touring Pakistan asked, "Is there sometimes unconscious 'collusion' between Pakistani policy makers eager to adopt high-status Western ideas and British educationalists eager to spread 'good practice'? Do both connive (with the best of intentions) at Western 'solutions' which do not travel well - or which need to be adapted to local conditions before doing so?" (Peter, 1987). Doubtless the answer is affirmative. The *British Council* advisors (1987, p. 3) saw it as their role "to get people to ask their own questions, even if we don't like the questions. We must invent strategies to encourage questions, not collude with others' ideas of our own authority." Yet the advisor may be bounced into giving answers which are then taken as authoritative. (She can then be blamed when things go wrong).

Governments hope to find solutions that cost little to start and almost nothing later, make a good show of solving a social problem, tread on nobody's cultural or religious sensibilities and require no political commitment beyond a few photo-opportunities with grateful rehabilitated families. Such answers have not been found by the Government of Pakistan, which finally grew weary of entertaining a succession of short-term advisors. It now has some 20 Western volunteers, Peace Corps and British VSOs, sharing their skills in government and voluntary agency schools. The DGSE Director General, welcoming some of the volunteers, informed them (in a kindly way) that he did not expect them to achieve anything during their stay. Presumably he felt they could do no harm and might lay the piping for an inflow of foreign funds.

The directors of 14 special education institutions, responding to a trends survey, gave a mixed response to the suggestion that mental handicap activities in Pakistan are "mostly dominated by Western ideas/methods, with insufficient cultural/conceptual adaptation." Half of them (seven) agreed with this multiple-choice option, five preferred the formula that there was "a suitable blend of Western/Pakistani ideas and methods," while four felt there should be "more ideas/methods from Western countries to provide a framework for local experience to grow." Some from each group, eight altogether, also thought that "more input is needed from other, non-Western countries." (Miles, M., 1991). The idea of South-South exchange, while attractive, would not avoid the problem if, as Hutt (1979) remarks of India, ". . . the uncritical acceptance of Western pedagogic models has meant that there has been no systematic conceptual analysis of the goals and strategies of learning, nor formulation of a philosophy of education that is consonant with the aspirations of the culture."

But What Would Be Appropriate?

Special needs services are late-comers in the development game. When nations have organized food and water, housing, roads, schools, health services, communications, they may tackle social problems hitherto seen as marginal or insoluble. Most basic developments require some attitude change and the learning of new skills, but the mass of people can be motivated if they see broad and visible benefits. However, the general benefits of helping some 10-15% of the population affected directly or indirectly by disability are less obvious. Economic arguments count for less in countries where there is much unemployment and under-employment. Among the masses, humanitarian motivation may not go beyond the idea that disabled people "should be pitied," "there should be a place for them," and "the government should do something" (Miles, M., 1983).

The problem is that Western special education is based on ideas about children, childhood, development and learning that differ substantially from those common in Pakistan. Ordinary people can quite quickly get used to modern technology like telephones, tractors and water-flush toilets, which do not require them to alter their basic idea of who they are and how they relate to their kin. But it is not clear that middle-class, NENA notions of childhood and learning *can* be absorbed in less than several decades - regardless of whether they *should* be. In 12 years of close contact with Pakistanis in special education, often in a training role (Miles, C., 1991), the present authors saw little absorption of these notions. Some semblance of Western special education could be carried out, against the grain. It remained an alien import.

Within Pakistani cultures, half the population (females) are treated on an everyday, practical basis as being inferior in intelligence, physical strength, spiritual worth, and general esteem. This estimate is easily and confidently maintained, despite a growing discontent among some of its victims. There is also widespread discrimination against people of darker skin color, despite the contrary teaching of Islam and the irrationality of this attitude. The *similarly negative attitudes* toward disabled people, or toward childhood, will probably resist criticism and pressure, since people with disabilities and children in general appear in Pakistan to be "self-evidently" inferior in ability and worth. However, at least one Government workshop targeted, "the responsibility of special educators . . . to change the attitudes of society" (Report of the National, 1987, p. 42).

Serpell (1984, p. 23) suggests that "rather than assuming the need to import wholesale a specialised system which was developed elsewhere, the basic parameters of local patterns of child care and socialisation should be examined for their strengths and weaknesses in relation to the special needs of disabled children." So, can special needs education effectively develop on an alternative, Pakistani cultural and conceptual base? This remains to be seen. Certainly, there are indigenous special education developments outside the wealthier Western nations. 'The West' itself was not 'wealthy' nor uniformly 'developed' when special education began in earlier centuries. Britain now sends trainees to the Peto Institute in

Hungary, where GNP is a fifth of that of Britain. Brazil has a vast network of active parents' organizations for handicapped children. Traditional therapies are integrated with modern methods in China (Zhuo, 1988). Japanese 'daily life therapy' for autism is being tried in the USA (Gurry and Larkin, 1990). In India, yoga therapy is used in special schools, with its accompanying mental attitude and philosophy (Vijay Human Services, 1988). Billimoria (1986) notes the existence "in ancient ayurvedic literature [of] a science known as 'Vikritanga' wherein the mentally retarded and the mentally ill were clearly differentiated and specific etiological factors and remedies spelt out. Unfortunately we have not only been unable to build on our earlier knowledge but we have totally abandoned it."

Whether the use of these indigenous practices will lead to the development of a full-blown non-Western style of special education, or whether there will be a convergence across many cultures, is not clear. Ansari (1989b), discussing the need for indigenisation of psychology in Pakistan, sagely notes that

Indigenous concepts have to be relevant and appropriate also. . . . We must learn from the past, but should not be a prisoner to the past. . . . Indigenous concepts must be critically evaluated for their relevance and usefulness. True indigenization means freedom, self awareness and ability to perceive and evaluate different models. Rather than parochialism, narrow-minded nationalism or revivalism.

Some reviewers of the 'non-Western development' idea believe that "the world is becoming so small that one cannot even think of purely indigenous practices, especially in a heavily colonialized society like Pakistan" (Jaffer, R., 1990, personal communication). Seeing that the early Western developments and current Third World practices take place in completely different historical circumstances, G. Freyhoff considers that the influences of intercultural contacts "*may not have the results that we are expecting*--colleagues from developing countries may incorporate into their conceptual base some parts of our experiences and knowledge that we would not have thought of" (1990, personal communication). However, Freyhoff notes that this process has its risks, in that while taking different directions "they will make different mistakes which are not predictable and therefore also not avoidable."

One Practical Step

A neglected strategy would be to reinforce culturally normal activities already practised with disabled children in Pakistan. For example, a study in the North West Frontier (Miles, M., 1985a) found that among 43,416 pupils enrolled in 103 ordinary schools, 825 (1.9%) were reported as "disabled" by their teacher. With class sizes varying from 30 to 80 pupils, disability of a noticeable level will be much exceeded by unnoticed mild impairments. Across Pakistan, at least 200,000 children with appreciable disability are already enrolled in ordinary schools, with no extra help, i.e. at least 20 times the number in special schools. The study advised the government to devote resources to help these children, many of whom drop out after a year or two. When this study appeared, government officers were also hearing about integration from foreign advisors, but apparently they found the idea merely confusing at the time. They were trying to accommodate the notion of children who were somehow different, or who learned differently; whereas the ideal of Western integration involves a paradigm shift, towards schools that enable all children to fulfill their potential, rather than sieving out the weak and assigning them their place on the scrapheap.

Nevertheless, by 1989 the government of Sind was piloting inservice training of teachers to cope with casually integrated disabled children. Similar activities are reported by Jangira (1988) in India. Despite the poor start to planned integration in India already quoted by Narasimhan and Mukherjee, casual integration has long been noticed by aware observers such as Nimbkar (1979), discussing physically disabled children around 1960. Discussion of planned integration is normal in India's professional journals. Victor (1982), Parikh and Dhylon (1988) and Fazelbhoy (1989) on children with impaired hearing, developmental disabilities and visual impairment, are cautiously positive. Though there is a strong tendency to gloss over the problems and report the successes in this sort of article, yet these authors evidently have enough confidence to admit some difficulties.

To Be Continued

Many practical steps could be listed for Pakistan to take, but to do so would be pointless. The *first* steps needed are those that mid-level practitioners, e.g. school heads and provincial education directors, have themselves conceived and could implement. Some realignment of national economic priorities would help. The government has long known this, but has not significantly increased education budgets. Judging by its actions, it does not seriously believe in education. Maybe it believes, but does not think that the present system could deliver, however much money were allocated.

Pakistanis in their various cultures must themselves decide how they will educate special needs children. It is tempting to compare features of Pakistan with aspects of Western societies in earlier years, and to predict Pakistan's evolutionary path. 'They can avoid making the mistakes we made' is the naive slogan. Yet when 'we' were making them, the services later considered 'mistaken' were not necessarily so, and seldom felt mistaken. Seen with attitudes and resources then current, the 'mistakes' usually felt quite good. The difference of viewpoint works not only on the Western/Asian axis. Some drug, race, and crime issues are 20 years further evolved in parts of the USA compared with Britain. This leads American visitors to predict developments in Britain and to point out the flaws in the current British measures. Their advice is seldom heeded.

It is unlikely that the British are much stupider than Americans, or that Pakistanis are stupider than the British who try to advise them. When a problem in one's own society has been adequately examined and conceptualized in terms familiar within the language and context of that society, and it seems that there is a technological solution, the advice and help of technicians who have been using the technology in another society can be of benefit. But where the problem is still unfamiliar or is conceptualized differently, outside help is less likely to be of immediate use. If Western special education is ill-adapted for Pakistan, it may also be a poor fit in many other countries. It is also still very poorly understood among many immigrants and less educated people in western countries.

The authors spent 12 years demonstrating, publishing and mobilizing resources for rehabilitation and special education with Pakistani colleagues who in turn explained and demonstrated in national workshops. Our concept of special education (which was of course subject to our personal limitations and hardly represented the full range of Western experience) did not seem to be widely absorbed. In recent years we began to see why, as described. Latterly we gave priority to making available relevant information (Miles, M., 1987, 1989b, 1989c, 1990) and field-testing strategies for skill transfer (e.g. Miles & Frizzell, 1990; Miles,

1991). Our colleagues achieved some good results with what they learned and what they knew already. Their onward transmission to their peers has some credibility. The process may continue for another decade or two before an indigenous Pakistani version of special education takes shape. If it happens that quickly, they will have been smarter than the Europeans who learnt their special education over about 200 years.

Acknowledgements. Over the years, the authors were educated and befriended by many Pakistani colleagues, children and families. In the special education field, Rafiq Jaffer, Irfan Malik, Laeeq Mirza, Khalida Tareen, Oliver Caleb and Mahjabeen Agha were particularly informative. However, they bear no responsibility for the views expressed in this chapter. We also gratefully received review comments from Mel Ainscow, Caroline Currer, Geert Freyhoff, Rafiq Jaffer, Marja-Liisa Murdoch and Susan Peters.

References

Abdullah, Tahira (1981). *The Situation of Disabled Children in Pakistan.* Islamabad: UNICEF (P.O. Box 1063).

Adams, Carol (1982). *Ordinary Lives. A Hundred Years Ago.* London: Virago.
Includes detailed description of daily lives of working class children in late nineteenth-century Britain. Many similarities with poorer children in Pakistan now.

Ahmad, A., Jan, H., & Nisar (1989). Child Labour and Exploitation. *Report of the seminar "Child Abuse in Pakistan",* p. 26. Peshawar: Pakistan Pediatric Association NWFP (Khyber Medical College) & UNICEF (P.O. Box 476).

Ahmed, Akbar S. (1988). *Discovering Islam: Making Sense of Muslim History and Society.* London: Routledge & Kegan Paul.

Ahmed, Akbar S. (1990). Foreword. *Pakistan. The Social Sciences' Perspective.* A.S. Ahmed (Ed). Karachi: Oxford University Press.

Ahmed, Syed Nasir (1988). Part of the Government for Uplift of Disabled in Pakistan. *Aadarsh Monthly,* 2 (17-18) pp. 48-50.
A short summary by Pakistan's (then) Director General of Special Education.

Ajmal, Mohammad (1978). The Value of Creative Playing and Cultural Experiences. *The Pakistan Times,* (22 Dec. 1978.)

Ajmal, Mohammad (1986). Interiority. In *Muslim Contributions to Psychotherapy and Other Essays,* pp. 21-27. Psychological research monograph No. 5. Islamabad: National Institute of Psychology (P.O. Box 1511).
A senior psychologist/philosopher discusses the importance of the child archetype in Islamic Humanism.

Akbar, Raja M. (1989). *A Survey of Special Education Facilities for the Handicapped Children in Pakistan.* M.A. thesis, Dept. of Educational Planning and Management, Allama Iqbal Open University, Islamabad. 102 pp.
Useful recent survey of institutional facilities and development.

Akhtar, Tasleem (1989). Child abuse--What needs to be done. *Report of the seminar "Child Abuse in Pakistan"*, pp. 38-43. Peshawar: Pakistan Pediatric Association NWFP (Khyber Medical College) & UNICEF.

Alam, Anis (1990). Education crying for government's help. *The Frontier Post*, (16 Nov. 1990), p. 12.

Alam, Iqbal & Shah, Nasra M. (1986). Population Composition, Mortality and Fertility. In N.M. Shah (Ed.), *Pakistani Women. A Socioeconomic & Demographic Profile*, pp. 53-86. Islamabad: Pakistan Institute of Development Economics (Quaid-i-Azam University).

Ali, Isfana Juzar (1988). Child and Adolescent Psychiatry. In S.H. Ahmed (Ed.), *Psychiatry in Pakistan*, pp. 22-24. Karachi: Pakistan Psychiatric Society (Jinnah Postgraduate Medical Centre).

Ansari, Z.A. (1989a). Research on Child Development in the National Institute of Psychology. In Seema Pervez (Ed.), *The Pakistani Child: Educational and Psychological Research*, pp. 142-170. Islamabad: National Institute of Psychology (P.O. Box 1511).

Ansari, Z.A. (1989b). Indigenisation of Psychology in Pakistan. *National Institute of Psychology Newsletter*, 8(1):4-6. (P.O. Box 1511, Islamabad).

Anwar, M. & Naeem, M. (1980). *Situation of Children in Rural Punjab.* Lahore: Dept. of Sociology, University of Punjab, with UNICEF.
Interview survey, largely descriptive, focusing on women and young children, maternal and child health, schooling.

Anwar-ul-Haq, M.; Ahmad, Ashfaq; Cheema, M. Asghar; Zafar, M. Iqbal & Tahir, G.G. (1989). Family Size and Sex Preference Among Women in Rural Pakistan. *Journal of Rural Development and Administration*, 21(3):41-58. (Pakistan Academy for Rural Development, Peshawar).

Aries, Philippe (1973). *Centuries of Childhood.* Harmondsworth: Penguin. French original, 1960, Libraire Plon, Paris.
Influential account of historical ideas of childhood. Some of Aries's views are attacked vigorously by S. Pollock (q.v.).

Asberg, R. (1973). *Primary Education and National Development.* Stockholm: Almqvist & Wiksell.

Bano, Maher (1988). A Thematic Analysis of Children's Stories in Urdu in Terms of Achievement, Affiliation and Power Motives in Pakistan. *Pakistan Journal of Psychological Research*, 3(1-2):33-41. (National Institute of Psychology).

Bhatti, K.M. (1986). *Annotated Bibliography of Social Research in Pakistan.* Peshawar: Pakistan Academy for Rural Development.
540 annotations in 141 pp. Stronger on rural development and administration.

Bhatti, M.A., Khalid, H., Shireen, S. & Saeed, F. (1988). *Female Teachers in Rural Pakistan (Problems and Remedies).* Islamabad: National Educational Council, Ministry of Education, Government of Pakistan.

Billimoria, Roda B. (1986). *Attitude-Reality: The Situation of the Mentally Retarded in India.* Paper presented at Rehabilitation International Asia Regional Congress, Bombay, September 1986.

British Council (1987). *Pakistan Special Education Seminar, 6-7 July 1987, Lucas Institute, University of Birmingham.* London: The British Council.

Bude, Udo (1990). *Improving Primary School Teaching. An Evaluation of the Field-based Teacher Development Programme in the Northern Areas of Pakistan.* Dok 1597 C/a. Bonn: Deutsche Stiftung für internationale Entwicklung.
Detailed report covering many aspects of current teaching practice. 228 pp.

Cambridge University Asian Expedition (1962). *The Budhopur Report. A Study of the Forces of Tradition and Change in a Punjabi Village in the Gujranwala District, West Pakistan.* Lahore: Social Sciences Research Centre, University of Punjab.

Channer, Yvonne & Parton, Nigel (1990). Racism, Cultural Relativism and Child Protection. In *The Violence Against Children Study Group, Taking Child Abuse Seriously,* pp. 105-120. London: Unwin Hyman.

Chaudhary, Muhammad Iqbal & Khan, Mushtaq Ahmed (1969). *Sociology. An Introduction.* Lahore: Noorsons.

Chaudhary, Muhammad Ashraf (1979). Problems of Kidnapping. In *The Problems of Children in Pakistan.* Islamabad: National Council of Social Welfare.

Coupe, J. (1987). *Teaching Mentally Retarded Children. Report of a Training Workshop, Hyderabad, April 1987.* Islamabad: Directorate General of Special Education.

Currer, Caroline (1983). *Pathan Mothers in Bradford. Some Facts about their Everyday Lives; and Some Views Concerning Having a Baby; Rearing Children; Health and Illness, Happiness and Sadness and Health Services.* Coventry: Dept. of Sociology, University of Warwick.

Daniel, Arzu Edgar (1990). A Non-Year for the Girl Child. *The Pakistan Times* (28 Dec. 1990), Magazine Section pp. I & V.

Directorate General of Special Education (1988). *Special Education Bulletin.* Islamabad: Author.

Education and Care of Handicapped. Report of the Delegation which Visited the U.K., Denmark, FRG, Kuwait and India to Study their Systems for Education and Care of Handicapped. 1986. Islamabad: Directorate General of Special Education. 192 pp.
Largely descriptive report of a tour which preceded formulation of the National Policy for the Education and Rehabilitation of the Disabled.

Emanuel, R. (1987). *Notes on Two Visits to Pakistan by a Speech Therapist.* Consultant report. London: The British Council. *(May be restricted).*

Ezzaki, A., Spratt, J.E., Wagner, D.E., (1987). Childhood Literacy Acquisition in Rural Morocco: Effects of Language Differences and Quranic Preschooling. In D. Wagner (Ed.), *The Future of Literacy in a Changing World.* Oxford: Pergamon.

Farooqi, S. (1988). Educational uplift of the disabled. *The Pakistan Times* (6 April 1988), pp. 4, 5.
Short summary by Pakistan's (then) Director General of Special Education.

Fayyaz, Fayyaz Ahmad (1990). Rehabilitation of the Handicapped: Centres to be Formed in Rural Areas. *The Pakistan Times* (30 April 1990), Sports & Youth Section, p. B.

Fazelbhoy, R.S. (1989). Integrated Education in India: Benefits and Problems. *J. Visual Impairment & Blindness*, 83(1):47-50.

Federal Bureau of Statistics (1986). *Survey of Disabled Persons 1984-85.* Karachi: Author.

Fraser, B.C. (1987). *Education for Deaf Children in Pakistan.* (Pak/999/29) Consultant report. London: The British Council. 16 pp.
Detailed and perceptive report, based on a short tour.

Ghuman, P.A.S. (1975). *The Cultural Context of Thinking.* Windsor: National Foundation for Education Research.

Giladi, Avner (1989). Concepts of Childhood and Attitudes Towards Children in Medieval Islam. A Preliminary Study with Special Reference to Reactions to Infant and Child Mortality. *Journal of the Economic and Social History of the Orient*, 32(2):121-152.

Grotberg, Edith H. (1977). Child Development. In E.H. Grotberg (Ed.), *200 Years of Children*, pp. 391-420. Washington, DC: US Department of Health, Education & Welfare, Office of Child Development.
Indicates the quite recent growth of "modern" views of the child in USA.

Grotberg, Edith H. & Badri, Gasim. *(Badri mistakenly printed "Bardin")* (1989). Shifting from Traditional to Modern Child-Rearing Practices in the Sudan. *Early Child Development and Care*, 50, 141-150.

Gul, Gulzar, A. (1979). The Learner-Centred Approach in Education as a Function of Our National Objective. In Z.A. Ansari et al. (Eds.), *New Directions in Pakistani Psychology*, p. 170. Islamabad: Pakistan Psychological Association (P.O. Box 1773).

Gurry, Susan & Larkin, Anne (1990). Daily Life Therapy: Its roots in Japanese Culture. *International Journal of Special Education*, 5(3):359-369.

Handbook of Statistics on Disabled Persons in Pakistan (1981). Islamabad: Ministry of Health, Special Education & Social Welfare.
The handbook gave district-wise guesstimates and population census figures. Probably unavailable now.

Haq, Ikramul (1989). Little Hope for Children of Poverty. *The Pakistan Times*, (2 Oct. 1989), p. 6.

Haque, Abdul (1987a). Some Implications of Sex-Trait Stereotypes Research. *Proceedings of the Sixth Conference of Pakistan Psychological Association*, pp. 77-82. Islamabad, P.O. Box 1773: Pakistan Psychological Association.

Haque, Abdul (1987b). Social Class Differences in Perceived Maternal Acceptance-Rejection and Personality Dispositions Among Pakistani Children. In Cigdem Kagitcibasi (Ed.), *Growth and Progress in Cross-Cultural Psychology*. Lisse: Swets & Zeitlinger BV.

Haroon, Ayesha (1989). Unspoken Plight. *The Frontier Post* (8 Nov. 1989), p. 9.

Hasan, S. Sibte (1988). The Influence of Culture on the Development of Thought. In S.H. Ahmed (Ed.), *Psychiatry in Pakistan*, pp. 12-16. Karachi: Pakistan Psychiatric Society.

Hassan, I.N. (1979). General Features of Psychopathology Found Amongst Primary School Children of Federal Areas Schools, Islamabad. In *Proceedings of Fourth Session, Karachi 1979*, pp. 34-45. Islamabad: Pakistan Psychological Association (P.O. Box 1773).
Pilot study of 82 pupils with problems. Discusses need for guidance and counselling services in Pakistan.

Hassan, I.N. (1985). Psychological Profile of Pakistani Women in the Light of Developmental Social Stereotypes. In Z.A. Ansari et al. (Eds.), *New Directions in Pakistani Psychology*, pp. 17-21. Islamabad: Pakistan Psychological Association (P.O. Box 1773).
Elementary questionnaire study of 200 urban and rural schoolgirls. Discusses women in Pakistani cultures.

Heath, Shirley Brice (1989). The Learner as Cultural Member. In M.L. Rice & R.L. Schiefelbusch (Eds.), *The Teachability of Language*, pp. 330-350. Baltimore: Paul H. Brookes.

Heneveld, Ward, & Hasan, Parween (1989). *Evaluation of Sind School Improvement Programme*. Geneva: Aga Khan Foundation. 62 pp.
A detailed report of an imaginative project.

Hisam, Zeenat (1984). Neglect of Girls the Only Explanation for Pakistan's Unusual Male:Female Population Balance. *Children: Development Trends in Pakistan*, Special issue 1984, 10-11. Islamabad: UNICEF (P.O. Box 1063).
UNICEF published 11 issues of the journal *Children*, 1982-6, with a number of informative articles, some of which appeared also in national newspapers.

222   Education and Disability in Cross-Cultural Perspective

Honig, Alice Sterling (1982). Caregivers and Children Learning Together: A Cross-Cultural View. In L.L. Adler (Ed.), *Cross-cultural Research at Issue*, pp. 113-124. New York: Academic Press.

Hussain, Arshad (1990). *Erosion of Childhood*. Paper presented at the Eighth International Psychiatric Conference of Pakistan Psychiatric Society, Islamabad, December 1990.

Hutt, Corinne (1979). Early Education and Child Care in India and Sri Lanka: A Critical Review. *Bulletin of the British Psychological Society*, 32, 377-380.

Ikram, Tahir (1990). Tragedy of Missing Children Assumes Grave Dimensions. *The Frontier Post* (21 April 1990), p. 8.

Inayatullah (1989). Social Sciences in Pakistan. An Evaluation. *International Social Science Journal*, 41(4):617-633.

Isa, Begum Qazi (1990). The Status of the Girl Child in Baluchistan. *The Pakistan Times* (26 Oct. 1990), Magazine Section, IV.

Ishtiaq, Kishwar (1977). *Mentally Retarded Children: A Social-Psychological Study*. New Delhi: Chand & Co.
Published Ph.D. thesis, more useful as an indication of socio-psychological bias in a middle-class urban researcher than as a descriptive report.

Israr, Mohammad (1985). Cognitive Development of Pakistani Primary School Children: Salient Findings of a Research Project. In Z.A. Ansari et al. (Eds.), *New Directions in Pakistani Psychology*, pp. 67-74. Islamabad: Pakistan Psychological Association, P.O. Box 1773.
Useful summary of several years' work on Piagetian stages in Pakistani children. Indicates wide gap between cognitive demands of school textbooks and actual abilities of children.

Israr, Nargis (1987). A Cognitive Development Task Battery for Primary School Children of Pakistan. In M. Pervez & N. Durrani (Eds.), *Cognitive Development in Primary School Children of Pakistan*, pp. 19-57. Islamabad: National Institute of Psychology (P.O. Box 1511).

Israr, Nargis (1989). Researches on Learning Environment and Drop-Out of School Children in Pakistan. In Seema Pervez (Ed.), *The Pakistani Child: Educational and Psychological Research*, pp. 189-193. Islamabad: National Institute of Psychology.

Jaffer, Razia, & Jaffer, Rafiq (1990). The WHO-CBR Approach: Programme or Ideology--Some Lessons from the CBR Experience in Punjab, Pakistan. In M. Thorburn & K. Marfo (Eds.), *Practical Approaches to Childhood Disability in Developing Countries: Insights from Experience and Research*, pp. 277-292. St. John's, Canada: Project SEREDEC, Memorial University of Newfoundland.
Describes on pp. 289-92 a truly community-based special school in contrast to the artificial, top-down, WHO-style "community based rehabilitation."

Jaffer, Rafiq & Jafri, Qurat-ul-Ain (1989). *Special Education in Pakistan: Problems and Opportunities*. Paper presented at the Workshop on the Role of Psychologists in Mental Health Programmes, September 1989, Lahore.

Jaffer, Rafiq, Welle-Strand, Anne & Jaffer, Razia (1990). *Inside a Pakistani School. A Study of Primary Schools in the Nathiagali and Mansehra Regions of NWFP*. Oslo: IMTEC, International Learning Cooperative (Rosenhof skole, Dynekilgt. 10, 0469 Oslo 5). 56 pp.
Revealing report on the quality of teaching in typical rural schools.

Jafri, S.S. (1990). Books for Children and Youth. *The Pakistan Times* (22 April 1990), Sports & Youth Section, p. B.

Jahoda, Gustav & Lewis, I.M. (eds.) (1988). *Acquiring Culture: Cross Cultural Studies in Child Development*. London: Croom Helm.

Jangira, N.K. (1988). *Special Education for the Disabled: Designing a Model for Developing Countries*. Paper presented at UNESCO consultation meeting in the context of Third Medium Term Plan for 1990-1995, Paris, May 1988. New Delhi: National Council of Educational Research and Training.

Javed, M. & Asghar, M. (1988). *Research Studies at Quaid-i-Azam University, Islamabad: Theses Submitted to the University up to 1986*. Lahore: Al-Waqar Publishers.

Johnson, B.L.C. (1979). *Pakistan.* London: Heinemann.
A comprehensive geography of Pakistan by a perceptive Westerner.

Kakar, Sudhir (1979). Childhood in India: Traditional Ideas and Contemporary Reality. *International Social Science Journal,* 31(3):444-456.

Kakar, Sudhir (2nd Ed., 1981). *The Inner World. A Psycho-Analytic Study of Childhood and Society in India.* Delhi: Oxford University Press. 241 pp.
Insider view of Indian childhood, place of the child in Indian society and myth.

Kalwar, Peer Baksh & Ahmed, S. Haroon (1989). Child Rearing Practices in Various Ethnic Groups in Pakistan. *Proceedings of Seventh International Psychiatric Conference,* pp. 89-98. Karachi: Pakistan Psychiatric Society.

Kasi, Abdul Malik; Pervez, Yousaf; Bahadri, Taimur; Dotana, A.R.; Iqbal, Aftab (1988). Opium Intake and Its Implications Among Infants and Children. *Pakistan Pediatric Journal,* 12(1):31-38.

Kazi, Aftab (1987). *Ethnicity and Education in Nation-Building. The Case of Pakistan.* Lanham: University Press of America. 185 pp.
Scholarly exposition of the neglect of ethnic/cultural factors in Pakistan's education system.

Khan, Mazhar-ul-Haq (1972). *Purdah and Polygamy. A Study in the Social Pathology of the Muslim Society.* Peshawar: Nashiran-e-Ilm-o-Taraqiyet.
Detailed, impassioned polemic against current child-rearing practices in the purdah household (pp. 102-146). Apparently based on general observation rather than research.

Khan, Mushtaq (1985). Keynote Address. *Report of a Seminar on Iodine Deficiency Disorders in Pakistan.* Islamabad: UNICEF (P.O. Box 1063).

Khan, Shaheen (1986). Labour Force Participation of Children: A Case Study. In Ijaz Nabi (Ed.) *The Quality of Life in Pakistan,* pp. 329-350. Lahore: Vanguard.

Khan, Sohaila (1987). Sex Differences in Field Dependence and Socialisation in a Group of Pakistani Children. *Pakistan Journal of Psychological Research*, 2(1-2):3-16.

Khan, Yousuf Ali (1990). *Academics Versus Activists--A History of the University of Peshawar (1950-88)*. Peshawar: Khyber Printers.

Khattak, Nasreen (1990). The Girl Child: 1990 is Her Year. *The Pakistan Times*, (10 April 1990), Midweek Section, C.

Klitgard, Robert; Siddiqui, Khalil Y.; Arshad, Muhammad; Naiz, Naheed; Khan, Muneer A. (1986). The Economics of Teacher Training. In Ijaz Nabi (Ed.), *The Quality of Life in Pakistan*, pp. 253-286. Lahore: Vanguard.

Kraan, J.D. (1984). *Religious Education in Islam. With Special Reference to Pakistan*. Rawalpindi: Christian Study Centre (P.O. Box 529).

Kumar, Krishna (1987-88). What a Child Looks for in Early Learning. *Future. Development Perspectives on Children*, 22-23, pp. 35-37. New Delhi: UNICEF.
Indian professor of education pleads for a modern child-oriented approach to early learning in Indian schools. *Future* is an informative source on children's health, welfare and education in South Asia over the past decade.

Kumar, Krishna (1989). Revived Policy Interest in Education. Issues at Primary Level in India. *Future. Development Perspectives on Children*, 26-27, pp. 27-30.

Lari, Z.S. (1988). *The Provision and Development of Special Education in Pakistan*. M.Ed. dissertation. Cardiff: University of Wales.

Malik, Irfan (1987). *Special Education in Pakistan Today*. Paper presented at the Pakistan Special Education Seminar, July 1987, Birmingham. London: The British Council.

Malik, S. (1988). Situation of the Physically Disabled in Pakistan. *Report of DPI Asia/Pacific Leadership training seminar for women with disability. Islamabad, November 1987.* Islamabad: Disabled People's Federation of Pakistan.

Marsden, Bill (1990). "Mrs. Walker's Merry Games for Little People: Locating Froebel in an Alien Environment. *British Journal of Educational Studies,* 38(1):15-32.

Miles, Christine (1986). *Special Education for Mentally Handicapped Pupils: A Teaching Manual.* Peshawar: Mental Health Centre & Palo Alto: Hesperian Foundation.

Miles, Christine (1991). Mobilising Skills for Special Education in Pakistan: A Personal Cross-Cultural Experience. *International Journal of Special Education.* 6(2):201-212.

Miles, M. (1982). Teachers for Mentally Handicapped Pupils. *Journal of Rehabilitation in Asia,* 23:46-47.

Miles, M. (1983). *Attitudes Towards Persons with Disabilities Following IYDP (1981). With Suggestions for Promoting Positive Changes.* Peshawar: Mental Health Centre, for National Council of Social Welfare, Government of Pakistan, Islamabad. 104 pp.
Attitude survey of 286 urban and rural respondents, with third world literature review. Available ERIC ED 236 826 and Lib. Cong. P-E-84-931173.

Miles, M. (1985a). *Children with Disabilities in Ordinary Schools. An Action Study of Non-Designed Educational Integration in Pakistan.* Peshawar: Mental Health Centre, for National Council of Social Welfare, Government of Pakistan, Islamabad. 85 pp.
Situation of casually integrated pupils and follow-up, with recommendations for Government action. Available ERIC ED 265 711.

Miles, M. (1985b). Problems of Definition & Categorization of Mental Retardation in Pakistan. In *Report on National Coordination Conference on Education of Mentally Handicapped Children, Islamabad, July 1985,* pp. 80-85. Islamabad: Directorate General of Special Education.

Pakistan 227

Miles, M. (1987). Handicapped Children in Pakistan: Targeting Information Needs. *Health Policy & Planning*, 2(4):347-351.

Miles, M. (1989a). Monitoring Polio Trends from Physiotherapy Records. *Tropical Doctor*, 19(1):3-5.

Miles, M. (1989b). Information Based Rehabilitation for Third World Disability. *Social Science & Medicine*, 28(3):207-210.

Miles, M. (1989c). Disability Policies in Pakistan: Is Anyone Winning? *International Journal of Special Education*, 4(1):1-15.
Discusses some of the "concept gap" between Asian governments and Western consultants, that hinders service development.

Miles, M. (1990). A Resource Center Developing Information Based Rehabilitation. In M. Thorburn & K. Marfo (Eds.) *Practical Approaches to Childhood Disability in Developing Countries: Insights from Experience and Research*, pp. 261-276. St. John's, Canada: Project SEREDEC, Memorial University of Newfoundland.

Miles, M. (1991). Effective Use of Action-Oriented Studies in Pakistan. *International Journal of Rehabilitation Research*, 14(1):25-35.

Miles, M. (1991). *Mental Handicap Services: Development Trends in Pakistan*. Peshawar: Mental Health Centre.

Miles, M. & Frizzell, Y. (1990). Handling the Cerebral Palsied Child: Multi-Level Skills Transfer in Pakistan. *Physiotherapy*, 76(3):183-186.
Includes discussion of attitudes and capabilities of mothers in Pakistan and in London with cerebral palsied children.

Minturn, Leigh (1963). The Rajputs of Khalapur, India. Part II: Child-Training. In B.B. Whiting (Ed.), *Six Cultures. Studies in Child Rearing*, pp. 301-361. New York: Wiley.
Detailed account of rural children and child rearing, which, although the field-work is 30 years old and in the adjoining country, has many points of similarity and resonance with rural Pakistan in the 1980s.

Mubarak, Mohsin (1990). Health Coverage: An Evaluation for Future Strategy. *The Pakistan Times*, (24 Dec. 1990), p. 2.
Lengthy extract from a book (title not given) by a former research director of the Pakistan Medical Research Council.

Mumtaz, Khawar & Shaheed, Farida (1987). *Women of Pakistan: Two Steps Forward, One Step Back?* Lahore: Vanguard.

Nabi, Ijaz (1986). Introduction: The Socio-Economic Overview. In Ijaz Nabi (Ed.), *The Quality of Life in Pakistan*, pp. 1-19. Lahore: Vanguard.

Narasimhan, M.C. & Mukherjee, A.K. (1986). *Disability. A Continuing Challenge*. New Delhi: Wiley Eastern. 127 pp.
Detailed description of Government and NGO rehabilitation services and philosophy, by two of India's senior disability planners.

National Education Policy and Implementation Programme. (1979). Islamabad: Government of Pakistan, Ministry of Education. 114 pp.
Detailed education policy and rationale.

National Policy for the Education and Rehabilitation of the Disabled. (1988 Review). 1988. Islamabad: Ministry of Health, Special Education & Social Welfare, Directorate General of Special Education. 30 pp.
The current published policy of the Government of Pakistan on special education and ancillary services.

Newson, John, & Newson, Elizabeth (1968). *Four Years Old In An Urban Community*. London: George Allen & Unwin. 570 pp.
Detailed study of 700 children and their parents in Nottingham, UK.

Nimbkar, K.V. (1979). Compulsory Education and the Crippled Child. *J. Rehabilitation in Asia*, 20(1). (Reprinted, earlier date not given).

Pakistan Commission on the Status of Women (1989). *Report.* Islamabad: Government of Pakistan.
Frank views on the status of women in Pakistan, including girls and family conditions, in 1984. Publication was suspended by General Zia-ul-Haq, but the report appeared in 1989 when Benazir Bhutto gained power.

Pakistan Statistical Yearbook 1988. Karachi: Federal Bureau of Statistics, Government of Pakistan.

Parikh, Jyoti & Dhylon, Ram (1988). Integrating Handicapped Children in the Regular Class: An Evaluation. *Disabilities and Impairments,* 2(1):53-57.

Parviz, Fauzia (1988). Starting school. *The Frontier Post* (April 22 1988), p. 15.

Perkins, E.A. & Powell, M.G. (1983). *An Investigation into the Feasibility of Home-based Behavioral Intervention with Pre-School Handicapped Children of Asian Origin.* Birmingham: Community Mental Handicap Team, West Birmingham Health Authority.
Includes discussion (pp. 26-28) of child-rearing and play with handicapped children by 'Asian' mothers in Birmingham, UK.

Pervez, Seema (1984). *Personality Dynamics of Pakistani Children.* Psychological research monograph No. 3. Islamabad: National Institute of Psychology (P.O. Box 1511). pp. 43.
Children's Apperception Test, local adaption, with 200 primary school children divided into upper, middle and lower socio-economic status.

Pervez, Seema, (Ed.), (1989). *The Pakistani Child: Educational and Psychological Research.* Islamabad: National Institute of Psychology.
Report of a national seminar held in 1986. Useful summaries of past and current research in this field.

Peter, Margaret (1987). Military Leads Advance into the Mainstream. *The Times Educational Supplement,* (3 April 1987), p. 19.

Planning Commission, Government of Pakistan (1986). *Sixth Five Year Plan 1983-88.* Islamabad: Author.
Considerations of special education appear on pp. 430-431, 552-554.

Planning Commission, Government of Pakistan (1988). *Seventh Five Year Plan 1988-93 & Perspective Plan 1988-2003.* Islamabad: Author.
Includes general discussion of educational objectives and a caustic view of present achievements (pp. 243-254). Considerations of special education appear under "Social Welfare" (pp. 299-304).

Pollock, Linda A. (1983). *Forgotten Children. Parent-Child Relations from 1500 to 1900.* Cambridge: CUP.
Detailed study of changing Western concepts of childhood, challenging some theories about how change has occurred.

Pritchard, D.G. (1963). *Education and the Handicapped 1760-1960.* London: Routledge & Kegan Paul.

Qaisrani, Nasim & Khawaja, Sarfraz (Eds.) (1989). *Planning of Basic Education in Pakistan.* Islamabad: Academy of Educational Planning and Management, Ministry of Education.

Quddus, Naseem J. (1990). *Problems of Education in Pakistan.* Karachi: Royal Book Co.

Quddus, Syed Abdul (1989). *The Cultural Patterns of Pakistan.* Lahore: Ferozsons.

Rack, Philip (1982). *Race, Culture and Mental Disorder.* London: Tavistock.
Multi-cultural psychiatry in Bradford, UK, with more general considerations.

Rafiq, Razia (1979). *The Impact of Urbanisation on the Economic, Social and Political Structures of Shah-Di-Khui. A Case Study of a Village near Lahore City.* MA Thesis. Islamabad: Dept. of Anthropology, Quaid-i-Azam University.

Rauf, Abdur (1975). *Dynamic Educational Psychology*, 3rd Ed. Lahore: Ferozsons. 490 pp.
Detailed textbook, first published in 1958, heavily influenced by Western ideas of that era. Chapters on Child Development (pp. 29-32), Influence of Family (131-154), and Role of Culture (155-174), present a rather idealized and prescriptive view.

Rauf, Abdur (1988). *Islamic Culture in Pakistan*. Lahore: Ferozsons.

Report of the National Workshop on Development and Preparation of Teaching/Learning Materials for Mentally Retarded Children, March 1987, Islamabad, 1987. Islamabad: Directorate General of Special Education.
Includes a brief consideration (pp. 41-42) of cultural norms affecting child-rearing and handicap.

Riaz, Muhammad (1988). *Modern Techniques of Documentation and Information Work*. Lahore: Qadiria Books.

Rizavi, Sayyid Sajjad (1986). *Islamic Philosophy of Education*. Lahore: Institute of Islamic Culture.
Useful review of early Muslim thinkers on childhood education, pp. 97-108.

Roghani, Mehr Taj (1989). Female Children in Pakistan - The Deprived and Neglected. In *Report of the Seminar on "Child Abuse in Pakistan"*, pp. 30-37. Peshawar: Pakistan Paediatric Association NWFP (Khyber Medical College) & UNICEF.

Sachar, R.K.; Verma, J.; Prakash, V.; Chopra, A.; Adlaka, R.; & Sofat, R. (1990). The Unwelcome Sex--Female Feticide in India. *World Health Forum*, 11(3):309.

Sandgren, Bjorn & Asberg, Rodney (1976). *On Cognition & Social Change. A Report from a Pilot Study Regarding the Effect of Schooling on Cognitive Growth and Attitudes Towards Social Change in Pakistan*. Lahore: Institute of Education & Research, University of Punjab.

Sedgwick, Fred (1991). Playing is a Serious Game. *The Times Educational Supplement* (April 19), p. 10.

Serpell, Robert (1984). Childhood Disability in the Socio-Cultural Context: Assessment and Information Needs for Effective Services. (Mimeo). Later version published (1988) in P.R. Dasen, J.W. Berry & N. Sartorius (Eds.), *Health and Cross-Cultural Psychology*, pp. 256-280, London: Sage.

Shah, R.A. (1976) Preface. *Detailed Curricula for PTC (Primary Teaching Certificate) and CT (Certificate in Teaching) Programmes*, 1975. Islamabad: Ministry of Education, Curriculum Wing.

Shah, Syed Ashiq Ali (1989). Research Standards of Psychologists. *National Institute of Psychology Newsletter*, Volume 8, No. 4, p. 2. (P.O. Box 1511, Islamabad).

Shahid, Mohammad Shoiab (1987). Obsessive Compulsive Thought in a Repressed Society. In *Proceedings of the Sixth Conference of Pakistan Psychological Association*, pp. 83-86. Islamabad: Pakistan Psychological Association.

Shakil, F.M. (1990). Apathy of Education Department--II. *The Frontier Post* (25 Nov. 1990).

Shami, S.A. (1983). Inbred and Non-Inbred First Cousin Marriages. *J. Pakistan Medical Association*, 33 (1) 3-6.

Shanker, Uday (1976). *Exceptional Children*. New Delhi: Sterling Publishers.

Shehab, Rafi Ullah (1986). Treatment of Children in Islamic Society. *The Pakistan Times* (9 October 1986).

Sheikh, M.S. (1990). A Policy for Disabled. *The Pakistan Times*, (6 May 1990), Sports and Youth section, p. B.

Singer, Andre (1982). *Guardians of the North-West Frontier. The Pathans*. Amsterdam: Time-Life Books.

Singh, Suneet Vir (1984). The Young Child in Two Worlds. *Future. Development Perspectives on Children*, 11-12, pp. 47-49. New Delhi: UNICEF.

Special Education & Welfare Division (1990). *Performance-1989.* Islamabad: Author.

Staley, John (1982). *Words For My Brother. Travels between the Hindu Kush and the Himalayas.* Karachi: Oxford University Press.

Suvannathat, Chancha (1985). Past, Present and Future Directions in Asian Child Rearings: A Synthesis Chapter. In C. Suvannathat, D. Bhanthumnavin, L. Bhuapirom & D. M. Keats (Eds.), *Handbook of Asian Child Development and Child Rearing Practices,* pp. 408-415. Bangkok: Behavioural Science Research Institute, Srinakharinwirot University.
Summary chapter in a collection sponsored by UNICEF & UNESCO, based very largely on Western-influenced research in Thailand.

Tareen, K.I. (1983). *Epidemiological Study of Childhood Disability. Survey/Study in Punjab (Pakistan). Interim Report.* Lahore: UNICEF.

Tareen, Khalida; Bashir, Anjum & Nasar, Tanveer (1984). *A Study of Patterns of Psychosocial Disorders in Children Living in Katchi Abadis.* Lahore: POB 621, Society for Mentally and Emotionally Handicapped Children. 82 pp.
Elementary studies of children with psychiatric disorders, one clinic-based, the other door-to-door in slum areas. Some review of child-rearing practices.

Tariq, Pervaiz Naeem (1989). Researches on the Social Development of the Child in Pakistan. In Seema Pervez (Ed.), *The Pakistani Child: Educational and Psychological Research,* pp. 171-176. Islamabad: National Institute of Psychology.

Thanvi, Maulana Ashraf Ali (1981 in tr.). *Heavenly Ornaments,* transl. M.M.K. Saroha. Lahore: Sh. Muhammad Ashraf.

The Frontier Post (Editorial). Another Bestial Act (5 May 1989).

The Frontier Post (Editorial). What We Are Up Against in Education (27 April 1990).

The Hedaya (or guide). *A Commentary on the Mussulman Laws,* transl. Ch. Hamilton. Lahore: Premier Book House, 1963 (reprint).

The Koran. Transl. George Sale. London: Warne. (n.d.).

The Pakistan Times (Editorial). Admission Crisis, (13 Sept. 1981).

The Pakistan Times (Editorial). A Primary Issue, (26 Jan. 1989).

The Pakistan Times (Editorial). The Rights of the Child (2 Oct. 1989).

The Pakistan Times. 4m. Children Join Illiterate Pool in Pakistan Every Year. (4 Nov. 1989), p. 11.

The Pakistan Times (Editorial). Primary Failure (6 Nov. 1989).

UNESCO (1974). *Special Education Statistics.* Paris: Author.

UNICEF (1985, 1988b, 1991). *The State of the World's Children.* New York: Author.

UNICEF (1988a). *Joint UNICEF/Govt. of Pakistan Master Plan 1988-1993.* Islamabad: Author.

Victor, Prem (1982). Mainstreaming in India. In P. Victor & A. Loewe (Eds.) *All India Workshop for Teachers and Parents of Hearing Impaired Children. Selected Papers.* pp. 168-174. New Delhi: Max Mueller Bhavan.

Vijay Human Services (1988). *Teaching Yogasana to the Mentally Retarded Person.* Krishnamacharya Yoga Mandiram, 13 Fourth Cross St., A.K. Nagar, Madras.

Wadud, Sayed Abdul (1986). Why Islamic Order Could Not Be Introduced. *The Pakistan Times*, (28 March 1986), Magazine Section.

Zafar, Saeed Iqbal (1987). Sons or Daughters by Choice. *The Pakistan Times*, (27 Nov. 1987), Magazine Section, p. II.

Zaidi, S. Akbar (1988). *The Political Economy of Health Care in Pakistan*. Lahore: Vanguard.
Zaidi suggests (pp. 123-33) that the type and distribution of public service provision (health, welfare, education) are dominated by the needs of a small, unrepresentative elite, and unavailable or inappropriate to the needs of the mass of the population.

Zaidi, S.M. Hafeez (1975). Psychological Research on Social Change. In S.M. Hafeez Zaidi (Ed.), *Frontiers of Psychological Research in Pakistan*, pp. 43-59. Karachi: Psychology Dept. Karachi University.

Zhuo, D. (1988). Traditional Chinese Rehabilitative Therapy in the Process of Modernization. *International Disability Studies*, Volume 10, pp. 140-142.

CHAPTER 8

SPECIAL EDUCATION IN CROSS-CULTURAL PERSPECTIVE: PEOPLE'S REPUBLIC OF CHINA

by Dai-Hua Shen

DEMOGRAPHIC INFORMATION

China occupies one of the pivotal geographical regions of the earth, covering an area of 3,691,500 square miles. It is bounded clockwise from the north by Mongolia, the former USSR, North Korea, the Pacific Ocean, Hong Kong, Macao, North Vietnam, Laos, Burma, India, Bhutan, Sikkim, Nepal, Pakistan, and Afghanistan. China's location within the framework of the Eurasian landmass and the Pacific Ocean has influenced the country's history and is the basis of many of its present strategic, commercial, and climatic problems.

China's location has been of the greatest significance, for its vast north-south extent in the northern temperate zone gives it not only a great variety of climates, plants, and animals, but also some of the most productive agricultural regions of the earth. Northern Manchuria, a part of China lying on the latitude of southern Labrador, shares the intense cold of Siberia. But the southern extremity of China, Hainan Island, lies well within the tropics and grows coconut palms, coffee, and rubber trees. In between lie all the intermediate climates of the temperate zone. Each has its specialized effects upon vegetation and crops, providing a large array of products upon which the Chinese have used their ingenuity to create tasteful foods, artistic works, and functional objects.

China is the most populous country in the world, containing almost one fourth of the human race. According to the fourth census of July 1990, the mainland had a population of 1.133 billion (Liaowang, 1990), and of this number approximately 94% were Han-Chinese. The "men of Han"--referring to the Han Dynasty (202 B.C.-220 A.D.) under whom China came of age culturally and politically--are usually called the Chinese by Westerners, and have a common history, culture, and written language. The remaining 6% of the people is composed of various minority groups, usually referred to as "minority nationalities" because of their diverse ethnic and linguistic backgrounds. They are generally found in China's border areas or in its marginal agricultural lands (Moseley, 1965).

The population of China is heavily concentrated in the most arable areas--on the Great Plain of North China, on the fertile central plateau of Szechwan, in the river valleys and deltas, and in the coastal areas. The rate of growth and the ratio of people to arable land is more significant than the actual size of the population. The rate of growth is estimated at about 2.47% in the 1980s. Although this rate is not among the world's highest, if such a relatively moderate rate is applied to the large base population, the annual growth exceeds 24 million people. Based on the study of specific areas of population concentration, the population density of North China plain is over 1,200 people per square mile and the density of the Yangtze River delta is as much as three times these figures. This means that there are too many people for the available cultivable land-- over 1,500 people per square mile. The huge population has added to China's burden. To cope with the country's political, economic, and social development in the 1990s, China must implement its population policy in a more stable manner.

POLITICAL IDEOLOGY AND STABILITY

The modern political fate of China was shaped by the conflict with Japan (1937-1945). The devastating impact of the long, drawn-out hostilities on economically and militarily weak China was a more serious consequence. The toll in death and destruction after more than eight years of conflict was incalculable. Perhaps even more ominous for the Nationalists was their confrontation by a Communist Party whose ranks had been tremendously swelled during the Sino-Japanese struggle.

Since 1949 China had split into two parts. The Communists chased the Nationalists off the mainland, shrinking their domain to the Island of Taiwan. The establishment of the People's Republic of China was an epochal event in the long history of the Chinese people. In preceding centuries the founders of new regimes, while occasionally shaking up the prevailing way of life drastically, had nevertheless striven to revitalize and preserve the empire's social and cultural heritage. The new communist rulers however, were unswervingly committed to building an entirely new way of life in keeping with their ideological convictions. Under their forced draft programs major upheavals were inspired throughout the land. And with the passage of time an increasingly large percentage of the Chinese people were born and reared under conditions dissimilar to those known to the older generations. It is unlikely that these younger men and women can ever be inspired to return to a past which they have never known.

Since 1972 when U.S. President Richard Nixon visited China, the mystery of the iron curtain has been revealed. In recent years, due to the policy of opening the door to the outside world, contact between China and the Western world became more frequent. Meanwhile the ideology of democracy gradually spread throughout the whole country. This connection surely will accelerate political reform as well as help China work toward modernization.

Socio-Economic Conditions: Goals and Priorities

China's basic national conditions are characterized by a vast territory, abundant resources, a weak political foundation, and a large population. The heavy population burden is affecting the progress of China's modernization drive, so the problem of overpopulation will be the top priority issue needing to be addressed. The population problem is mainly a rural population problem because it accounts for nearly 80% of the national population. In the vast rural areas, the backward production mode has caused the traditional consciousness that has continued for several thousand years to remain in the minds of peasants. Such old child-bearing concepts as "many children, many blessings" and "raising children as a safeguard against old age" are the greatest obstacles to the work of implementing family planning in rural areas. To carry out education at each level from top to bottom is very important, so that the broad masses of peasants can truly understand the close relationship between population control on the one hand and improvement of family life and realization of national modernization on the other.

The issue of rural population is not merely one of quantity. More important, it is one of quality. In the past, the level of the rural economy was low, communications facilities were poor, culture and education were very backward. After over 10 years of reform and development, the peasants' living standard as well as cultural level have greatly improved. In recent years, rural literacy classes have been flourishing. The work to eliminate illiteracy in rural areas is a long term and arduous task and it will develop simultaneously with the modernization drive in the rural areas, complementing each other (Renmin Ribao, 1990).

China is the world's biggest developing country with a large population but a relatively small acreage of arable land for its size. The most important priority to more than one billion Chinese people at present is to have adequate food and clothing and access to medical care and education. Through common efforts by its people of all nationalities over the past forty years and more, China has turned itself from a formerly backward agricultural state into a country with the beginning signs of prosperity. Rapid progress has been made in economy and culture. Between 1953 and 1989, the gross national product increased by an average of 7 percent annually while the national income increased by an average of 6.8 percent annually. In 1989, compared with the peak year before 1949, China's grain output increased 2.7 times, cotton 4.5 times, and cloth 6.8 times, all rising to first rate status in the world.

In 1989, the number of students in colleges, middle schools, and primary schools was 17.8 times, 39.8 times and 5.1 times respectively that of 1949. The working people not only have enough food and clothing, but also have seen a remarkable improvement in their living and health standards. In 1989, China's life expectancy reached 70 and population and infant death rates dropped to 7 and 40 per thousand respectively. The illiteracy rate dropped to 15.85 percent in 1990 from 80 percent in 1949 (*Beijin Review*, 1991).

Beginning in 1991 China will implement another "Eight Five Year Plan." The reform of the economy will be carried out with more vigor and the pace for opening up to the outside world will make greater strides.

Public Health and Welfare

China has a quarter of the world's population. Since 80% of these people live in rural areas, primary health care services are given priority in these areas. The rising health status of the Chinese people can be illustrated through a comparison of some principal health indices in 1949 (the founding of the People's Republic of China) and 1985, as provided in Table 1 (Zhu, 1990).

Table 1. Mortality & Life Expectancy Rates

		1949	1985
Mortality (per 1000 population)		25	6.37
Infant mortality (per 1000 live births)	rural	200	25.1
	urban	120	14
Maternal mortality (per 1000 deliveries)		150	5
Average life Expectancy (years)		35	68.9

By implementing the principles of putting prevention first and controlling diseases in a phased manner, serious infections and endemic diseases have been effectively brought under control.

In the 1950s, concerted efforts were made in this respect, leading to the eradication of smallpox and dramatic reductions in plague, cholera, malaria, and endemic goiter. Work has continued on the control of endemic and frequently occurring disease. Because of the immunization program, the incidence of diphtheria, pertussis, measles and poliomyelitis has been greatly reduced as shown in Table 2 (Zhu,1990).

Table 2. Incidence per 100,000 population of four infectious diseases in 1959 and 1986

	Diphtheria	Pertussis	Measles	Poliomyelitis
1959	22.4	240	1432	2.60
1986	0.07	7.97	18.9	0.17

The rural water supply before the founding of the People's Republic in 1949 was inadequate in both quantity and quality, but by 1985 some 0.4 billion out of 0.8 billion rural population had been provided with improved drinking water, and tapwater had been made available to 30% of them.

The government has devoted much attention to the building up of medical and health institutions and the training of health professionals to provide a solid foundation for the development of primary health care. The rural three-tier medical service network is composed of the medical and health institutions of the county, the town, and the village. It has been found appropriate to the rural situation, in which the areas are vast, the inhabitants are scattered, and medical and health services are inadequate (Zhu, 1990).

Medical and health institutions at the county level not only act as training centers for health staff but also provide technical guidance. In towns these institutions play a pivotal role in the organization of medical and health care services. The health centers in the villages act as a foundation of the entire system and undertake the great bulk of primary health care activities carried out in the country. With the establishment of the three-tier network, health services have become both accessible and affordable.

CULTURAL NORMS AND VALUES

The Confucian tradition and ideology have welded the Chinese People into a single civilization for over 2,000 years. Therefore, if we are to understand the nature of the changes taking place in China today under communism, we must first understand what traditional Chinese society was like.

Confucian ideas, the enunciated values of Chinese society up until the Cultural Revolution (1966-1976), are grounded in the life and teachings of Confucius, the great Chinese sage and philosopher, who was born in 551 B.C. The period when Confucius lived was one of social chaos, and he hoped to alleviate suffering among the people by restoring order and peace through moral and political reforms. The all-pervasive concerns of this doctrine were social order and personal dignity, to be derived from right conduct and hence from social approval. In its acknowledgement that not all people are equal in their capabilities, Confucianism divided society hierarchically, the individual being subordinated within the family and within society by an established system of graded relationships. A scholar elite was expected to take the reins of political and social leadership and by example spread the Confucian morality through out every segment of society.

Through the centuries Confucian teachings set a pattern, or ideal, for the structure of the family and of Chinese society at large. In Confucian's famous theory about the ideal nation, he once said ". . . the whole country should belong to the people of this country. Persons who are able and virtuous need to be elected to serve the country." This theory is the earliest form of democratic ideas in the world. In order to have a harmonious human society, he also mentioned, "Let all the senior citizens have happy remaining years; the capable men and women can devote themselves to the society, children will grow healthily, the widows, widowers, the weak and the handicapped all will be taken good care of."

In traditional China the institution of prime importance was the family and the dominant principle of a righteous life was considered to be allegiance to one's parents. (Hsiao, translated "filial piety," was one of Confucious' cardinal virtues.) Confucian teachings regarding the sanctity of relationships between family members and setting forth mutually protective functions for them were at bottom the same as his ideals for government, which he conceived of as a kind of large family.

The family, as idealized in traditional China, was a joint family made up of several small related units, covering perhaps five generations. This family lived under one roof and functioned as a single cooperating unit in all its activities--economic, religious and social. Its members might work at a combination of occupations--agriculture, business and government and by such concerted effort the united family might be able to achieve wealth and prestige. The structure of this ideal family was hierarchical, according to generation, age and sex. It was headed by the eldest male, who wielded complete power over all the family members. The headship usually passed to the eldest son, or sometimes to the son adjudged most worthy. Wives, brought into the husband's joint household through family rather than individual decision were subservient to the husband's mother and to other family members.

Since the ninteenth century the Chinese traditional way of life began to face the pressures of the commercially aggressive western powers. The impact of their technological culture challenged China's very existence. As early as the first two decades of the twentieth century, many of the scholar class were reacting against the traditionalism and asserting that China must reform or cease to exist. In their view, much of the Confucian ideal of the family-oriented society was incompatible with the requirements of the modern state and could only impede China's economic and political development. These men advocated sweeping changes in the codes that affected marriage, divorce, and the status of women, all so important to the nature of the traditional family system, and presented the first serious challenge to the system (Lang, 1964). After communists took over mainland China, the foundation of the traditional system was completely destroyed during the Cultural Revolution (1966-1976). Many activities were directed against traditional religions and the education system. Educators and scholars were facing an unheard-of catastrophe. These were the "dark ages" for Chinese people.

In order to work toward modernization, political reforms have been carried out by the Chinese government after the Cultural Revolution.

Although the political situation has changed from time to time, through historical observation the way of Chinese life has always been affected by the traditional system in some aspects, especially among the five human relationships: ruler and minister, father and son, husband and wife, brothers, and friends.

In regard to marriage, Chinese people believe those people who carry the same family name are blood related. Considering the risk of genetically transmitted handicap, marriage between these people as well as marriage between first parallel cousins is strongly discouraged. Throughout Chinese history, traditional views which promoted discriminatory practice toward the disabled have been quite powerful. During the Shang Dynasty, illness was conceived as a problem between living individuals and their ancestors, where harmony between living and dead was disrupted. Ancestor worship included the assumption of reciprocity though, for when the health of an individual became suspect in spite of the payment of deference to ritualistic norms, it was the ancestor who lost his power to protect future clan members from demons, and his memory would no longer be worshipped (Unschuld, 1985).

Later, neo-Confucian value claims, which stressed the importance of maintaining harmony and balance between heaven and this world, through practicing obedience to the proper norms of social behavior (Li) within the household, did little to positively address the needs of those with special infirmities. The expectation of reciprocity, whereby children would care for their aged parents in return for their parents' initial protection during their formative years, worked against those children who because of disability would be hard pressed to contribute to family sustenance and thus fulfill their assumed obligations. Confucian doctrines further argued for a perfectionistic view of mental health, which was equated with mental equilibrium and harmony, virtue and the absence of inner restlessness and apprehension. The importance of classical learning through master canon further assumed that distinctions in individual learning capability were insignificant. It is not surprising that the disabled were subjected to shaming techniques, and that many disabled children continue to be hidden by their parents (Epstein, 1989).

In some areas with minority nationalities such as the Yunnan Province which has many remote and undeveloped areas, attitudes are backward and there is inbreeding that leads to congenital birth defects. Statistics show 6.35 percent of its population of 37 million as handicapped, a higher percentage than any other province in China. One family in four in Yunnan includes a disabled person (Kristof, 1991). Concerning this situation, provinces like Zhejian and Gansuh have passed legislation that prohibit retarded children and close relatives from marrying or raising families.

Educational Ideology

The Chinese People have traditionally set a high value on education and accorded respect and position to educated people. Since the earliest time education has been considered a major function of government in China.

The concept of education was not unlike that of liberal education in the Western World. The content of the curriculum was broad. Its core was the "six arts," which may be comparable to the trivium and quadrivium of the liberal arts of western education. They consisted of rituals, music, archery, charioteering, writing, and mathematics. Rituals meant the observance of customs and traditions as well as the laws of the land; they were the expression of good manners and propriety of conduct. Music included poetry and songs and dancing; it was supposed to have a salutary effect on the emotions and the inner spirit. The other arts indicated a concern for the development of both body and mind and the concept of the educated person as one having many-sided interests, including sports, physical skills, and artistic expression.

Examination plays an important role in Chinese education. Advancement from lower schools to higher schools was determined by examinations. The most important examinations were administered by the state for the purpose of selecting competent scholars to fill government posts. Thus began the competitive examinations that laid the groundwork for the well-known civil service examination, and the selection of personnel by examination introduced a system of "government by scholars" that became a major characteristic of traditional China. This system of examination-led education caused a major problem. Passing of the examinations became the sole objective of studying, and anything not directly related to the examinations was of little concern.

Today, China's system of schools provides six years of elementary education, six years of secondary education on two levels, and a four-year college followed by graduate study, conforming with the American pattern. Education is free of charge in China, and compulsory education includes first grade through sixth grade. However, in most big cities compulsory education extends to nine years.

The percentage of students in China at various levels in 1988 were shown as follows (Greer, 1989):

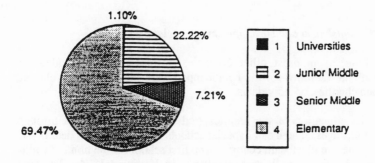

In the socialist modernization drive, it is necessary to take education as the foundation and rely on science and technology to invigorate the economy. Due to the social and political reform during recent years, the changing of social needs and the increased job competition have resulted in proper readjustment in China's education for economic take-off. The training of specialized technical personnel has become a new focus of China's secondary schools, polytechnics, and vocational schools. There are 458 two or three-year tertiary schools at present, compared to less than 200 in 1982, and over 1.78 million specialized personnel have been trained in the past decade. Statistics show that currently there are 16,000 vocational schools with over five million students. The number of vocational school students is 44.8% of the total students of the same age (Xinhua, 1990). China's education system is trying to adjust to the needs of the country's economic reform and social development. An effective system of vocational and technical education is now being formed, and raising quality will be the keynote of China's college and university education development for a long time to come.

SERVICE FOR SPECIAL NEEDS CHILD

Because China is burdened with one-fourth of the world's population, like most of the Third World countries, the education of handicapped people is not an urgent issue in China. While China is working toward the goal of modernization, Chinese authorities also have taken notice of the educational problem of over two million children with special needs. Special education has lately received much attention from Chinese authorities.

The Establishment and Development of Special Education

In China, as in most other countries, efforts to provide adequate educational facilities for the handicapped were initiated by the church, private charities, or individuals.

The education of the handicapped in China has passed through different stages. The idea of special schools for the blind and deaf began during the late nineteenth century. The first school for the blind in China was established with British assistance in Beijin in 1874. The first school for the deaf was established in 1887 in Shandong Province by Americans.

Before 1949 when the People's Republic of China was founded, the education of the handicapped was unorganized. Special education was not included in the national education system until 1953 when the Division of Education for the Blind and Deaf was established. Special classes for students with mental retardation first started in 1958. More recently the Department of Special Education was founded in 1980. Since then, the progress of special education in this country has become more steady (Zhongguo Jiaoyuxue Baekechyushu).

Today, China offers special education for three categories of physically and mentally handicapped children in two distinct forms: in special schools and in special classes within ordinary elementary schools. The former are directed at those who are blind, deaf, and mentally retarded, and the latter only at those who are mildly retarded. The severely handicapped are not being served in public school at the present time.

Identification and Eligibility

Due to the shortage of expert personnel, and insufficient standardized instruments, as well as the absence of national and provincial norms, the entire issue of assessment is complex. Most of the mentally retarded children are first noticed by their parents with respect to their subaverage general intelligence and deficits in adaptive behavior. Students with mild disability problems in most cases are not identified until they are already in regular class and after a period of time when they start to demonstrate continuous academic failure that is in some way significantly different from their peers. These students are most often criticized for being lazy or absentminded. People seldom notice their special needs, and they usually stay in the regular class with very limited learning. Children with other physical disabilities can be examined by physicians. Basically all disabled students except those who have serious conditions are eligible for special education.

Because of the diversity of Chinese culture, family members fulfill their responsibilities to disabled children with varying degrees of effectiveness and compassion. Many parents hide their disabled children from public view, demonstrating their extreme reluctance to admit to their child's infirmity publicly. Other than this, lack of transportation service as well as handicapped access in the school building, even when the education itself costs nothing, forces the majority of exceptional children to stay at home. A few of them study with home teachers, and others learn with family members.

Special Schools

As mentioned above, China only offers special education for three categories-blind, deaf and mild mental retardation-at the present time.

Education for the blind and deaf was the earliest form of special education in China. Before 1949 (the founding of new China) there were only 42 schools for the blind and deaf in China; the number of students was estimated at around 2,500 (Piao, 1986). During the past forty years the government gradually took over all of the private special schools. Today, there are 450 special schools for the deaf, 18 for the blind, and 40 for the deaf and blind, serving over 50,000 students. Since 1949, students who receive special education have increased as much as 20 times (Zhongguo Jiaoyu Bao, 1988).

The education of blind and deaf persons is focused on vocational training. Chinese leader Deng Xiaoping once said in a national education meeting that China's national power and the stamina of economic development will more and more depend on the quality of the labour force and quantity of China's intellectuals. The object of vocational education is to help the disabled become producers instead of a burden to society.

Vocational training has emphasized some specialities which include work in the fine arts, carpentry, iron work, woodwork, tailoring, knitting and basketwork. Traditional finger massage technique was taught to the blind children. Besides vocational training, deaf students are given course work in daily conversation, movement to music rhythm, narration, and training in improved auditory facility. The blind children learn the new braille which uses an international alphabet (Epstein, 1989). Within each school there is a workshop providing students with opportunities for hands-on experience. Usually profit is made through the workshop which also becomes the major financial resource of the school.

Before students graduate, schools must ensure that they have had at least one speciality. Since it is difficult for Chinese people to accept the social integration of the handicapped at this moment, most of the employment opportunities are only available at special factories which are founded either by voluntary organizations such as the China Disabled Persons' Federation (which is led by Deng Pufang, Deng Xiaoping's disabled son) or the Civil Affairs Bureau of the Ministry of Public Security at the provincial and national levels.

With regard to educating students with mental retardation, traditionally, people do not even think the retarded can be educated. Education for the mentally retarded did not exist until after 1958. The first provision was a special class for them. At present, there are over 100 special schools throughout the country and 1,885 special classes are organized in ordinary schools. Although the number of special schools and classes has grown, approximately 0.5%-1% of the country's school-aged population are mentally retarded (Zhongguo Jiaoyu Biao, 1987). Clearly, the educational needs of the children are not being met.

At the beginning stage, education emphasizes helping the mentally handicapped to learn general adaptation to everyday living. Moreover attention is also concentrated on assisting these children with academic ability by having them repeat easy lessons in the various classes, such as reading, writing and mathematics. Meanwhile vocational education is also offered to mentally impaired individuals. Students are taught handwork such as assembling parts. Similar to other types of handicapped students, most of the employment is limited to special factories.

Although special schools and classes increased several times since 1949, the enrollment rate of the school-aged (7-15) blind students is only 3%, and 5.5% for the deaf students (Zhongguo Jiaoyu Bao,1988). The low enrollment rate is due to several factors: (1) Because of China's vast territory and population, the special education school system does not have the capacity to meet the needs of disabled children adequately. Moreover, special schools are unbalanced in distribution. For example, no special schools exist in provinces like Guangxi, Zhejian, Tibet, Ningxia and Qinghai; (2) Almost all the special schools are located in big cities. These schools are usually boarding facilities, which serve to separate youth from family as well as peers; (3) Lack of a transportation service makes the situation more difficult for the large number of students who come from rural areas to receive special education; (4) Traditionally, the handicap itself is considered a kind of disease by Chinese people. It was conceived as a problem between living individuals and their ancestors. People even believe a handicap is contagious, and are afraid to get close to them. Parents also think it is a shame to have disabled children, and these children are usually shielded by their family, so that they hardly have any social contact at all; (5) There are an insufficient number of special facilities and with no handicapped access in school buildings, students can hardly learn independently.

Special Education Teacher Training

The severe shortage of teachers is one of the major obstacles to developing special education in China. Currently there are about 9,500 special education teachers in the whole country. Among them most of the teachers are not even qualified. The ratio between special education teachers and students is 1 to 5.58. According to the statistical information, the school-aged handicapped children were estimated at about 3.88 million in China. If only half of them received special education, over 38 thousand teachers would be needed. Table 3 provides the statistical number of special school students and teachers from 1953 to 1987 (Piao, 1988).

Table 3. Special School Students & Teachers

Year	No. of students	Staff	Teachers
1953	5260	797	444
1955	5312	763	433
1957	7538	1103	718
1958	10101	1338	902
1959	17764	2772	1755
1960	26701	4345	2587
1962	17500	3195	2103
1963	18024	3285	2157
1965	22850	3722	2613
1973	24940	4915	3244
1976	28519	5954	3745
1978	30934	6930	4244
1980	33055	8002	4791
1981	33477	8596	5131
1983	35729	9631	5642
1985	41706	11482	7250
1986	47175	13013	8186
1987	52876	14483	9480

In order to recruit special education teachers, Chinese authorities from central to local levels gradually adopted several training programs. For example: (1) short-term training classes are supported by the provincial government in Heilongjiang and Shandong; (2) special education courses are offered at teacher's colleges; (3) special education teacher's colleges have been established in Naning, Shandong and Liaoning; (4) a special education major at the university level has been offered in Beijin Normal University, as well as East China Normal University since 1986; (5) international academic exchange programs are offered.

Through the above training programs, special education in several provinces such as Liaoning, Shandong, Heilongjiang, Jingsu and Jyilin have had tremendous improvement. Other than this, the first special education research center was founded at Beijin Normal University in 1988 to provide information on special education including: fundamental theory and application, history, present situation and future trends, curriculum, and teaching techniques and facilities, among others (Zhongguo Jiaoyu Bao, 1988).

National Policy

In China, treatment of the handicapped is only in its infancy. The national policy of special education has one basic objective, namely, to improve the early identification and treatment of handicapped children. Shortly after the People's Republic of China was established, the communist leadership reaffirmed a commitment to the education of the disabled at all levels. A document was signed in 1951 by Prime Minister Chou Enlai which called for the establishment of schools for "deaf-mutes, the blind, and other handicapped people and to provide education for children, juveniles as well as adults with physical defects." Over the past four decades China has made progress in its work for the handicapped.

A survey in 1987 found that there are over 50 million handicapped people in China. They constitute a difficult and special group in social life. Based on the idea that handicapped people should enjoy the deep love of their families as well as the concern, protection, and respect of society, experts from legal and other fields hold that it is necessary for China to have a specific law for the handicapped. "The PRC Disabled Protection Law" (which came into effect on 15 May 1992) examined and approved by the 17th Session of the Seventh National People's Congress Standing Committee on 28 December 1990, marks the legalization of China's undertakings concerning the handicapped. The law consists of 9 chapters and 54 articles which address issues concerning rehabilitation, education, employment, cultural life, welfare services, environment and legal responsibilities (Xinhua, 1990). This is a major event in the Chinese people's social life.

Since the founding of New China, its undertakings concerning the handicapped have developed rapidly under party and government care. With the help and support of the entire society, marked improvements have been made in the living conditions of the handicapped, but sometimes handicapped people's rights are neglected and violated, and some of them are even deprived of their rights. For example, based on the old regulation, physically handicapped students (even if they were academically prepared) were denied from continuing their education in colleges. Undertakings concerning the handicapped are falling behind social and economic development. The Chinese Constitution and law as well as the experience in running programs for the handicapped urgently necessitated the formulation of a special law regarding the handicapped. The law has not only created a good weapon with which handicapped people and their family members can fight against illegal practices, but also a guideline for the development of welfare for people with disabilities in China. This is also a practical step taken by China to safeguard human rights and respond to the UN "World Wide Action Program on the Handicapped" (Xinhua, 1991).

In line with the principle of "equality and participation" the PRC Disabled Protection Law provides that handicapped people enjoy equal rights with others, and protects these rights from being violated. It also stipulates that the government will use supplementary methods to support and develop programs concerning the handicapped and at the same time encourage the handicapped to take part in social life and enjoy their achievements.

Future Plans and Priorities

China has the largest number of handicapped people in the world. Statistics shows that 18.1 percent of Chinese families have a disabled member (*China Daily*, 1990). The Chinese government has always held that developing welfare for the handicapped is an important task. This is not only important for economic development and political stability but also for the development of spiritual civilization and the normal life of tens of millions of families.

When we look at the progress of special education in China, it is hard to make comparisons with Western society, not only because of the difference between social-economic and political systems but also due to the cultural diversity. However, China has the capacity to accept Western thinking. In order to develop an effective special education system, it is important for China to draw on the experience of the Western world and adapt it to Chinese characteristics. The recently passed PRC Disabled Protection Law is the best example of borrowing and interpreting ideas and experiences from Western countries. Concerning the future goals for handicapped people, several suggestions need to be considered by Education and Civil Affairs authorities as follows:

(1) Establishing research centers and welfare organizations to be responsible for the identification, education, welfare and employment opportunities of all disabled individuals. (2) Obtaining financial support from local government or enterprises instead of central government taking the full responsibility for funding. (3) Gradually increasing the educational opportunities and implementing the idea of mainstreaming by integrating special classes into regular schools. (4) Developing handicapped access in school and public buildings to allow them to participate in social activities. (5) Training special education teachers in all needed areas by sponsoring all types of schools and special programs; setting up special education departments at ordinary teacher-training schools; and helping teachers of regular education to master knowledge about special education. (6) Reflecting the life of the handicapped through public mass media, to raise public awareness of the handicapped conditions and their capabilities.

China's work for the handicapped started relatively late, but its development rate is relatively quick. For several decades, 41,000 welfare enterprises of various kinds have been set up across the country and more than 700,000 handicapped people have been employed. In recent years, there has been an obvious change in educational opportunity for the handicapped. Today China has more than 4,000 disabled young people studying in colleges and universities (Renmin Ribao, 1990). According to the State Council's "Various Suggestions on the Development of Special Education" the educational pattern is gradually developing in all localities. Other than these, the China Disabled Persons' Federation and its local organizations have been playing an important role in implementing the "PRC Disabled Protection Law" and doing a great deal of arduous work over the last few years.

Due to the policy of opening the door to the outside world, and the frequency of international cultural and academic exchanges, overseas visits and short-term training courses have increased. Moreover, some international conferences on special education as well as special athletic contests have also been held in China. We believe special education in China will certainly make new progress and reach a higher level.

References

Beijin Review (28 Jan.-3 Feb. 1991). *Government Work on Human Rights Viewed,* as translated in Foreign Broadcast Information Service, FBIS-CHI-91-031.
Useful review of legal protection, basic rights to existence, family planning, minority nationalities, religious freedom, and protection of civil rights. (pp. 12 - 17)

China Daily (24 Dec. 1990). Handicapped Law Ready for Passage by NPC (National People's Congress), as translated in Foreign Broadcast Information Service, FBIS-CHI-90-248.
The proposed law promised the disabled preferential treatment in rehabilitation education, employment, cultural life, welfare, and environment.

Epstein, I. (1989). *Special Education in Japan and China.* Delivered at the VIIth World Congress of Comparative Education. Uses the cultural diversity to view the special education system in both countries.

Greer, C. E. (1989). *China, Facts & Figures Annual* Vol. 12, education section. Statistical information in the field of education.

Kristof, N. D. (30 May 1991). China's Disabled Get Helping Hand in High Places. *New York Times.*
The improvement in the status of the handicapped took place mainly in the years since Deng Xiao Ping achieved supreme power in 1978. The prime advocate of handicapped in China is Mr. Deng's eldest son, Deng Pufang.

Lang, O. (1964). *Chinese Family and Society,* New Haven, Conn.
Detailed information about traditional Chinese family and society.

Liaowang (10 Dec. 1990). Article Views Population, Family Planning, as translated in Foreign Broadcast Information Service, FBIS-CHI-90-002.
A Chinese journal focuses on domestic political and economic affairs. This article provided the answers which indicated tremendous achievements have been made in family planning work, but the population situation is still grim. (pp. 16-17).

Moseley, G. (1965). China's Fresh Approach to the National Minority Group, *China Quarterly*, No. 24.
Useful review of the role of the minorities and their early development.

Piao, Yong Xin (Feb. 1986). *Shyhluenn Woguo Teshu Jiaoyu De Fajaan Hann Puuyi* (The Development and Research of Special Education in China). Beijin: Beijin Normal University Press. (Social science edition, in Chinese.)
Critical issues about special education development and how to work with it in the present situation. (pp. 59-64)

Piao, Yong Xin (June, 1988). Zhongguo Teshu Jiaoyu Shytzy De Peiryeang (Special Education Teacher Training in China). Beijin: Beijin Normal University Press, (pp. 64-68). (Social science edition, in Chinese.) (pp. 64 - 68)

Renmin, Ribao (28 Dec. 1990). Article Stresses Issue of Rural Population, as translated in Foreign Broadcast Information Service, FBIS-CHI-91-006.
From a Chinese daily newspaper, this article focuses on the rural population problem as mainly a problem of quality of education.

Renmin, Ribao (22 Oct. 1990). Tangible Results Reported in Work for Handicapped, as translated in Foreign Broadcast Information Service, FBIS-CHI-90-212.

Unschuld, P. U. (1985). Medicine in China: A History of Ideas, Berkeley: University of California Press, pp. 24-28.

Xinhua (28 Dec. 1990). Roundup Views Development of Education, as translated in Foreign Broadcast Information Service, FBIS-CHI-90-002.
The training of specialized technical personnel has become a new focus of China's secondary schools, polytechnics and vocational schools.

Xinhua (29 Dec. 1990). Law on Protection of Handicapped Cited, as translated in Foreign Broadcast Information Service, FBIS-CHI-91-003.
List of contents includes nine chapters and 54 articles.

Xinhua   (15 Jan. 1991).   Beijin Symposium Studies Law for
    Handicapped, as translated in Foreign Broadcast Information Service,
    FBIS-CHI-91-011.
    Over 60 law experts, social welfare workers, officials, and people
with disabilities attended the meeting and expressed their views on the
significance, function, educational aspects, and application of the law.

Zhongguo Jiaoyuxue Baekechyushu (China Education Encyclopaedia).
    Beijin: People's Education Press, p. 368. (In Chinese.)

Zhongguo Jiaoyu Bao (China Education Journal) (8 March 1988). (In
    Chinese.)Tsarnjyi ertong ing hann jengcharngren i yang show jiaoyu
    (Disabled Children Should Have Equal Opportunities to Receive
    Education).
    Government works hard to increase education opportunities for
disabled children.

Zhongguo Jiaoyu Bao (Feb. 26, 1987).   (In Chinese.) Shyy ruohjyh
    ertong showdaw lianghao jiaoyu (The Mentally Impaired Students
    Should Have Opportunities to Receive Special Education).

Zhongguo Jiaoyu Bao (24 Nov. 1988).   (In Chinese.) Woguo teshu
    jiaoyu luohhow miannmaw jyidye gaejinn (Special Education in
    China Needs Urgent Improvement).

Zhongguo Jiaoyu Bao (3 Nov. 1988).   (In Chinese.) Beishyda teshu
    jiaoyu yanjiow zhongshin chernglih (Special Education Research
    Center was Founded at Beijin Normal University).

Zhu, Ao-Rong (1990).   China: The Goal Is Attainable. In Achieving
    Health for All by the Year 2000. The World Health Organization.
    Includes useful information about the main achievements and basic
experiences in the development of primary health care in China. (pp. 55-
57).

CHAPTER 9

EDUCATION AND DISABILITY IN CROSS-CULTURAL PERSPECTIVE: THE UNITED STATES

by Susan Peters

INTRODUCTION

The population of the United States totals 220,099,000--the fourth largest in the world. The geographic and demographic characteristics across all 50 states and territories are greatly diverse. One-fourth of the population lives in rural areas (2,500 or less). Seventy-five percent live in urban and suburban areas. The largest cities are losing population, while small and medium-size cities are gaining. Large cities such as Detroit, Los Angeles, Chicago, and New York contain large numbers of poor, unemployed, non-English speaking ethnic minorities. While the GNP is approximately $10,000 per capita, rural and urban variations are widespread. The diversity of conditions thus pose different problems for adequate schooling within as well as across states.

Today, nearly one out of four Americans attend school, or approximately 56.6 million. Most of these schools are public schools-- 87.6% of all elementary and secondary schools; 77.7% of all post-secondary education schools (Center for Educational Statistics, 1988). When measured by GNP, the United States spends more on education than any other nation except Canada and the Netherlands (Clabaugh & Rozycki, 1990). However, spending on education is allocated disproportionately to post-secondary institutions. Total expenditures for elementary and secondary education in 1990 were $221.6 billion (*U.S. News and World Report*, September 16, 1991). Of this amount, federal funds for all education expenditures totaled 25.7 billion dollars out of a total operating budget of 990.9 billion dollars. Thus, federal funds are only a small part of the revenues allocated to schools. The bulk of funding comes from local and state revenues and thus the amount spent per child can vary considerably as well, from district to district and state to state, depending as it does on the relative wealth (measured by its tax base) of each school district. (The national average expenditure per pupil is $4,713.) In the past few years, a growing number of school districts in the U.S. have declared bankruptcy, as local, state, and federal revenues have not kept pace with needed expenditures.

Elementary and secondary education in the United States is typically divided into six years of elementary school (grades Kindergarten through 5), three years of "middle" school or what is termed Junior High School (grades 6-8 or 7-9), and three or four years of secondary schooling (grades 9 or 10 through 12). Free, universal, compulsory school attendance is required from ages 6 to 16 (although this may vary somewhat from state to state), or grades 1-12. In addition, a growing number of young children ages 2-4 attend private pre-schools. Relatively low-cost post-secondary education is available in some form or another to virtually every American citizen, although many do not take advantage of it. Options include vocational-technical schools, two-year community colleges, and four-year university programs and beyond. Many post-secondary programs cater to non-traditional students, as a growing number of women and minorities return to school to upgrade skills and/or change careers after time out from work in the market place (e.g., during child-rearing).

Schools at elementary and secondary levels in American education are organized by school districts which vary in geographical size as well as demographic size. Traditionally, local school districts have maintained a great deal of autonomy in all facets of their operations-from curriculum to teacher salaries. Taken as a whole, the school system in America is significantly decentralized in its organization, loosely coupled in its operations, and diverse in quality of programs and demographic make-up. When current societal trends are introduced into the picture of school organization, the complexity of the issues affecting schools for all children becomes apparent.

CURRENT SOCIETAL TRENDS

The Politics of Schooling

Schooling in a democratic multi-party system such as the United States is highly sensitive to political pressure from competing interest groups. Today's increasingly technological and service-oriented economy has placed education in the center of business and legislative attention as the focal point for preparing our nation to compete "effectively" in the world. Our country has a history of public outcries for broad-based education reform in response to socio-economic conditions. In the 1950s, the Russians' success in launching Sputnik prompted a move away from a decade of child-centered reforms in public education to an academic curriculum focused primarily on science and math. Then, in the late 1960s, as a response to massive student protests (the Vietnam War and civil rights discrimination against blacks were two of the key issues), schools embraced a humanistic curriculum and sought social relevance (Gross, 1985). Today's educational reform movements, spearheaded by commissioned reports, most notably *A Nation At Risk* (1983), characterize American education as threatened by a "rising tide of mediocrity." A direct link is drawn between falling student scores on national achievement tests and our declining position in the world economy. A pendulum swing to the 1950s' focus on higher standards is rapidly occurring, but with a significant difference. Then, schools were seen as failing the individual. Now, the schools are accused of failing society.

In the words of the Deputy Secretary of Education and former Xerox Chairman, David Hearns, "Education is not a priority to compete with the national defense, the trade deficit, the federal budget deficit, drugs or AIDS. We must think of it as the solution to the rest of those problems." (Perry, 1989: 138). Once again in our history, the clarion call is going out for "nothing less than a complete restructuring of U.S. schools" (Perry, 1989: 138). The purpose of this restructuring is said to be: "To compete in a global marketplace where mental might is increasingly the quality that separates winners from losers . . ." (Perry, 1989: 137).

An indication of just how far legislatures will go in placing the blame and responsibility for society's problems on schools is Governor Engler's proposal for the state of Michigan. In the Fall of 1991, he asked lawmakers to pass a "Michigan Education Warranty Program." Under this plan, high schools would "verify to employers that graduates have attained basic skills in reading, writing, mathematics and problem-solving. If the employer finds a graduate lacks these skills, he or she may be sent back to high school or another educational institution, public or private, for remedial training" (Hornbeck, 1991: 1A). This remedial training would be at the high school's expense, with no cost to the graduate or employer!

One word that dominates in the plethora of educational reform reports (well over 350 since 1983) regarding the solution for "mediocrity" in our nation's schools is excellence (often equated with efficiency and its links to economic productivity). Many see this focus on excellence as a retreat from the commitment to equality which dominated American education in the 1960s and 1970s (Gross, 1985). The result has been a tension between raising standards of excellence through standardization of curriculum and teacher certification at national and state levels, and the increasing societal trend toward diversity and equal opportunity. This trend has been brought on not only by a super-symbolic economy which demands specialization (one increasingly dependent on brain power and information verses industrialization and manufacturing), but by changing demographics.

Demographic Diversity

The second significant trend affecting education today is the fact that our demographics are rapidly changing. Historically, the United States has assimilated large numbers of immigrants from diverse minority and ethnic backgrounds. By the year 2000, one in three Americans will be nonwhite. California has already passed the 50% mark for minority children in K-12 schools. Numbers of poor, working mothers, single head of households are growing as well. Of every 100 children born in the United States today:

*12 will be born out of wedlock
*40 will be born to parents who divorce before the child is 18
*5 will be born to parents who separate
*2 will be born to parents of whom one will die before the child
    reaches 18
*41 will reach age 18 "normally"
*between 21-25% of school children live in poverty
(Hodgkinson, 1985)

The number of teenage pregnancies is also growing. Every day in the United States, 40 teenage girls give birth to their THIRD child. Approximately 700,000 babies out of an annual cohort of 3.3 million babies born to teenage mothers "are almost assured of being either educationally retarded or difficult to teach" due to the tendency of teenage mothers to give birth to children who are premature (Hodgkinson, 1985).

Legislation and the Courts

A third societal trend is that the United States has increasingly become a litigious society with 5 percent of the world's population but 70 percent of the lawyers (Gergen, 1991: 72).

Unfortunately, laws have not been effective in legislating behavior and economic realities. This problem is exemplified in the situation of blacks in American society. Since racial integration was mandated by federal law in 1964, legislation of social policy has been undermined by prejudicial attitudes and social conditions. In a feature story, "Black and White in America," Harrison Rainee asserts, "Race fatigue grips America as the fight over a once revered value has become mired in haggling over numbers and racial balances" (Rainee, 1991: 18). According to the latest census data, of more than 9 million blacks, about 30% still live in almost complete racial isolation, the median wealth of black families is only one-tenth that of white families, and 63 percent of black school-age children still attend segregated schools.

Despite the limited success of litigation in bettering the circumstances of blacks, handicap groups have chosen the same path. Using the landmark case of *Brown v. Board of Education* (1954) which challenged segregation of blacks in public schools, these groups have established precedence in their own landmark cases, including *PARC v.*

the Commonwealth of Pennsylvania (1972) and *Mills v. Board of Education* (1972). In both of these cases, U.S. district courts handed down decisions requiring individual states to provide free appropriate education to students with disabilities. The principles of equal opportunity and the notion of inferiority inherent in segregation established in *Brown* provided the basis for these legal arguments.

Litigation efforts to combat discrimination against persons with disabilities culminated in the 1991 passage of the Americans with Disabilities Act (ADA). Known as the civil rights act for people with disabilities, the law specifically addresses discrimination on the basis of disability in the areas of employment, public and private transportation, public accommodations, local and state level government jobs and services, and availability of telecommunication devices for deaf people. Joseph Shapiro, in an article entitled "Liberation Day for the Disabled," comments: "For the first time, America is saying the biggest problem facing disabled people is not their own blindness, deafness or other physical condition but discrimination" (Shapiro, 1989: 20). This observation harks back to the central argument contained in *Brown* (1954): "Segregation of minority children solely because of race 'generates a feeling of inferiority as to their status in the community that may affect their hearts and minds in a way unlikely ever to be undone'" (Peters, 1987).

In addition, political protest tactics such as the civil rights marches and sit-ins of the 1960s were used by disabled groups two decades later to pressure for change. In 1988, for example, when officials of Gallaudet University (whose majority student enrollment is deaf or hearing impaired) attempted to hire a hearing president, student protesters took over the University, grinding classes and business as usual to a virtual halt and attracting international attention to issues of discrimination. As a result, the first deaf president in the history of Gallaudet University was hired.

Finally, a new group of individuals-those with Acquired Immune Deficiency Syndrome (AIDS)-have added hundreds of thousands more to the population of people with disabilities in the United States. AIDS policy advocates have also taken to the courts in highly publicized cases, for redress against employment discrimination, the right to attend public school, and to challenge health insurance companies who withdrew health coverage.

Overall, the civil rights movement of the 1960s helped reconstruct the inequalities inherent in a segregated system of education for black students. Spurred by the impetus of legal cases such as *Brown*, parents of handicapped students began to demand their rights as well. Debate surrounding minority groups, including those labeled as handicapped, has thus become overtly political through the mechanism of legislative struggle in the courts. As a result, legal theory and the precedents established in court cases have achieved ascendency over educational theory and practice, and economic conditions.

IDEALS, THEORY AND PRACTICE IN EDUCATION

The American Creed

Historically, education in America has rested on three root concepts: merit, opportunity, and equality. In essence, these concepts are part of what socialist Gunnar Myrdal called the American Creed: ". . . ideals of the essential dignity of the individual human being, of the fundamental equality of all men and of certain inalienable rights to freedom, justice and a fair opportunity" (Rainee, 1991: 18). The Horatio Alger meritocratic ideology whereby success can be attained through individual effort or merit has been instilled in generations of Americans, so that even today a surprising 60 percent of blacks said that "if blacks would try harder, they could be just as well off as whites" (1989 ABC News-*Washington Post* poll, 1991: 21). In addition, Anglo-American teachers, for the most part, reflect the American Creed as well in their belief in mastery over nature, scientific objectivism, and the individual's ability to "climb the ladder of success" (Brantlinger and Guskin, 1987).

These ideals and root concepts demand the twin competing goals of democracy and efficiency. American Progressivism in the period between 1900 and 1950 failed to reconcile these competing goals. American society has been torn "between the ideal of meeting the legitimate needs of every individual and the goal of securing the national welfare [social justice]. We struggle with the legacy of Progressivism today because *the same conflicts have gone unresolved*" [emphasis added] (Stevens and Woods, 1987: 345).

Today's educational reform proposals call into question the same American Creed and meritocratic ideology. Once again, we struggle with the historical question, "What are schools for?" (the individual? civic culture? workplace? national defense?). The same conflicts exist between quality and equality, social utility and individual need, and between social policy and economic priorities. The scales are currently tipped in favor of the workplace and efficiency with an equal opportunity caveat. Specifically, President Bush in February, 1991, unveiled an "Opportunity Action Plan" for education which emphasized delivering services more "effectively" (i.e., raising national standardized test scores) while "retaining key protections in current laws" (e.g., protection of the disabled) (*Michigan Counterpoint*, Summer 1991: 7).

Historically, the concepts of merit, opportunity, and equality have been translated variously into practice. Currently two proposals for educational practice stand out as exemplifying the American Creed. The first proposal receiving a large amount of media attention is "Schools of Choice" whereby students may no longer be required to attend their neighborhood schools, but may choose freely which school to attend. This policy is said to make the practice of schooling more responsive to market demand and free-enterprise in a democratic economy, and as such, corresponds with the concept of merit.

A second related practice that is growing in popularity is the "magnetizing" of American education. In the U.S. today, there are approximately 5,000 magnet schools attended by as many as 20% of high school students (Toch, 1991). These public schools limit admission and teach specialized curriculum in order that "promising" students may profit from the opportunity provided. Opponents of magnet schools believe their policies raise some difficult questions about equity. Proponents respond that magnet schools are "no different than any other special program designed to serve the needs of a select population" (Toch, 1991: 64). Programs for students with disabilities that spend two to three times more per capita than typical students are often pointed to as the prime example.

Effective Schools Research

From the above discussion, it would seem that educators have negligible influence over the conditions of schooling as well as over the outcomes. Businesses, politically appointed commissions, legislatures, and the courts appear to be setting the agenda for educational reform. While the current reform proposals do represent a significant power shift away from schools toward interest groups (notable among them, parents), there is a body of U.S. literature known as the Effective Schools Research which is having an impact as well. Several years of school-based research have resulted in a checklist of factors that are said to lead to effective schools: 1) educational leadership, 2) orderly school climate, 3) high achievement expectations, 4) systematic monitoring of student performance, and 5) an emphasis on basic skills (Bickel & Bickel, 1986: 490).

Unfortunately, the effective school research has been manipulated by politicians who have their own agendas for school reform. Effective schools research calls for school-based reforms, and deregulation to spur innovation through greater local flexibility to achieve excellence. But in spite of the research and political rhetoric, several large school systems in the last few years have been subject to take-overs by the state. In 1989, the authorized takeover of the 28,000-student Jersey City schools in New Jersey cited "deep and chronic problems that include widespread political patronage, nepotism and cronyism; corrupt management, and *academic failure*" [emphasis added] (Toch, 1989: 69). Known as "academic bankruptcy laws," no fewer than eight states have enacted these laws permitting takeover of any school system failing its students. "Failure" is subject to political interpretation.

Amidst the "rattling of bones" of the Effective Schools Research, findings by a minority number of school researchers are falling on deaf ears. Argulewicz (1983) undertook a study of 9,950 Anglo, Black and Hispanic students in Kindergarten through sixth grade in order to examine the probability of being labeled as disabled and placed in special education programs outside the mainstream of typical classrooms. The study found that "cultural/linguistic variables were more influential in the probability of special education placement than the often cited socio-economic variable" (p. 198). While the context of schooling (e.g. cultural factors) is acknowledged as a variable in the research on effective schools, this variable appears to have been down-played by public officials and the media.

In a comprehensive review of Effective Schools Research, Bickel & Bickel (1986) contend that the findings show that schools do make a difference as compared to earlier research (spearheaded by the well-known Coleman Report) that contended that schools are relatively powerless when compared to effects of socio-economic background. However, the second major contention of the Effective Schools Literature, which has largely been ignored, is that "instruction and learning take place in a larger social environment" (Bickel & Bickel, 1986: 491).

In a comprehensive overview of research in the referral, assessment and placement of minority and/or low-income children in Special Education classes, Brantlinger & Guskin find convincing evidence that "acculturation is the most important characteristic being evaluated in a child's performance on a test" (1987: 9). A whole host of other variables also found to be affected by cultural differences include: assessment, assigning, grades, making referrals, classifying deviance, recommending services, teacher expectancy, and teacher behavior towards students.

The central message in this alternative line of relatively overlooked research is that societal attitudes underpinned by cultural values and beliefs play a dominant role in what goes on in schools. Failure, from this perspective, is not only school failure, but societal failure. School experiences are influenced by and interdependent with societal conditions. As Alvin Toffler states, "The 'education' problem is not a problem of education alone, but of several interlinked problems-alcoholism, drug abuse, unemployment, mental illness, etc. Each is the concern of a different bureaucracy, none of which can deal effectively with the problem on its own, and none of which wants to cede its budget, authority, or jurisdiction to another" (1990: 263).

Seymour Sarason supports this view in his recent book, "The Predictable Failure of Educational Reform." He asserts that we must shift our focus from schools to a comprehensive view of reform that focuses on the impact of society on schools. By his standards, "Any action that stays within the system--based only on its own resources, personnel, decision making processes, and planning--is misconceived, parochial, and likely to fail" (1991: 35-36). The majority of those who look to the Effective Schools Literature for solutions to educational problems fail to grasp this essential point.

From these alternative viewpoints and societal trends, it is this author's observation that schooling and education are more than a forum for "winners in the global market place." Those who espouse this view of schooling miss the point, and doom education reform to failure. The "education problem". . . is not technical. Nor is it motivational. Nor is it moral. The problem inheres in unreflective acceptance of assumptions and axioms [about schooling] (Sarason, 1991: 148). Schooling is a form of cultural politics drawing its meaning from social, cultural and economic contexts in which schools operate. The democratic ideals of merit, opportunity and equality are not simply linked to domestic production and their current emphasis on efficiency/excellency but reveal schools as sites of cultural re-production of societal norms. That is, schools are agents that reproduce cultural values.

The societal trends discussed here have a direct bearing on treatment of people with disabilities with important consequences for schooling. The politics of schooling, demographic trends, and litigation/legislation bring powerful influences to bear on education for people with disabilities. It has been said that conditions at the edge of a society reveal more about the state and progress of society than conditions in the middle. The situation of education for people with disabilities reflects the true ideals of American education and society in general. "Special" education for people labeled as disabled says important things about the nature of commitment to education and the cultural politics of schooling.

CULTURAL NORMS AND VALUES

The Cultural Politics of Schooling: Historical Context

Americans hold the ideal of wellness-sturdy, healthy bodies and keen alert minds. Good health, active learning, a wholesome environment, and equality of opportunity make up a considerable portion of American societal ideals. When individuals do not present in their physical well-being the ideal of sturdy and active participation in all that modern life offers, the fault has been traditionally placed with the child and the child's background characteristics, not with the school and its environments.

School norms emphasize levels of function within a prescribed range of behaviors, capabilities and developmental markers. Teachers in typical classrooms have been trained to function within these norms. Students who do not meet the norms have become the purview of special education teachers who are trained on separate tracks and teach students labeled as disabled in separate classrooms, as if these students are fundamentally and innately different. Recently, people with disabilities and their advocates perceived that special education classes had become dumping grounds for students who did not fit the expectations and structure of typical students in typical classrooms. How this came to pass is not surprising, given the history of schooling in America.

Since the second half of the nineteenth century, Americans have become accustomed to segregating people with disabilities who did not measure up to societal norms of health and well-being. People with disabilities have been institutionalized in settings where they could be better cared for with their own kind. The prevailing notion of a handicap has been one of incompetence and inability. "A child's handicap was seen as an unalterable characteristic of the child. . . . Given this, and the conviction that the handicapped were different in kind from the rest of children, it made sense to develop separate educational systems" (Hegarty, Pocklington & Lucas, 1984: 8). These separate institutions and educational programs have gone about their business of "maintenance" for decades with no mechanism for accountability. Institutions of social welfare, rehabilitation, and education are essentially holding tanks for those considered non-productive citizens.

In the twentieth century, special education became an organized and recognized profession among educators. Several groups, such as the Convention of American Instructors for the Deaf, the American Association of Instructors of the Blind, and the American Association on Mental Deficiency organized and applied pressure to the National Education Association (NEA) to create a department within NEA to meet these children's needs. Such a department was formed in 1897 and became known as the Department of Special Education. This department was an instrumental force behind the first public school classes for handicapped children in the United States. However, World War I and the Depression interfered with its growth.

World War II and its aftermath had a significant effect on the prevailing notions of handicap and the provision of education for exceptional children. Disabled veterans of the war returned home in large numbers and were visibly leading productive and useful lives. They were a sizeable minority whose need for social rehabilitation programs began to change attitudes with respect to handicapped people. Spurred by the impetus of returning veterans and no longer ashamed, parents of handicapped children began to demand access to educational resources for their children in the early 1970s. Many parents felt their children's needs were not being met in segregated schools where, removed from the educational mainstream, their children received little preparation for a normal adult life (Garwood, 1979).

Labeling as a Social Construction

As numbers of children who were failing in the mainstream of education increased (due to demographic trends noted earlier), separate programs proliferated, including bi-lingual and compensatory education and programs such as Headstart. For students with perceived disabilities, eligibility for receiving services was based on increasingly sophisticated systems of labeling. In the early 1900s, Binet developed the intelligence test which allowed psychologists to classify retarded children into three categories: idiots, imbeciles, and morons. In the mid 1900s, Alfred Strauss developed a neurological theory of abnormality in children with abnormal behavior who were otherwise considered intelligent. His work led to the creation of the category emotionally disturbed. The category of learning disabilities was established in 1963 at the first Association for Children with Learning Disabilities conference. By the time of the passage of the comprehensive Education for All Handicapped Children Act of 1975, the United States recognized and defined 10 categories of disability in school age children. In the 1990 Amendments to the Act, two more categories were added.

The medical model of disease is predominant in the schools' biological and reductionist labeling of children. In all recognized definitions, the unchallenged axiom is that a disability is innately debilitating and can be objectively defined. But classification by medical criteria does little to illuminate the social and educational needs of students. In addition, labels are not usually assigned until a child enters school. Then, at the earliest stages of schooling, students are tracked in programs such as Headstart for young pre-school and kindergarten students based on a "theory of contagion": The assumption is that, "When underprivileged children entered schools, they caught a cognitive virus that was inimical to healthy development; Headstart would inculcate them against the virus" (Sarason, 1991: 72).

In this way, the classic pattern of mild mental retardation was conceived, known as the "six hour retardation" syndrome.

This classic pattern for the mildly retarded involves little or no recognition of any handicapping condition during the preschool years; increasing incidence of mild mental retardation during the school years up to about age 14; decreasing frequency of mild mental retardation from age 14

on, with most persons earlier classified as mildly retarded
during their school years adjusting sufficiently to adult
demands so that they are no longer regarded as retarded as
adults. (Reschly, 1988: 27)

Interestingly, labeling first began to be challenged in the 1970s and early
1980s, not as an illegitimate practice in and of itself, but in its
consequential discrimination against racial minorities. Blacks and
Hispanics were found to be overrepresented in certain categories of
disability compared to the total population. For example, the National
Center for Education Statistics published a report in 1985 which found:

The proportion of black pupils in classes or training
programs for the mentally retarded is two-to-three times
higher than the proportion of white pupils in such classes
and programs. The proportion of blacks in classes or
schools for seriously emotionally disturbed students is
higher by two-thirds to three-quarters than the comparable
proportion of whites. By contrast, the proportion of blacks
in programs for the gifted and talented is 40-to-50 percent
lower than the proportion of whites in such classes. (p. 29)

As a result of these findings in earlier court cases such as *Larry P. v.
Riles* (1979) and *Diana v. State Board of Education* (1970), as well as
other reports with similar findings (Finn, 1982; Heller et al., 1982;
Mahon et al., 1981; Manni et al., 1980), the politics of labeling became
an issue which challenged the ostensibly objective nature of disability.
States responded by manipulating classification of students in two
significant respects. First, eligibility criteria were manipulated.
California changed its Intelligence Quotient cut-off score for mentally
retarded students from 79 to 70, which reduced the numbers of students so
labeled by half. Changes in Texas and Illinois involving the types of
tests used to classify students led to virtual elimination of mildly
mentally retarded students (Reschly, 1988). Table 1 demonstrates the
change in numbers due to changes in policy for the 4 most populous
states.

TABLE 1: No. of Children Served Under EHA by Selected
Handicapping Conditions

STATE	1978-1979			1988-1989			% CHANGE		
	LD	MR	ED	LD	MR	ED	LD	MR	ED
California	92,957	41,023	23,199	237,344	23,230	11,099	+255	-56	-48
Illinois	70,931	46,977	28,721	96,093	16,572	14,697	+14	-283	-195
New York	19,410	48,566	39,403	156,850	18,767	35,253	+808	-258	-11
Texas	129,784	36,259	9,729	166,873	22,742	23,485	+13	-159	+241

NOTE: LD = Learning Disabled; MR = Mentally Retarded; ED = Emotionally Disturbed
SOURCE: U.S. Department of Education, 1980 and 1990

A noticeable shift in school policy from biological to environmental reasons (i.e., cultural disadvantage) for labeling students became evident as schools responded to court cases and research findings. But the solution remained the same--pull-out from typical classes on the basis of assessment of student deficits. Labels changed, but there was no change in the environment served. Table 2 shows the relationship between labels and the environments in which students with particular labels are served.

TABLE 2: Percentage of Handicapped Children Served
in Different Environments (All Conditions)

STATE	# Served in All Environments			% Served in Reg. Class/ Sep. Class		
	1977-78	1982-83	1987-88	1977-78	1982-83	1987-88
California	332,013	361,047	388,747	67/30	69/30	66/29
Illinois	226,258	261,769	215,241	61/27	58/32	61/30
New York	215,968	263,775	280,103	51/42	42/41	47/41
Texas	330,530	286,165	283,196	84/11	78/15	83/11

NOTE: Data for 1987 separates regular classes into two categories: Regular Classes and Resource Room. This breakdown is as follows:

	% Served in	
	Regular Class	Resource Room
California	25	41
Illinois	26	35
New York	8	39
Texas	3	80

SOURCE: U.S. Dept. of Education, 1980, 1985, 1990

The separate environments in which most students with disabilities were being served began to be challenged as well, as it became evident that these students were not succeeding in separate classes. In a comprehensive review of program outcomes for special education, Gartner and Lipsky find: "There is no compelling body of evidence demonstrating that segregated special education programs have significant benefits for students. On the contrary, there is substantial and growing evidence that suggests the opposite is true" (Lipsky & Gartner, 1989:19). Specifically, a review of over 50 efficacy studies on special education placement find:

1. consistently little or no effects for students of all levels of severity placed in special education settings;

2. mean academic performance of integrated mildly handicapped students is in the 80th percentile of their peers in general education, while their peers in segregated settings score in the 50th percentile;

3. full- or part-time placement in regular classes is more beneficial for students' achievement, self-esteem, behavior and emotional adjustment;

4. the drop-out rate is at least 10 percent greater for special education students than for general education students.

The practice of labeling for the purpose of segregating students is the operational result of viewing disability as an innate difference of an individual. All labeling practices place the burden of school success on the student and blame the victim. The label pegs the student as having a deficit or disorder outside the normal range of behavior--both academic and social. As has been noted earlier, throughout the 1980s, problems with labeling became more and more apparent. Evidence that labels were social constructions of deviance rather than innate characteristics of students was most apparent in the education of students with learning disabilities. Each school district in the United States has been allowed to develop its own definition of learning disability. In addition, these definitions are subject to interpretation by educational professionals. According to Ysseldyke (1986), eighty percent of all children in typical classes could be labeled as learning disabled as a result of these variations.

Since the landmark legislation at the federal level, Public Law 94-142, 1975 (known as the Education For All Handicapped Children Act or

EHA), the number of children with learning disabilities has risen from 750,000 to 2,000,000, or an increase of 267%. While changes in the number of learning disabled students are dramatic, the total identified population of special education children has changed relatively little (increase of 5%) since passage of the law. These changes in specific handicapping conditions over time are so abrupt that they cannot be explained by changes in the number of students in the total population. The explanation must therefore lie in changes in educational procedures for identification and classification of students. The Office of Special Education and Rehabilitative Services notes: "It is likely that the decreases in the mentally retarded count are in part related to increases in the learning disabled count" (Weiner & Hume, 1987: 88). It is also likely, the OSERS Report continues, that decreases in the number of children classified as mentally retarded "are the result of an increasing sensitivity to the negative features of the label itself and to reaction on the part of local school systems to allegations of racial and ethnic bias as a result of the use of discriminatory or culturally biased testing procedures" (Weiner & Hume, 1987: 88). Table 3 below provides examples of these changes in the learning disability population since passage of PL94-142 for the four most populous states.

TABLE 3: No. and % Change in No. Served Under EHA Annually Since School Year 1976 Learning Disabled

STATE	NUMBER			% CHANGE IN NO. SERVED	
	1976-77	1982-83	1988-89	1976-77-1982-83	1982-83-1988-89
California	74,404	198,696	237,344	267	16
Illinois	53,328	96,805	96,093	181	-1
New York	34,514	116,753	156,850	338	26
Texas	50,890	150,768	166,873	296	10

In summary, political pressures were brought to bear as a result of findings that schools were discriminating on the basis of cultural differences through the practice of labeling and segregating students in special classes. The practice of labeling has its roots in traditional notions of disability as a deficit. Children who were failing the norms of societal achievement were removed from regular classrooms. The process for making decisions in schools is thus lodged within a powerful framework of economic, political, and cultural conditions.

The Economic Context of Disability

As more and more students became labeled and shunted off to special education classrooms and programs, available resources began to be strained. While special education personnel were available, the intensity and length of time a child's deviant behavior was tolerated in typical classrooms was lowered, raising the likelihood of referral to a self-contained or segregated setting. When the system reached its saturation point and budgets were stretched beyond their capability to serve special education students, educators began to call for a shared responsibility between special education and regular education (Will, 1986). Known as the Regular Education Initiative (REI), this proposal and variations of it call for elimination of the EHA classification system and the pull-out approach.

Strained economic conditions, combined with issues of discrimination brought to the courts, provided the impetus for a growing movement toward inclusion of students with disabilities in typical classes. Ironically, this movement is based on the values of equal opportunity-the same argument used to segregate students in the first place. However, the economic issue and the moral issue must be carefully separated. "To recognize the moral problem but to have its resolution depend solely on economic considerations is tantamount to reinforcing the implicit assumption that schools are primarily for nonhandicapped children." (Sarason, 1982: 256).

Parents and advocates who support "inclusive education" argue that all children can learn. Preparation for life in a democratic society demands that schools value individual worth and equal opportunity. The growing diversity in the society as a whole, they argue, requires that schools represent this diversity within the typical classroom.

SERVICES FOR SPECIAL NEEDS CHILDREN

Incidence and Prevalence

Thirty-five million Americans-one in seven-have physical or mental impairments that interfere with their daily activities (National Center for Health Statistics, 1989: 32). Of these, approximately ten to twelve percent are school-age children. However, national data on classification and school placement practices for these children suggest little clarity or agreement about who is disabled for virtually every category of disability (Biklen, 1989: 10-12).

A partial explanation for this disagreement lies in current demographic characteristics which have forced a broadening of the role schools play in a democratic society. A new category of "at-risk" students has emerged. Students at-risk for school failure or for dropping out of school are those with minority status, those in poverty, those with language differences, and those who have disabilities. Often, several of these characteristics are present in one student. Education is experiencing a strong reform movement as a result of these growing numbers of at-risk students. As the diverse characteristics of school children has grown, education has begun to show signs of reconceptualization. "Special" education is being transformed to a concept of education for all diverse students.

Prior to 1975, school children identified as handicapped were either excluded from public schooling or segregated in special programs. Since 1976 the total number of children from birth to age 21 who were identified and served in special education has risen from 3,600,000 to 4,687,620 (Twelfth Annual Report to Congress, 1990). These children have been served under federal legislation entitled Part B of EHA (Education of the Handicapped Act-PL94-142) and Chapter 1 of ESEA (Elementary and Secondary Education Act) (U.S. Department of Education, 1990: xiii). Approximately one out of ten students is assigned to special education programs. These students fall into the recognized categories of disability presented in Table 4 below.

**TABLE 4:   Children Age 6-21 Counted Under EHA,
School Year 1988-89**

Handicapping Condition	No. Counted
Learning Disabled	1,973,291
Speech or Language Impaired	957,739
Mentally Retarded	522,864
Emotionally Disturbed	336,760
Hard of Hearing & Deaf	41,049
Multihandicapped	65,096
Orthopedically Impaired	41,514
Other Health Impaired	46,639
Visually Handicapped	17,116
Deaf-Blind	792
All Conditions	4,002,860

Source: U.S. Dept. of Education, 1990

The Present Situation

Four types of handicaps account for 94% of children served: Learning Disabilities, 48%; Speech Impaired, 23%; Mentally Retarded, 14%; Emotionally Disturbed, 9%. Ninety-three percent of all children with disabilities are served in typical school buildings: 30% in typical classes; 38% in resource rooms; and 25% in self-contained classrooms. However, as can be noted from the previous Tables, there have been sharp changes over time, as well as wide variations among all 50 states (Lipsky & Gartner, 1989: 16).

Funding for services to special needs students amounts to about two times that of per pupil spending for typical students. Per pupil excess cost for special education students on a national average amounts to $3,652. Nationwide, states pay the bulk of these costs or about 57.8%. Local districts contribute about 34.4% of excess costs, and federal monies about 7.8%. Total costs are rising, as recent amendments to federal law have increased the kinds of related services deemed necessary for an appropriate education for these children. The most recent additions include services to infants and toddlers, and transition services from school to work for school leavers. As an example, in New York one in every eight students is assigned to special education. The costs are

$16,746 annually per student as compared to $7,107 for typical students in regular education. Three thousand of those special education dollars per student go to testing annually in order to label the student. The results? Only 5 percent of all students accepted into special education programs are ever returned to the mainstream. Only 17 percent graduate from high school (Berger, 1991).

The Integration Imperative

Parents of children with disabilities sought redress from segregation in the legislature as well as in the courts. Change in societal attitudes and social policy was thus spearheaded by a minority of dedicated advocates who chose to rely on the courts rather than on the schools for their integration goals. As a result of parental pressure, supported by various special interest groups, Public Law 94-142, the Education for All Handicapped Children Act of 1975, was passed and integration became the major issue in special education. PL94-142 contains within it legalistic mechanisms for insuring a free appropriate public education for children with disabilities. The implicit message is a moral indictment against schools and a commentary on the limited alternatives that were available for these children.

The mechanism of due process inherent in the law was based on the fifth and fourteenth Amendments to the United States Constitution and is carried out through the Individualized Education Plan (IEP). Parents must agree in writing to the identification and subsequent placement of students perceived as needing special education. When parents and school authorities disagree, parents are entitled to a due process hearing and if not satisfied, may pursue their disagreements through the courts. This legalistic mechanism for ensuring an appropriate education was carefully crafted as part of federal legislation. The reason for this is that parents did not trust the ability of school systems to address the educational needs of their children. However, the IEP is contrary to the autonomy of individual teachers and has become rife with conflicts over the status of general and special education personnel.

PL94-142 also introduced the concept of Least Restrictive Environment (LRE), or placement of students with disabilities in an educational setting with nondisabled age-appropriate peers to the extent possible. However, school systems interpreted LRE to conform with institutional custom and practice. The result was to restrict placement of children labeled as disabled in general education classrooms.

Services for special needs children since the mid 1970s have been characterized as categorical programs administered by separate systems. Students are labeled and placed in programs with other students carrying the same label. Those who are mainstreamed for all or part of the school day are still the main responsibility of special education teachers and support personnel. The IEP spells out the services to be provided, the intensity and duration of these services, and these services are reviewed and evaluated annually by a committee that includes the parents, teachers and other relevant personnel.

A least restrictive environment continuum of services is available to provide options for these students. This continuum ranges from full-time placement in typical classes with support, to segregation in separate facilities. Allocation of financial resources comes from separate sources. Personnel are separately trained. Organization and administration is managed separately. This system is changing, however, based on the arguments discussed above. The continuum of services is now considered to be provided in one setting rather than across multiple settings. Support services are being offered within the typical classroom rather than in pull-out programs.

Current Practice

There are a growing number of schools, school districts, and state-wide programs that have adopted "inclusive education" practices. In these systems, the commitment is to educate all children (including the most severely handicapped) together with typical students full-time in regular education classrooms with the support services necessary for all students to succeed. These "pockets of excellence" provide promise for the system as a whole. The most well-known programs of full integration at the state level are the Homecoming Model adopted by Vermont (Thousand & Fox, 1986) and Project Merge in the state of Washington (Hunter & Wood). At the district level, well-known successful programs include Ed Smith Elementary School in Syracuse, New York, and selected programs in Johnson City, New York (Lipsky & Gartner, 1989: 278).

In addition, several teaching practices have been adapted for successful use in integrated classrooms. These include models of collaborative teamwork (Vandercook & York, 1990), cooperative learning (Sapon-Shevin, 1990), mastery learning (Wang, 1989) and the Adaptive Learning Environments Model (ALEM) developed by Margaret Wang (Wang, 1989).

Another project which holds great promise is the Accelerated Schools Project directed by the Center for Educational Research at Stanford (Levin, 1990). This effort consists of 54 schools with large "at-risk" populations, including students labeled as disabled. The driving concept in these schools is that all students are gifted and talented. In order to raise achievement, teachers accelerate learning rather than slow it down. This approach has proven especially successful with children who have acting-out behaviors who normally would have been labeled as emotionally disturbed and shunted off to special education programs.

Three basic elements are present in all of the inclusive education practices: 1) commitment to the success of including all children, 2) careful planning and coordination among all the teaching and support personnel, and 3) staff involvement at all levels, including in-service training and preparation for adaptive strategies to include all students. Other best practices that are incorporated in these models include age-appropriate school placement, attention to social as well as physical integration of students, home-school partnerships to utilize the resources of parents, systematic instructional decisions, and systematic ongoing program evaluation.

One such model is the program in Saline, Michigan known as CONCEPTS (Collaborative Organization of Networks: Community, Education, Parents, The Workplace and Students). CONCEPTS was developed as an outgrowth of the school improvement program for the Washtenaw School District. The mission statement, adopted by the Board of Education, recognizes that all students can learn. From this mission statement, common goals were developed:

1. Students, regardless of disability, will have the opportunity to attend school with non-handicapped peers. Students who previously would have attended a self-contained special education program in a school outside their community may be able to be educated with other students from their neighborhood.

2.   Students with special needs will be grouped with peers
of approximately the same chronological age within regular
education classrooms.
3.   Every effort will be made to provide special education
and supportive services within regular classes, using a
classroom-based model, to maximize the benefits of special
and adapted instruction for all students in a classroom.
Services will be put into regular classrooms rather than
pulling students out to receive services.   (Source:
Washtenaw Intermediate School District, 1990)

Next, the district obtained grant money to train personnel. They began
with a cadre of volunteer teachers who were interested in and committed to
the goals of inclusive education.

Implementation of CONCEPTS began in school year 1989-90.
Twenty-five students were integrated full-time in their home schools.
Support services within these students' classes included a teachers' aide
and a special education teacher who team taught with the general
education teacher. These personnel were able to work with all students in
the classroom. More cooperative group learning strategies were utilized.

Along with this direct classroom support, a Building Planning Team
meets monthly to discuss the student's program. The team has a
potential of twenty members (including an occupational therapist; a
physical therapist; a social worker; speech, reading and music teachers;
the principal; parents and senior citizen tutors) who are called upon when
needed. Another essential component of the program is the Circle of
Friends. A group of eight volunteer students meet once a week for lunch
and to plan after school activities. Facilitated by the classroom teacher,
the group shares feelings and raises children's awareness.

Overall, CONCEPTS is seen as a collaborative effort between special
and general education. Students continue to receive special education
support but within the context of the general education program in what
is called a classroom-based model. Services are focused upon teaching
students new skills within the typical classroom. General and special
education teachers share responsibility for adapting classroom activities to
meet the needs of the student. Individualization, support, and caring are
emphasized over categorization and labeling.

After one year, outcomes for everyone involved in the program are reported as positive. From the Superintendent's perspective, ". . . this new opportunity for students to remain in their home communities and receive appropriate instruction is in response to students and parent interest, and the value our communities place on attempting to create schools where every child belongs" (WIDS, 1990: 7). According to the fifth grade teacher, "The impact on the students has been unbelievably positive, because of the staff-support level in the room (WISD, 1990: 7). A parent responds: "Inclusion is critically important. And not just for Dana, but for the community as well. The more youth of this generation experience the reinclusion of inconvenienced children like Dana into not only school but all facets of the community and life, the more it will become a natural and expected activity in the generations that follow" (WISD, 1990: 10).

Conclusion

PL94-142 mandated a free appropriate education for all handicapped children. The years immediately following this legislation saw a rise in number of students served. The expectation that students who did not meet norms of the typical classroom were better served in pull-out programs was reinforced by interpretation of the LRE to coincide with customary school practice. The general education system in turn was buttressed by special education personnel who collaborated in this implicit contract by accepting these children. A number of factors in the ensuing years caused a reexamination of these practices. First, the classification procedures pointed to flaws in the system, especially with regard to students of minority backgrounds and those suspected of having a learning disability. Second, there was growing evidence that these children were not succeeding in separate environments. Third, dwindling resources forced a second look at separate administrative systems and a search for alternatives of shared responsibility. Finally, the values of equal opportunity and individual worth provided the impetus for progressive inclusion of students with disabilities. This impetus was supported by the need to provide an appropriate education for growing numbers of "at-risk" students in the general education population.

THE FUTURE: ISSUES AND PRIORITIES

In considering the education of students with disabilities, one must ask questions and challenge assumptions about ideals, theory and practice. Beginning at the grass roots, with practice, it would appear on the surface that special education should be effective. After all, who would not want smaller class sizes, explicit learning contracts (IEPs), multidisciplinary teaching and planning, and instructional strategies geared to individual students' capabilities? The problem lies in the fact that benefits are only available to a select few who are labeled as having disabilities. As a result, students are devalued, assigned to separate routines and spaces, and experience discontinuity and segregation. The outcome for such students is discrimination, lowered expectations, and ultimately school failure.

The challenge for the future is to find ways to provide educational programs that do not require labeling and segregation. Educators must begin to build programs on children's strengths, rather than on their weaknesses, in order to achieve real education progress for all students, not just those considered disabled. The United States is headed in this direction with the movement toward inclusive education. But to date, those schools that have integrated students have had to do so on "special" time-limited monetary grants and with legal "waivers" to accomplish their goals. Often, the current structure is part of the problem rather than the solution. If students are to be educated without labels, then school programs and teachers must be delabeled and desegregated as well. Specifically, university programs that train teachers to be "special" or "regular" on separate tracks can hardly be expected to produce teachers prepared for diversity in today's classrooms.

Practice is underpinned by ideals. Public Law 94-142 was based on a goal of equal opportunity. The law's imperative to educate students with disabilities in the mainstream to the extent possible with their peers succeeded not in abolishing inequality, but in extending it. Schools set up a structural arrangement to coincide with customary practice based on societal beliefs in meritocracy, and meritocracy depends on inequality of outcomes. However, outcomes for students with disabilities are dismal by anyone's standards. In 1989, the United States Census Bureau reported that "disabled Americans are less likely to hold jobs now than earlier this decade, and those who do work have lost earning power" (Schmid, 1989). Further, a 1985 national survey by Harris found that "70 percent of working-age disabled people were unemployed. Of those, two-thirds said they wanted to work but were prevented from doing so because, among other reasons, they found discrimination in hiring or lacked transportation" (Shapiro, 1989: 22).

Educational reform must be tied to larger societal reform. Societal conditions that impact students in schools must be addressed as priority, not the least of which are broken families, drugs, teen pregnancies, homelessness, crime, and poor or non-existent schools. Specifically, school climate as a factor in effective schools must be acknowledged as holding complex relationships with the political culture of society as a whole.

Addressing educational problems as a subset of societal problems will require new collaboration among researchers, and new relationships between agencies and organizations, both public and private. In the United States, programs and services have experienced uneven and incremental development, resulting in an unintegrated set of programs that "are not unlike immiscible liquids that defy integration. Adapted from varying traditions (but mostly European in origin), the programs as a body are characterized by serious gaps and unnecessary overlaps" (CNAPD, 1991: 310).

Finally, education will always be in need of reform. The essence of life is change. The problems facing the United States today will only grow more complex as we continue to diversify-not only demographically, but politically and socially. World-wide economic interdependence exacerbates the complexity of the issues facing education today. However, conditions at the margin of society for those who are relatively weak and powerless will ultimately condition our responses to society as a whole. The answer to the question, what are schools for has important future consequences for us all.

References

ABC News-Washington Post Poll (1989), in Black & White in America. *U.S. News and World Report*, July 22, 1991.
The magazine from which this Poll is taken publishes issues twice monthly and is an excellent source for a wide range of issues.

Algozzine, Robe & James Ysseldyke (1983). Learning Disabilities as a Subset of School Failure: The Over-Sophistication of a Concept. *Exceptional Children*, pp. 242-246.

Argulewicz, Ed N. (1983).   Effects of Ethnic Membership, Socioeconomic Status, and Home Language on LD, EMR, and EH Placements. *Learning Disabilities Quarterly*, Vol. 6, pp. 195-200.

Berger, Joseph (1991).   Costly Special Classes Serve Many with Minimal Needs. *New York Times*, April 29.

Bickel, William E. & Donna Diprima Bickel (1986).   Effective Schools, Classrooms and Instruction: Implications for Special Education. *Exceptional Children*, Vol. 52, No. 6, pp. 489-500.

Biklen, Douglas, Dianne Ferguson & Alison Ford (eds.) (1989). *Schooling and Disability*, Chicago, IL: University of Chicago Press.

Brantlinger, Ellen A. & Samuel L. Guskin (1987).   Ethnocultural and Social-Psychological Effects on Learning Characteristics of Handicapped Children. *Handbook of Special Education: Research and Practice*, Vol. I. Margaret C. Wang & Herbert J. Walberg (eds). Oxford: Pergamon Press.
Several of the citations in this chapter come from the three volume Handbook.   An excellent source for a wide range of topics, it brings together many of the best known U.S. writers in special education.

Brown vs. Board of Education (1954).   347 U.S. 483 Topeka.

Center for Educational Statistics (1988). *Digest of Education Statistics*.

Clabaugh, Gary K. & Edward G. Rozycki (1990). *Understanding Schools: The Foundations of Education*. New York: Harper & Row, Publishers.

CNAPD (Committee on a National Agenda for the Prevention of Disabilities) (1991). Disability in America: Toward a National Agenda for Prevention. Washington, DC: *National Academy Press.*
While politically commissioned, this text thoroughly covers the topic of incidence and prevalence and the problems in identification of disability, with chapters on analytical methods employed.

Diana vs. State Board of Education (1970). C.A. No. C-70-37. (N.D. Cal., July, 1970) (consent decree).

Fierman, Jaclyn (1989). Giving Parents a Choice of Schools. *Fortune,* December 4, 1989, pp. 147-152.

Finn, J.D. (1982). "Patterns in Special Education Placement as Revealed by the OCR Surveys," in K.A. Heller, W. Holtzman & S. Messick. *Placing Children in Special Education: A Strategy for Equity.* Washington, DC: National Academy Press.

Garwood, S. Gray (1979). *Educating Young Handicapped Children: A Developmental Approach.* London: Aspen Systems Corporation.

Gergen, David (1991). America's Legal Mess. *U.S. News and World Report.* August 19, 1991, p. 72.

Gross, Beatrice & Ronald (1985). *The Great School Debate: Which Way for American Education?* New York: Simon & Schuster, Inc.
An authoritative source book on the controversy over the quality of U.S. schools. It contains the full report of *A Nation At Risk* by the National Commission on Excellence in Education.

Hagerty, George J. & Marty Abramson (1987). Impediments to Implementing National Policy Change for Mildly Handicapped Students. *Exceptional Children,* Vol. 53, No. 4, pp. 315-323.

Hegarty, Seamus, Keith Pocklington & Dorothy Lucas (1984). *Educating With Special Needs in the Ordinary School.* Windsor, Great Britain: NFER-Nelson.

Heller, Kirby A., Wayne H. Holtzman & Samuel Messick (eds) (1982). *Placing Children in Special Education: A Strategy for Equity.* Washington, DC: National Academy Press.

Heshusius, Louis (1986). Paradigm Shifts and Special Education: A Response to Ulman and Rosenberg. *Exceptional Children*, Vol. 52, No. 5, pp. 461-465.

Hodgkinson, Harold L. (1985). *All One System: Demographics of Education-Kindergarten through Graduate School.* Washington, DC: The Institute for Educational Leadership, Inc.

Hornbeck, Mark. Engler Pushes for Warranty on Graduates. *Detroit News*, September 9, 1991, p. 1A & 6A.

Hunter, Richard D. & Stillman W. Wood (198-). "Project Merge: Maximizing Educational Remediation Within General Education. A Discussion and Review of an Alternative Service Delivery Model for Mildly Handicapped Students." Washington: Olympia School District.

Jenkins, Joseph R., Constance G. Pious & Mark Jewell (1990). Special Education and the Regular Education Initiative: Basic Assumptions. *Exceptional Children*, Vol. 56, No. 6, pp. 479-491.

Larry P. vs. Riles (1984). United States Court of Appeals, Ninth Circuit, No. 80-427. January 23, 1984. Trial court decision affirmed.

Levin, Henry M. (1990). *Building School Capacity for Effective Teacher Empowerment: Applications to Elementary Schools with At-Risk Students.* Stanford, CA: Center for Policy Research in Education.

Levin, Henry M. (1985). *The Educationally Disadvantaged: A National Crisis.* Stanford, CA: Stanford Ed. Policy Institute Program Report No. 85-B1.

Lilly, M. Stephen (1987). Lack of Focus on Special Education in Literature on Educational Reform. *Exceptional Children*, Vol. 53, No. 4, pp. 325-326.

Lipsky, Dorothy Kerzner and Alan Garner (1989). "The Current Situation," in *Beyond Separate Education: Quality Education for All*. Dorothy Kerzner Lipsky and Alan Gartner (eds.). Baltimore, Maryland: Paul H. Brookes Publishing Co.
Used as a text in university classes on special education policy, this book presents research on inclusive education.

Mahon, H.J., J.M. First & W.A. Coulter (1981). An End to Double Jeopardy: The Declassification/Transition of Minority EMH Students. *Integrated Education*, Vol. 18: 16-19.

Manni, J.L., D.W. Winikur & M. Keller (1980). A report on minority group representation in special education programs in the state of New Jersey, 225 W. State Street, Trenton, NJ 08625 (ERIC No. Ed 203 575).

Michigan Counterpoint (1991). "President Bush Again Pushes for School Choice, Excellence." Vol. II, No. 4. Alexandria, VA: National Association of State Directors of Special Education. A quarterly newsletter with coverage of innovation in education.

Mills vs. Board of Education (1972). 348 F. Supp. 866 (D.D.C. 1972).

National Association of State Directors of Special Education (1991). Critic Says IEPs Should Treat Every Child as Gifted and Talented. *Michigan Counterpoint*, Vol. II, No. 4, p. 21.

National Center for Ed. Statistics (1985). *The School Age Handicapped: A Statistical Profile of Special Ss in Elementary and Secondary Schools in the U.S..* Washington, DC: U.S. Government Printing Office.

National Center for Health Statistics (1989). Current Estimates from the National Health Interview Survey, 1988. Vital & Health Statistics, Series 10, No. 173. DHHS Pub. No. (PHS) 89-1501. Washington, DC: U.S. Government Printing Office.

National Commission on Excellence in Education (1983). *A Nation At Risk: The Imperative for Educational Reform.* Washington, DC: Government Printing Office. Stock #065-000-00177.

290   Education and Disability in Cross-Cultural Perspective

(PARC) *Pennsylvania Association for Retarded Children vs. Commonwealth of Pennsylvania* (1972). 343 F. Supp. 279 (E.D. Pa. 1972).

Perry, Nancy J. (1989). How to Help America's Schools. *Fortune,* December 4, 1989, pp. 137-142.

Peters, Susan (1987). *Mainstreaming and Socialization of Exceptional Children.* Ann Arbor, MI: UMI Dissertation Service.

Rainee, Harrison (1991). Black & White in America. *U.S. News and World Report,* July 22, 1991, pp. 18-21.

Reschly, Daniel J. (1988). *Minority Mild Mental Retardation Overrepresentation: Legal Issues, Research Findings and Reform Trends,* Vol. 2. New York: Pergamon Press, pp. 23-41.

Reynolds, Maynard C., Margaret C. Wang & Herbert J. Walberg (1987). The Necessary Restructuring of Special and Regular Education. *Exceptional Children,* Vol. 53, No. 5, pp. 391-398.

Sarason, Seymour B. (1991). *The Predictable Failure of Educational Reform.* San Francisco: Jossey-Bass Publishers.

Sarason, Seymour B. (1982). *The Culture of the School and The Problem of Change.* Boston, MA: Allyn & Bacon, Inc.
For those who want a perspective on schooling in America that is grounded in historical, social, political and cultural understanding, this book is an excellent place to begin.

Schmid, Randolph E. (1989). Census Report: Disabled in U.S. Losing Jobs, Money. *Lansing State Journal,* August 16, 1989.

Shapiro, Joseph P. (1989). Liberation Day for the Disabled. *U.S. News and World Report,* September 18, 1989, pp. 20-24.

Shapiro, Joseph P. (1989). Uncle Sam's NIMRY Attack. *U.S. News and World Report,* September 18, 1989, pp. 24-25.

Shepard, Lorrie A. (1987). The New Push for Excellence: Widening the Schism Between Regular and Special Education. *Exceptional Children,* Vol. 53, No. 4, pp. 327-329.

Skrtic, Thomas M. (1991). The Special Education Paradox: Equity as the Way to Excellence. *Harvard Educational Review*, Vol. 61, No. 2, pp. 148-206.
One of the most comprehensive analyses of special education from an organizational systems perspective.

Stevens, Edward & George H. Wood (1987). *Justice, Ideology and Education*. New York: Random House.

Thousand, Jacqueline (1987). Best Educational Practices of 1987: Effective Integrating Ss with Moderate/Severe Handicaps into Their Local Schools and Communities. *The Decision Maker*, Fall.

Thousand, Jacqueline S. & Wayne L. Fox (1986). *The Homecoming Model: Educating Students Who Present Intensive Educational Challenges within Regular Education Environments*. Burlington, Vermont: Center for Developmental Disabilities.

Toch, Thomas (1991). Schools That Work. *U.S. News and World Report*, May 27, 1991, pp. 58-66.

Toch, Thomas (1989). Seizing Control of School Disasters. *U.S. News and World Report*, October 23, 1989, p. 69.

Toffler, Alvin (1990). *Powershift*. New York: Bantam Books, p. 263.

United States Department of Education (1990). *Twelfth Annual Report to Congress on the Implementation of the Education of the Handicapped Act*.
Published annually since 1977, these reports contain statistics on special education, including numbers of students and range of placement for all recognized disabilities.

United States Department of Education (1985). *Seventh Annual Report to Congress on the Implementation of the Education of the Handicapped Act*.

United States Department of Education (1980). *Second Annual Report to Congress on the Implementation of the Education of the Handicapped Act*.

U.S. News and World Report, September 16, 1991, p. 13. Paying to Learn.

Vandercook, Terri & Jennifer York (1990). "A Team Approach to Program Development and Support" in *Support Networks for Inclusive Schooling*. William Stainback and Susan Stainback (eds). Baltimore: Paul H. Brookes Publishing Co.

Wang, Margaret C. (1989). "Adaptive Instruction: An Alternative for Accommodating Student Diversity through the Curriculum," in *Beyond Separate Education: Quality Education for All*. Dorothy Kerzner Lipsky & Alan Gartner (eds.). Baltimore: Paul H. Brookes Publishing Co.

Washtenaw Intermediate School District (1990). *Including Students in Neighborhood Schools: Washtenaw County's Inclusive Education Options*. Ann Arbor: Washtenaw Intermediate School District.

Weiner, Roberta & Maggie Hume (1987). *. . . and Education for All-- Public Policy and Handicapped Children*. Alexandria, VA: Education Research Group.

Will, Madeleine (1986). *Educating Students With Learning Problems--A Shared Responsibility*. Washington, DC: Office of Special Education and Rehabilitative Services.
   A seminal piece which is attributed as beginning the debate regarding restructuring of special education in the U.S.

Williams, Jane Case (1991). Special Education and Related Services to Minority Populations with Disabilities. *OSERS News in Print*, Vol. III, No. 4, pp. 20-23.

Ysseldyke, James E. (1986). "The Use of Assessment Information to Make Decisions about Students." In *Special Education Research and Trends*. R. Morris and B. Blatt (eds.). New York: Pergamon Press.

CHAPTER 10

EDUCATION AND DISABILITY: CHALLENGE AND OPPORTUNITY

by Susan Peters

EDUCATION AND DISABILITY:
CHALLENGE AND OPPORTUNITY

The authors of this book have examined the educational experiences of people with disabilities with the assumption that these experiences should be analyzed within the context of the cultures (systems of meaning expressed by patterns of behavior) in which they live. The authors hold the belief that the perceived cultural competence of people with disabilities has historically been distorted and undervalued. Images of cultural competence (or the ability to be seen as an active, contributing societal member) are products of deeply ingrained attitudes and beliefs that have evolved through centuries of lived experiences. These images include notions of disability held by individuals in families, organized groups, and society in general. Cultural ideology, structure, and practice within and across nation states interact with perceptions of disability to produce images of culturally competent individuals. Currently, these perceptions are undergoing a new phase of re-production.

The World Health Organization's International Classification of Impairments, Disabilities and Handicaps of 1980 and numerous other attempts to objectify disabling conditions cross-nationally were never very successful, and make increasingly less sense in an emerging "world polity" that is characterized by rapid change. This new world polity (or

293

system of creating value through collective conferral of authority cross-nationally) is characterized by codependence-economically, politically, and socially-and is producing changes in the way we think about disability to reflect notions of interdependence with contextual factors in the environment. In many of the countries included in this book, the growth of national legislation concerning individuals with disabilities reflects the growing sense cross-nationally that these individuals can and should be an integral part of community life. These changes are imperative, not only because of the resultant effect on quality of life for those with disabilities themselves, but for all people who must increasingly turn to formerly disenfranchised groups to contribute to the overall productivity of developing and developed but economically faltering countries.

The voices of these authors join the voices of a growing number of people with disabilities who are speaking out against oppression, stigmatization, and stereotyping. They are demanding a place in society for disabled people with equal rights, privileges, expectations, and opportunities for work and participation in all aspects of societal activities.   Understanding perceptions of disability and their interrelationship to structure, ideology and practice cross-nationally provides new cultural borders (historically constructed and socially organized maps of the world) that influence changes necessary to accomplish this growing sense of community and equality.

This book is a beginning. It begins the work of unpacking the traditional notion of people with disabilities as the "other." The study of education and disability in cultural context forces us to see people with disabilities no longer as a homogeneous, "deviant" group. Their individual characteristics of race, gender, ethnicity, age, abilities and beliefs begin to surface. From this perspective, a world view of disability begins to emerge that bears striking similarities as well as differences across widely diverse cultures and nation states. The interconnectedness of people, sensitivity to cross-cultural beliefs and values, and the new notion of disability as socially constructed and historically/culturally mediated systems of meanings provide an interpretive framework from which educators can begin to re-examine the purpose of schools, who benefits from schooling and what individuals should aim at in their lives. This interpretive framework is necessarily a moral framework from which to examine the ways in which individuals and groups produce collective memories, knowledge, social relations and values within historically constituted relations of power.

Specifically, cross-cultural applications of the models of disability that were presented in Chapter 2 allow us to understand how differing perceptions of disability interrelate with varying cultural conditions to produce new understandings of disability that will hopefully influence how educators think about schooling in significant ways.

Consequences of the Medical Paradigm of Disability

The underlying assumption in this paradigm is that disabled people possess an innate characteristic apart from the causes or consequences of this characteristic. The notion of "health" from this perspective is the absence of disease or infirmity. The assumptions of this paradigm are most influential in countries such as Japan and the United States. Both have highly advanced industrial and service sector economies where the infrastructure is in place to identify and serve any category of students that a large cadre of trained education professionals wishes to identify. The tendency is toward highly centralized service delivery models, and standardized methods of identification and assessment. These characteristics allow the traditionally ingrained assumptions of a medical paradigm to be played out to a very high degree within the educational system. Highly trained and specialized education professionals have the ability to classify students in an ever growing sophistication of techniques. Where the prevailing ideology emphasizes individual ability and meritocratic values, such as in the United States, this institutional and structural ability to classify students as disabled and to educationally segregate them is encouraged.

Both Japan and the United States have governmental policies that focus on education's contribution to economic development. These policies rely on individual and collective productivity. Japan's political ideology has been characterized by Itagaki and Toki in this volume as an "ability dominant society." However, in contrast to focusing on individual ability and meritocracy as in the United States, Japan's cultural expectations can be characterized as emphasizing group identity and conformity. Political ideology and cultural expectations in combination with a pervasive infrastructure have lead Japanese to a classification of students as socially deviant known as "Doya." (This classification may be considered simultaneously as a medical and social paradigm perspective because those that don't conform to the norms of group identity are considered as innately different-although there is arguably a fine line between the two.)

By the same token, the American emphasis on individual productivity combined with the expertise to label those who are not "productive" has led educators to classify a large number of their students as "learning disabled." In both cases, the medical paradigm has been carried to the extreme-classifying ever growing numbers of school children as disabled whose only disability is school failure. The tendency in this paradigm is to "blame the victim." The student is believed to be the cause of failure rather than the symptom of a failed school system. As a result, these students are seen as incapable of future ability to produce goods and services, whether by individual or group norms, and they are categorized and placed in segregated educational programs.

From these examples, we see that the classifications are different, but the underlying assumptions are the same, as are the consequences: People with disabilities are viewed as innately different, unable to effectively contribute to economic solutions to social problems, and subsequently are segregated and tracked through an elaborate system of medical classification within the respective educational systems. This practice of labeling based on norms of "individual productivity" and subsequent segregation in tracked programs insures that people with disabilities will be unable to become productive members of society.

Consequences of the Social Paradigm of Disability

The assumption here is that people with disabilities are socially deviant, and as such socially unacceptable, rather than innately or medically different. This assumption is very similar to that held in the medical model in its reliance on deviance or deficiencies to explain disability. The difference lies in the fact that people perceived as socially deviant do not have to be classified to attain this status. It is interesting that this model of disability has its most influential consequences in countries such as China, Pakistan, and Iran. In these countries, with large numbers of people living in rural areas, the access to centralized and standardized services is nonexistent for most. Here, the infrastructure is not in place to label and sort individuals in relation to a medical condition. All three countries lack adequate education and health services. Pakistan has a 70% non-literate population, Iran 38%, and China 16%. Less than 1% of the disabled school-aged population in these countries receive a formal education, but a considerable number of non-disabled children also do not.

As a result of these conditions, the social model of disability is most influential in private sector groups, not the least of which are families. In Pakistan, the concept of "Izzat" (individual face/family honor) is dominant. This concept influences the ways in which families treat the education of their children. In addition, education (especially in the early formative years) is left to family child rearing practices which are based on the belief that a child's personality is genetically determined, so that formal child development practices are not necessary. This belief bears striking resemblance to the medical paradigm. However, the way in which this is handled is through social paradigm strategies. Children are expected to be submissive and conformist to parental wishes. Children who do not conform are considered disobedient, an economic liability, and their condition, "the curse of God" (divine punishment). The concept of Izzat is not upheld by these children. As a result, these children are feared and pitied. They are denied social roles.

In Iran, with an Islamic government, education services and religion are closely intertwined. The principles and teachings of Islam are an integral part of the school curriculum. Islam teaches a "positive" and protective attitude toward disabled individuals. It is a social honor to serve them. Afrooz reminds us in his chapter that Muhammed teaches, "Serving handicapped people is like being in the service of the prophets of God" and the Koran states, "If any one saved a life, it would be as if he/she saved the life of the whole people." While the assumptions are the same in Iran and Pakistan (people with disabilities differ from the norm and are helpless in the sense that they are seen as incapable of socially responsible roles), the outcomes are different in some ways and similar in others. In Iran, the physical treatment of disabled people may be significantly better than in Pakistan because of the honor that Afrooz asserts is associated with serving them, but people with disabilities are still likely to be protected and sheltered in Iran. The result is similar in both countries: disabled people's social roles may be denied and taken over as the responsibility of others.

In China, cultural attitudes include expectations of reciprocity (children are to take care of the elders when they become adults). Neo-Confucianism teaches obedience to norms of social behavior, and holds a perfectionist view of health. A disabled child is considered to have disrupted the harmony from the ancestors, and to have brought shame on the family. In this case, health is not the absence of disease as such (in the medical paradigm) but entails the broader concept of spiritual, mental, family and physical harmony. This intertwining of the medical and social paradigms' assumptions makes it very difficult for people with disabilities in China. They are both innately and socially invalidated based on very strong traditional beliefs.

The interesting point to be made here, is that differences in cultural attitudes and ideology are apt to result in very different outcomes for people with disabilities, even though the level of available services is similar. In Iran, the disabled child is often protected and educational and habilitation services are offered to the extent possible. In Pakistan, they are most likely to be oppressed, and educational and habilitation services withheld. In China, most disabled people are hidden and considered undeserving of educational and habilitation services. These same similarities and differences played themselves out in the medical paradigm above, where similar assumptions lead to different categories, but consequentially similar outcomes.

In addition, the relatively lower level of resources in poorer countries such as Iran, Pakistan, and China provide a context in which the social paradigm may be dominant as an educational sorting device, while richer countries such as the United States and Japan may have the luxury to rely on the medical paradigm (which requires an infrastructure and specialized educational professionals) to sort individuals into separate educational programs. The allocation of resources (whether plentiful or scarce) is thus interdependent with the prevailing paradigm.

Consequences of the Political Paradigm of Disability

This paradigm contains the assumption that disabilities are social/political constructions, and that people perceived as disabled are oppressed minorities. While the previous two paradigms are built on a consensus of disability as deficient (either through disease or social deviance), this paradigm is built on conflict. The prevailing notions are challenged, setting the stage for political struggle. This assumption is still only held by a minority of people, but is gaining in acceptance throughout the world.

Some evidence of this paradigm is surfacing to differing degrees in all of the countries discussed in this book. The most concrete evidence is in the growth of national legislation to provide increased services to ensure equal opportunity rights to education for those with disabilities (i.e., The People's Republic of China Disabled Protection Law of 1992, The Americans with Disabilities Act of 1990, the 1988 National Welfare Visions policy of Japan, and Hungary's 1985 Education Act). A similar theme of treatment from this perspective can be seen in Hungary, Great Britain, and the United States. Each of these countries has a philosophy of government regarding education of people with disabilities that is stated in formal policy documents as the desire to equalize societal participation through equal educational opportunities provided to students labeled as disabled.

Hungary has a socialist welfare state that is predominantly centralized, even though it is currently undergoing changes toward a more decentralized form of governmental control over educational goals. The United States has a constitutional democracy that is characterized by a predominantly decentralized system of education at the state level with some federal level controls. Barton, in his chapter on England and Wales, argues that their educational systems, while in theory are decentralized, are still highly influenced by central governmental control over education. Although their governmental structures differ, these governments all expound the doctrine of equal opportunity for people with disabilities. For example, England's Warnock Report of 1978 "confirmed the perspective that the purpose and goals for all children are the same."

Implicit in this doctrine is the assumption that the environment-physical and social-is the key factor that determines a disabled person's ability to succeed. These policies therefore indirectly accept the notion that people with disabilities are socially oppressed. As an example, the language currently used in Hungary differentiates between vokkant (medically invalid) and Korlatozett (socially handicapped). The United States and England have similar differentiations in the language they use.

The outcomes for people with disabilities within the assumptions of this paradigm however are inherently contradictory. Students are segregated to "protect their rights." In all of these countries, the "mildly handicapped" whose innate disability is questionable at best, are by far the largest group. Also, minority groups are overrepresented: in the U.S., blacks and Hispanics are overrepresented in the population of school children labeled as disabled. In Hungary, the Gypsies make up 5% of the population, but 30-40% of Gypsy students are categorized as mentally retarded by school authorities.

The idea dominates that students must be labeled and segregated in order to provide educational services. While rights are extended, they must be earned through proving disability status (i.e., deficiencies). And in many cases, such as an overrepresentation of minorities labeled as disabled, this status is politically determined. In his chapter on England and Wales, Barton makes this point very powerfully and suggests that the inherent contradictions are covered by "diversionary rhetoric." Specifically, he points out that while the manifest function of labeling may be beneficial (to provide needed educational services), the latent functions impair academic and social competence, destroy independence, and actually produce dependency.

While the official policies of equal educational opportunity are similar in the three countries noted above, the differences in governmental structure appear to play a key role in the extent to which the political model has an ability to dominate. In England, where the central governmental influence is high, Barton notes that the past decade has experienced unprecedented interventions by government with "deliberate attempts to destroy the role of the Local Authorities in the administration and control of educational, welfare and housing provisions." The Warnock Report "represents a conservative political perspective" that is ambiguous in its support of integrating students with disabilities in mainstream schools. As a result, the number of special segregated schools in England has not been significantly reduced since 1978 when the report was finalized.

In Hungary, bureaucratic centralization in the sphere of education is changing, but Kozma and Illyes assert that "state bureaucracy tries to stop some local efforts in order to keep educational services throughout Hungary on the same level of development." Also, teachers' attitudes and practices are still highly influenced by decades of a nationalized school system characterized by a highly centralized curriculum, officially required methods of teaching and learning, and a socialist pedagogy emphasizing the collective good. These circumstances significantly inhibit the acceptance of alternative methods of instruction so important for the effective education of disabled students-especially those who are blind, deaf or developmentally delayed learners.

On the other hand, political conservatism in the United States over the past decade has led to a central government policy of deregulation. More and more, impetus for school reform has been turned over to state and local authorities. As a result, local school districts are allowed the flexibility to create alternative educational programs. Under these new conditions, a few districts whose members value full participation of disabled students are developing integrated educational programs for these students. As the successes of some of these programs are becoming widely documented and substantiated, the number is growing. A definite trend toward integration is becoming evident, albeit still highly contested, even though the courts and federal law are upholding a pattern of integration in most cases.

In the Social Paradigm, differences in ideology about the rearing and education of children brought about similar consequences-denial of social roles necessary for cultural competence and equal educational opportunity. In the Political Paradigm, similar educational ideologies carried out through different governmental structures still resulted in widespread oppression in the form of educational segregation of disabled students, or at best, pockets of full educational integration (as in the United States). The practice of educating students under a politically dominant paradigm, while introducing conflict necessary for change in the level of educational opportunity for disabled students still contains within it the assumption of disability as difference. The educational experiences of students with disabilities are compromised under this paradigm by the latent functions of labeling: labeling bestows rights while at the same time stigmatizes and often results in impaired competence from segregation in special classes.

Consequences of the Pluralistic Paradigm of Disability

This paradigm holds the assumption that a continuum of diversity exists across the whole spectrum of societal members. People with disabilities are only one part of that continuum. All members have positive attributes to contribute because they are different. Difference becomes one of the common characteristics that we all share.

This notion is best nurtured in a flexible, decentralized structure where individuals are interdependent and can hold multiple roles simultaneously, so that disability is not the single overriding characteristic of an individual. In those cultures where the family is still the main source of spiritual, educational, and economic resources, the Pluralistic Paradigm has the best chance of flourishing. Out of necessity, families must assign multiple roles to their members. A disabled child who is unable to work outside the home may become a caregiver for a younger sibling and in the process become socialized to responsible roles.

At the broader level, this same multiplicity of roles and self-sufficiency is seen in the trend toward community based services, especially in rural areas where existing services may be many miles away and thus virtually inaccessible. In this respect, the more advanced industrialized and wealthier countries which provide a wider range of formal services are not always better off. Formal services often result in greater and greater narrowing to specializations that ultimately result in gaps in services and "crack" children (those who fall through the cracks in a system that has become so standardized and specialized that few can meet eligibility requirements for services).

In recognition of this state of affairs, there is an effort to move away from formal service provision to greater use of informal systems and natural environments. As Miles points out in his chapter on Pakistan, the attempt to impose model programs from other countries on Pakistan's educational system has failed miserably because it does not take into account the local context, or the ways in which families function and their belief systems. This imposition is yet another attempt to standardize services, only on a cross-national basis. Diversity becomes a liability in these attempts. Similarly, China's recent legislation, modeled after the United States' civil rights bills will fail unless attention is paid to implementation strategies that take into account the traditional belief systems regarding disability.

Examples of the Pluralistic Paradigm are few and far between and are not as institutionally pervasive as the examples from the Medical and Social Paradigms. The forces of standardization and centralization of educational services constrain development of the assumptions contained in this paradigm. Three examples that stand out among the countries included in this volume are Pakistan's experience of "casual integration," the CONCEPTS program of integration in the United States, and Japan's experiment in the Tokyo slum area of Sanya.

First, "casual integration" of students with disabilities in Pakistan's ordinary schools occurs when class sizes vary from 30 to 80 students, so that many disabilities go "unnoticed." C. and M. Miles assert that at least 200,000 children with appreciable disabilities are already enrolled in ordinary schools with no extra help (or at least 20 times the number in special schools). The presence of these children in ordinary schools provides teachers with an opportunity to examine their teaching and learning practices. As a consequence, a few have embraced a child-centered approach to teaching versus "a view of schooling as obedience and memorization reinforced by fear" (See C. and M. Miles' chapter). Where experiments and innovation have been encouraged, a child-centered approach has emerged. C. and M. Miles go on to add, "This may happen without direct Western influence." Parameters of local patterns of child care and socialization may adjust in these cases out of necessity to accommodate the diversity inherent in large classes.

Second, in 1989, a small school district in a rural community of the United States developed a model integration program called CONCEPTS-Collaborative Organization of Networks: Community, Education, Parents, The Workplace and Students. The goal was to have students with disabilities remain in their neighborhood schools based on the agreed upon community-based value that "every child belongs." The overall emphasis is on collaboration among diverse groups both internal and external to the school. The model is child-centered. "Individualization, support, and caring are emphasized over categorization and labeling." The impact has been "unbelievably positive," with inclusion becoming a natural and expected activity.

Third, in the slum area of Tokyo, an independent school was established by "administrative fiat" because the socially handicapped children of seasonal and daily laborers had been rejected by the public schools. Largely ignored by the system because of their marginal status, the employees of this newly formed Taiei Public School were left to their own creative and innovative strategies. According to Itagaki and Toki: "The teachers who taught in this school were happy because they were involved in creative teaching free from standardized curriculum. They could develop their teaching ability without enforced institutional restrictions. The service seemed very effective within the school." Japan's experiment in the Tokyo slum area of Sanya had the following characteristics: creative teaching free from standardized curriculum; commitment and positive motivation of teaching staff; expanded role of teachers-including consulting parents on financial problems, completing legal registrations, and listening to complaints.

In sum, these isolated examples seem to flourish under structural conditions of flexibility and commitment and collaboration among educators. They perceive the concept of diversity as positive and central to education of all students, including those with disabilities. Non-traditional roles for both teachers and students are encouraged in this paradigm.

Lessons Learned

By now, it should be fairly clear that education for people with disabilities is a very complicated issue that goes well beyond focus on providing "special" education service delivery systems. It is argued here that cultural ideology, structure and practice combine with perceptions of disability to create educational experiences for students labeled as disabled. In addition, cultural borders and perceptions of cultural competence that affect these educational experiences are products of the wider environment in which culture is "lived." Each of the chapters in this book begins with a contextual description of the overall demographic, socio-economic and political conditions that have influenced issues of education and disability. For example, in her discussion of China, Shen points out that because there are too many people for the available cultivatable land (over 1,500 people per square mile) "overpopulation is the top priority issue needing to be addressed." In addition, 80 percent of Chinese people live in rural areas where primary health care is a major concern. Pakistan is similar in its population growth and distribution, increasing from 33 million people in 1951 to approximately 115 million people today with 70 percent living in rural areas. Iran's growth rate is 3.2 annually compared to a world average of 1.9 with 50 percent living in rural areas. These conditions strain the entire country, forcing attention on basic needs.

Besides rapidly growing populations, wars have greatly influenced the general conditions of most countries in this book, including Iran's prolonged war with Iraq, the Sino-Japanese struggle of World War II, and the European Theater in which 53 percent of Hungary's schools were bombed. The problem of disability is central to these conditions. Disease prevention, proper nutrition and health care are critical factors in ameliorating the conditions of disability and hunger caused by war. Many people with disabilities (caused directly or indirectly by war) need access to adequate health care for prevention as well as rehabilitation.

The conditions of overpopulation and war and the corresponding focus on meeting basic needs constitute constraints on countries' ability to provide education to disabled students. As C. and M. Miles point out, "When nations have organized food and water, housing, roads, schools, health services, communications, they may tackle social problems hitherto seen as marginal or insoluble." However, the problem of limited resources will always be a factor in human development. How we allocate limited resources is a matter of values. Market economies are based on ideologies. In a real sense, they are "enterprise cultures" (See Barton's chapter). "How resources are socially distributed, who has access to them, with what consequences are crucial political decisions." (See Barton's chapter). Education policy rests on values, and values are culturally determined-whether by an ability dominant society such as Japan, or an Islamic government such as Iran.

In the final section of each of the chapters in this book, the authors suggest that the positive future for education of disabled individuals rests on two factors: resources and their allocation. Positive application of these factors to education of disabled students requires stronger consumer control, pluralistic goals, and realignment of priorities. These factors are also dependent upon redefining cultural rules that ascribe meaning to the experience of being disabled. In their examination of world institutional structures, Thomas, et al. assert that Institutionalized cultural rules define the meaning and identity of the individual and the patterns of appropriate economic, political and cultural activity engaged in by these individuals. Application of this assertion to the issue of education and disability supports the argument that until negative perceptions of disability change, the conditions of disability will not.   Paradoxically, such worldwide conditions as war, hunger, poverty, and the AIDS epidemic increase the numbers of disabled people, and may to some extent force perceptions to change as it becomes increasingly difficult to ignore their plight--these people are no longer the "other," but our neighbors, friends, and relatives.

The cross-cultural examples given for each paradigm reveal a pattern: regardless of similar levels of service (as in countries with large hard to reach rural populations, or highly advanced technocratic societies), regardless of similar governmental goals and policies, different educational and quality of life outcomes occur depending on the cultural rules (Medical, Social, Political, Pluralistic) applied to the disabled person. These rules derive from cultural systems of meaning and become cultural borders that limit individual capacity and confine identities within them. Overall, the pattern is not linear. That is, the countries discussed in this book did not begin with a medical paradigm and progress through social and political paradigms to a pluralistic paradigm. Educational and political ideology, governmental structure and function, and school practice, combined with wider societal conditions play an influential role in educational treatment of disabled people, but may be viewed as secondary to the cultural values and assumptions that are used to make choices involving policy and practice.

All of these paradigms are present to a greater or lesser degree in each country described here. Each of the paradigms contains within it the capacity for creating and sustaining positive educational experiences for disabled people. It is when a particular paradigm dominates, to the exclusion of alternative perceptions, that it fails. When carried to extremes, each paradigm distorts its original goals and fails as well. As a result, the paradigms set forth in Chapter Two can no longer be conceptualized as single-cell phenomena, but as lying on a continuum from progressive to regressive as depicted in Table 1 below.

Table 1

Cultural Paradigms of Disability and Education

PARADIGM	PROGRESSIVE		REGRESSIVE
Medical	Provisions for prevention, habilitation in basic medical needs	Classification and labeling necessary to provide individualized education services	Focus on deficits Overrepresentation of minorities Questionnable categories of disability
Social	Social needs as defined by consumers are validated Consumers are provided resources they need for independence within their home communities	Increasing dependence on social services provided by professional gatekeepers who define needs of the client	Elaborate tracking systems segregate consumers Decision-making processes are top-down Social roles completely invalidated Consumers become welfare recipients
Political	Access to education guaranteed as inalienable right Resources provided to ensure equal opportunity within ordinary schools	Services provided through doctrine of separate but equal	Rights depend on acknowledging inferior status Constant struggle to maintain rights, with certain groups gaining over others
Plural	Diversity rewarded Seen as positive attribute Planned integration No minority status	Casual integration No real incentive/support provided	Some groups valued over others Increasing overt minority status Diversity becomes a mechanism for exclusion

The Medical Paradigm, as originally conceptualized by Gliedman and Roth in 1980, was depicted as virtually negative. However, this paradigm was based on assumptions of developed countries--i.e., basic health care needs are considered as a given. This assumption is arguable with regard to developing countries such as Pakistan and China. There are many significant ways that the medical profession can have a positive impact on the quality of life and access to education for those with disabilities, especially in the areas of prevention and rehabilitation. It is when the Medical Paradigm is carried to its extreme and begins to treat problems such as "learning disabilities" as primarily medical conditions, that the paradigm fails.

The Social Paradigm suffers from a tendency toward the same extremism as the Medical Paradigm. When social needs as defined by consumers are validated, then this paradigm may be seen as progressive.

However, when consumer-driven social goals are supplanted by professionals who alone have the power and "expertise" to define the educational needs of the client, the gate is opened for elaborate social welfare systems and client dependency.

By the same token, the assumptions of the Political Paradigm in its beginning stages of development were seen as the positive answer to the stereotyping and stigmatization of the Medical and Social Paradigms. The beginning assumption of equal rights for disabled people was seen as a progressive step toward their positive access to schooling. However, the experiences of England and the United States have disappointed disability advocates. Legislation under the Political Paradigm has created two classes of citizens: those "ordinary" people and those with "special" needs.

The Pluralistic Paradigm also has the capacity for regressive activities. While diversity may be celebrated as a positive attribute students bring to schooling, conditions of unequal power relations among various minority groups could become a mechanism for differential allocation of educational resources and ultimately, a mechanism for exclusion from educational services.

Challenges

The lessons learned from cross-cultural analysis of education and disability provide both challenges and opportunities. We began Chapter 2 with a quote: "Theory is a necessary myth that we construct to understand something we know we understand incompletely." The paradigms, or models of perception of disability, presented in this book were constructed to further our incomplete understanding of the experience of being disabled within an educational context. These paradigms allow us to challenge false assumptions that have heretofore gone relatively unchallenged. We must recognize "that dominant ideologies are neither natural nor unquestionably right" (See Barton's chapter). Challenging these false assumptions provides the opportunity to change-to move away from prejudice, discrimination and stereotyping toward social justice and equality. The six principles set forth below provide an interpretive framework for challenging these false assumptions and moving us toward positive change.

1. DISABILITY IS INTERPRETIVE.
This principle challenges the false assumption that disability is an innate and objective condition. A split between objective conditions and subjective experience is impossible due to the influence of environmental factors (not the least of which are perceptions of disability) on the causes and consequences of disability. There is a need to make problematic the scientific claims of "truth" in objective classification systems.

2. PROGRAMS ARE NOT RATIONALLY CONCEIVED.
This principle challenges the false assumption that nation states protect and guarantee the social welfare of disabled people through rationally conceived educational programs. Programs are politically conceived to serve the interests of dominant groups. They are underpined by values which are more than socio-political constructions-they include cultural rules (i.e., paradigms) that limit individual potential. There is a need to examine and redefine these paradigms.

3. INTERDEPENDENCE IS A VIRTUE.
This principle challenges the false assumption of individual autonomy and meritocratic values. Learners in today's world must be able to collaborate and problem-solve together. The educational system as a whole must reach beyond its traditional boundaries to consumers, parents, community, professional groups, government for collaboration at all levels-home, school, and society.

4. OPPRESSION COMES IN MANY FORMS.
This principle challenges the false assumption that oppression comes from "above" in the form of administrative fiat or structural conditions of schooling. Oppression can be based on innate, social, political, or cultural assumptions.

The Medical Paradigm carries potential for classifications that stigmatize. The Social Paradigm carries potential for benevolent humanitarianism that invalidates. The Political Paradigm carries the potential for legislation that segregates. The Pluralistic Paradigm carries the potential for diversity that lowers status and excludes. The negative potential of these paradigms, when carried to extreme, must be guarded against.

5. MORE IS NOT BETTER.
This principle challenges the false assumption that more resources, more technically advanced techniques, and more programs will solve the

education problems of people with disabilities. We need to support natural cultural activities that enhance participation of people with disabilities, to build community-based capacity for meeting their own needs rather than import "model programs" that do not take into account the cultural context within which they will operate.

6.   CONFLICT IS NECESSARY FOR CHANGE.

This principle challenges the false assumption that progress and justice are built on consensus and can be technically engineered. Change requires conflict-not superficial conflict over programs and services, but conflict over assumptions that drive our decisions about programs and services. The Medical and Social Paradigms have rested on a consensus approach to disability. The Political and Pluralistic Paradigms rest on conflict. They contain within them alternative assumptions about the power relations among disabled and nondisabled groups. These must be reexamined.

This chapter began with the assertion that a new world polity characterized by codependence is emerging that carries the opportunity for reconceptualizing perceptions of disability away from objectivist, rational, isolationist views toward an interactive, interpretive, subjectivist view.   Cross-cultural comparisons support the notion that ideology, structure, practice and beliefs in education of disabled individuals do not have national borders, but cultural borders which define disability and the consequential educational experiences of people with disabilities. This view of cultural borders in a world polity challenges educators to ask some basic questions when planning educational programs: What are the prevailing attitudes towards persons with disabilities within a particular culture? How are these attitudes reflected in educational policy? With what consequences? Which culturally specific practices and beliefs can be built upon to enhance educational opportunities for people with disabilities? Which must be discouraged or altered?

The best hope for the future in terms of education for disabled individuals may be to draw on the positive aspects of all four paradigms of disability, but the basic assumptions of the Pluralistic Paradigm should be central: People with disabilities are part of the diversity inherent in all cultures. They have positive attributes to contribute. Difference is to be celebrated, and is a common characteristic that we all share.

INDEX